Southbound Traveler

Southbound Traveler

An Outsider's Journey into the Heart of SEC Fan Culture

James March

Sailor Saint Press

Las Vegas

Copyright © 2017 by James March

All rights reserved. This book or any portion thereof may not be reproduced or used in any manner whatsoever without the express written permission of the publisher except for the use of brief quotations in a book review.

Layout by: Gerald Brennan

Cover Design by: Sarah Brookhart

Printed in the United States of America

First Printing, 2017

ISBN 978-0-692-93259-9 (print)

ISBN 978-0-692-93260-5 (epub)

SouthboundTraveler.com

Contents

Introduction 7
#21 Texas A&M vs. #9 South Carolina 13
#16 Clemson vs. #12 Georgia 37
#15 Ole Miss vs. Vanderbilt 53
Kentucky vs. Florida 75
Florida vs. #3 Alabama 95
Missouri vs. #13 South Carolina 121
#15 LSU vs. #5 Auburn 141
#2 Auburn vs. #3 Mississippi State 163
Tennessee vs. #3 Ole Miss 181
#4 Alabama vs. Tennessee 211
#3 Auburn vs. #4 Ole Miss 229
#5 Alabama vs. #16 LSU 239
#9 Auburn vs. #15 Georgia 259
#8 Ole Miss vs. Arkansas 275
LSU vs. Texas A&M 293
#15 Auburn vs. #1 Alabama 313
SEC Championship 331
The Sugar Bowl 341
Epilogue: The National Championship 353
Afterword: A College Football State of the Union 359

Introduction

I was experiencing a restlessness that I think most people can relate to. It was the spring of 2014, and I'd been feeling this way for a couple years. The particulars of my situation weren't disagreeable by any means: I was twenty-eight years old, three years out of grad school, teaching in a pleasant-enough community on the South Side of Chicago, at a school where I also served as athletic director and coach of the seventh-and-eighth-grade football team. But on the inside, I felt this gnawing, festering discontent, like I was being lulled to sleep by life; that the terms of my existence were being dictated to me as I quietly acquiesced. Social norms suggested I was fast approaching the age where I find a woman to marry and begin the seemingly inevitable march toward middle-class suburbia and children. I wasn't ready.

The next steps were still unclear, but I knew I couldn't dive into that great adventure until I'd scratched this existential itch. I put the intention out into the universe, and as with all things worthwhile in life, I was forced to wait. In the meantime, I sought relief where I could find it: by immersing myself in Chicago's heady improvisational comedy scene, attacking my fears head-on performing on stage; by toying with the idea of moving to the Pacific Northwest, making three trips in two years and fantasizing about a life rooted in the great outdoors as I applied for teaching jobs in Washington and Oregon; and, in perfectly clichéd twenty-something American fashion, by backpacking around Europe exploring off-the-beaten-path countries and learning to be comfortable alone with myself. While all valuable and thoroughly enjoyable, none of these experiences satisfied the undefined yearning I felt almost daily. I knew what I was feeling, but had the hardest time articulating my need to do *something* because I had no idea what that something was. Then, when I was least expecting it, that *something* blew in like a tornado and uprooted my life in a matter of 72 hours.

I'd been working through a 12-week writing program called The Artist's Way. Founded by the writer and filmmaker (and eccentric) Julia Cameron, it is designed to provoke a spiritual and artistic vision in the people who complete the course. Toward the end of the program, one of the writing prompts was to list five things you'd do if they weren't too "crazy." Among other ideas, my list included: 1) travel the United States by myself for an extended period of time; 2) write and publish a book; and 5) attend a football game at every school in the SEC (Southeastern Conference), arguably the most exciting conference in college football. There was a moment of instant recognition. Within five minutes, I understood that I'd be writing this book.

I'm not a particularly impulsive person by nature. I tend to look both ways before I cross the street. To my family, friends, and even my landlord Phil—who didn't understand why exactly I was asking to break my lease, but allowed me to anyway—this idea was sudden, and perhaps more concerning, vague. I, for one, was never bothered by the hastiness of the project or the repercussions of leaving my semi-comfortable Chicago existence. I never questioned the direction I was being pulled in. As someone given to second-guessing myself, I felt that my immediate, unwavering certainty only confirmed the rightness of the decision. Otherwise, the idea would've collapsed on itself in waves of self-doubt. *What are you thinking? This is ridiculous. This is impractical. Be realistic and do something constructive with your life. Why can't you just be normal like your friends?*

The lack of clarity and detail in what, exactly, the book would be about was a cause for concern. I knew the general focus—SEC fan culture—and I knew the guiding question: what don't I get about being a college football fan because I'm not from the South? But beyond that, there were process-related questions I had no answers for: What's my plan for uncovering Southern fan culture? Will this world be easier or harder to access as an outsider? What do I need to know about the South in a broader sense in order to understand why football means so much to so many Southerners? What are the similarities and differences between die-hards at different schools? Pesky logistical matters demanded a great deal of attention as well. To start, how much money would I need for this trip? How can I acquire said amount of money? How does one get a book published and find a literary agent? (My eventual answers to this question: do it yourself; don't.) Which games would offer the best opportunities to observe SEC fanaticism at its peak? How do I sequence game weekends and how do I find tickets to marquee matchups?

Most importantly, I had to answer a series of questions that had damning implications—for me, anyway: What do I do when I arrive in these towns? How do I approach people and get them to open up about what their school's football team means to them? Can I just walk up to tailgates and chat up complete strangers every weekend? These questions brought a few unpalatable truths to my attention. Namely, I had no idea how to write a book. Despite having two English degrees, I'd never written anything longer than twenty-five pages. Also, I'm not a journalist and I don't know the finer points of conducting interviews. Most worrisome, however, was the fact that I'm socially inconsistent. When I'm comfortable, there's no problem—I can be engaging, articulate, and, on particularly good nights, even charismatic. When I feel uncomfortable, though, I become withdrawn, quiet, and even standoffish. It's hard to carry a normal conversation when I feel anxious. Considering that putting myself in new and potentially uncomfortable situations constantly was the basic idea driving the book, this was a cause for concern.

In hindsight, two realizations dawned on me: 1) the above list of questions is significant and probably should have stopped me from moving forward; and 2), conversely, it doesn't matter how many process-related, logistical, or personal hurdles are in the way—when you're convinced that a life change is divinely inspired, the doors practically open by themselves.

Still, it was going to take a lot more than a flash of inspiration to transform an idea into a book. I had to figure out what, exactly, this story would be about. And, of course, I had to decide how to tell it.

🏈

If you're a college football fan, there comes a point every year in mid-August when there's nothing left to say. The preseason rankings have been published, the talking heads have shouted, we know who's up for a Heisman and which coaches are on the hot seat, and we're painfully aware of all our team's question marks heading into the season. The "talk" hits a saturation point about halfway through fall camp. Teams have been practicing for nearly two weeks, but there's still another two weeks until the season kicks off. To stave off the anxiety, we pacify ourselves with gossipy tidbits about who looks good in practice, which freshmen are in the mix for playing time, and who's earning starting jobs. Once in a while, we're lucky enough to have a quarterback controversy to keep ourselves occupied.

Let me clarify. When I say "we," I'm referring to the die-hards. I'm talking about the fans, real fans, who follow their college football team year-round. I'm talking about the people who don't miss a game and know which high school players are committed for next year. I'm talking about fans who watch, listen to, or read the transcript of the head coach's press conferences rather than waiting for the press clippings in the local paper the next day. I feel very confident including myself in this not-so-illustrious group. I consider myself someone who takes my college football a little too seriously.

Let me get it out of the way: I'm a Notre Dame fan. That means I've seen my share of ugly, disheartening football in my time. I was a kid the last time Notre Dame was a national power. That was when Lou Holtz stalked the sidelines for the Fighting Irish, laying down the law with a diminutive iron fist. I grew up in Chicago and I remember driving up to Delavan, Wisconsin, on the weekends to visit my grandparents. When my mom and sister and grandma went out to do whatever people who don't watch football do on a Saturday afternoon, I watched Notre Dame games on NBC with my grandpa. I didn't make a conscious choice to be a Notre Dame fan; it just happened. I've never stopped to question why I root for the Fighting Irish. And when college came around, attending another major Midwestern school—Marquette University—never shook my Irish fandom. (The fact that Marquette doesn't have a football team probably helped me sidestep any conflict of interest.) I really didn't give it too much thought when I started taking Notre Dame losses hard. I'm a die-hard fan. Thinking isn't required.

Midwest football has its share of true believers, but after years of reports about college football fans in the South trickled back to me, I started to see my fellow Midwesterners as comparatively tame. Fans down South are supposed to be a whole 'nother breed of fanatic. When I asked Southern transplants I knew in Chicago what makes college football fans down south so much more committed and impassioned, I never seemed to get a definitive answer. Usually, it came out something like this: "You have no idea. Until you've lived it, you can't possibly have any idea."

#21 Texas A&M vs. #9 South Carolina

August 28, 2014

Columbia, South Carolina

Scheduling the first weekend of the season was a no-brainer. South Carolina was a preseason top-10 team coming off three consecutive 11-win seasons, the only 11-win seasons in their 100-plus-year history. For their season opener they were squaring off against Texas A&M, a team playing its first game in the post-Johnny Manziel era. In case you haven't been on ESPN or TMZ the past couple years, Manziel is the Heisman Trophy-winning, hard-partying quarterback who put the Aggies back on the map nationally during their first two seasons in the SEC. #9-ranked South Carolina played #21 Texas A&M on a Thursday night in Columbia, South Carolina, and three hours down the road #12

Southbound Traveler

Georgia played #16 Clemson in Athens, Georgia, on the following Saturday afternoon. This power-packed one-two punch would make for a perfect trip initiation.

The drive from Chicago to Columbia spanned 800 miles over 13 hours. On the ride, I had plenty of time to get excited about the real journey ahead. But as I drove, initially, my thoughts rested in the past. Did I really quit my job and put all my possessions in storage? Is the hatchback of my Chevy actually filled with clothes and dry goods? Do my family and friends think I'm crazy? More importantly, am I crazy? An old Grateful Dead song[1] came on somewhere in Tennessee. The refrain blared as I turned the volume to full blast: *"Sure don't know / what I'm goin' for / but I'm gonna go for it / that's for sure."* As I sang along, a calm washed over me and I felt at ease. I turned to my right and noticed a pained look on my buddy Brandon's face; apparently my shrill, tone-deaf sounds didn't have the same calming effect on him.

Brandon tagged along for the first weekend of the trip. His defining characteristic is that he's an extreme extrovert, the kind of guy born to work in sales. I'm nowhere near as outgoing as Brandon; few people are. We're wired differently, but get along well. He'd always wanted to see SEC football, and I didn't object to company for the first week. So there we were. By the time we reached the place we were staying in Columbia,

---

[1] "Lost Sailor/Saint of Circumstance."

it was almost midnight. We met our Airbnb[2] hostess, Missy, and settled in for the night.

On the Tuesday before the game Brandon and I wandered around campus to get a feel for the university. Mopeds buzzed around South Carolina's campus like mosquitos at a summer bonfire. Mopeds cruising the streets, mopeds packed into bike racks with the front wheel chained, mopeds squeezed into tight parking spots between two cars. I've never seen so many mopeds in one place as I did on South Carolina's campus. Because fall semester was just underway, we happened upon a University-sponsored clubs and activities fair. Sawhorses blocked off either end of Greene Street and long fold-away tables lined both sides of the street. As representatives from various non-Greek service sororities, Bible studies, bowling societies, Frisbee-golf clubs, and improv troupes peddled their wares, students ambled about in Gamecock T-shirts, shorts, backwards caps, and backpacks while weaving in and out of conversations and picking up leaflets and pamphlets. More than anything, the scene made me feel like I'd missed out, especially since partying was the only extracurricular activity I picked up in college. It wasn't a full-blown regret. But still…

I walked through the Russell House bookstore where Gamecocks lined up two-dozen deep at the register, some purchasing textbooks but most grabbing new South Carolina gear. I was headed to meet up with a woman named Nancy at Starbucks to talk South Carolina football. We

---

[2] For so many reasons, Airbnb is how you want to find your lodging on the road. Between the access to insider information from locals, opportunity to meet new and interesting people, and chance to avoid corporate, cookie-cutter hotel and motel rooms, there are a million reasons to go Airbnb.

had begun chatting on one of the South Carolina football message boards over the summer and I thought she'd be a great introduction to Carolina football for a few reasons. First, she'd only recently moved to Columbia and become a USC fan, but the way she talked about the Gamecocks you'd think she was a backer from birth. Second, we grew up in the same neighborhood and attended the same grade school, St. Tarcissus[3], on the Northwest side of Chicago (albeit twenty-five years apart). I felt compelled to follow that "it's a small world" feeling and see where it led.

When she showed up at the coffee shop, Nancy had brought me a present: a metal drink bucket with an imprint of the South Carolina state tree, the palmetto, on the sides.[4] She had it custom made with the words "Fighting Gamecocks" printed on one side in garnet and "Fighting Irish" on the other in navy. Fresh-baked chocolate chip cookies and a little Cocky—the USC mascot—ornament sat inside the gift-wrapped bucket. I fumbled over my words. "Thank you" felt insufficient for such a heartfelt gesture, but I didn't know what else to say.

Nancy and her husband lived in Cleveland for thirty years before moving to Columbia four years ago. Going into her fifth football season, Nancy hasn't missed a home game yet. To be fair, it's probably easier to buy in when your team wins consistently. South Carolina finished each of the past three seasons ranked in the top-10, whereas I don't think Cleveland has been a playoff contender since Bernie Kosar. When she reminisced

---

[3] Shoutout to Raider Nation.

[4] Is it still Southern hospitality if she's only lived in the South a handful of years?

on thirty trying years as a Browns fan, I asked her what made being a Browns fan and a Gamecock fan different. "Well, we win—that helps. One thing here, you don't schedule weddings during football season unless it's on a bye week. And definitely don't die during the season; they might have to put you on ice until football's over in order to mourn you. Football is just so much more important here."

Right away, Nancy's wit and humor were apparent. It was also clear that she *gets it*: the indefinable something in Southern fans that makes them care about their team a little more than most other things in their lives. It flowed effortlessly from Nancy and seemed to linger around her like an aura. Clearly, a person needn't be born into this indefinable something to fully grasp it.

Like many fans, Nancy holds rites and rituals as inextricable parts of her game day experience. Among them are a carefully chosen, color-coordinated outfit and a weekly tailgate schedule. "It starts mid-summer, thinking about what I'm going to wear to the first game. I'll go through a few different outfits. This year I'm going with a garnet sundress and a black hat." But I realized the biggest draw for Nancy is that cheering for her team is an activity reminiscent of the past. It's "an old-time '50s or '60s innocent *Leave It To Beaver* enthusiasm," she explained. "The atmosphere is incredible."

The campy feel of bygone days is one of the main attractions for older fans coming back to the college game every fall. Another is the belief that their players are good guys on and off the field. Many college football enthusiasts cling to an undying certainty that their star athletes are great players and even better people. It's no different for Nancy, and it rang true in her words about the Gamecock players she's met over the years. "Jadaveon Clowney, Marcus Lattimore, Bruce Ellington, I've met all those boys and they're all very polite. 'Yes ma'am, no ma'am.' When I met Clowney at one of those 'meet the players' events, I told him, 'Make sure you go to class.' He just smiled and said 'Yes ma'am.'"

Her story made me laugh. A sweet, good-natured middle-aged lady walks up to this physical freak who runs a 4.5-second 40 yard dash[5] at 300 pounds, a surefire #1 pick in the NFL draft, and she tells him that school comes first. What else was he gonna say? Yes ma'am, indeed.

⚑

The most basic South Carolina football history lesson shows that winning is a relatively new phenomenon in Columbia. The Gamecocks spent decades toiling in the Atlantic Coast Conference (ACC) where many old-school fans felt they were treated like a redheaded stepchild by the North Carolina schools and Clemson, both on and off the field. Longtime Gamecocks still carry hatred and bitterness about being marginalized in the ACC. Younger Gamecocks don't remember what it was like watching South Carolina be the whipping boy in the conference, or their later stint as an independent, but for the older crowd the sense of persecution is acute. In fact, the only remnant younger fans seem to carry over from that era is a red-hot hatred for Clemson. If I could only take away one thing from my trip to South Carolina, it's that they despise Clemson. Of course, the feeling is mutual, and in terms of intrastate

---

[5] The average 40 time for NFL running backs, wide receivers and defensive backs is 4.5 seconds. The average time for NFL defensive ends is 4.8 seconds; for defensive tackles, five seconds.

feuds, this one rivals even Auburn—Alabama in it's all-encompassing fury.

Multiple Gamecock fans clued me in on how the animosity between the schools began. It seems the trouble started in 1890, when Ben Tillman became governor of South Carolina. Not a believer in the liberal arts education offered at USC, Tillman pushed for an agricultural and mechanical college in the state. According to Jerry Price, a lifelong South Carolinian, retired cop, self-published author and local historian, it happened like this: "To make a long story short, Clempson was created with the direct intention of destroying USC and this insanity seems to have become part of their DNA. Few, if any rivalries, can say that is the basis of it all. USC was reduced to 62 students, 2 professors, and barely had a plug nickel from the state to keep their doors open, while state labor was provided to build Clempson and a special fertilizer tax (no joke) to give Clempson extra money to thrive."

It's worth noting that nearly every Carolina fan I met pronounced Clemson as either *Clem-zinn* or *Clemp-son*. The idea is that Gamecock fans believe Clemson fans are so uneducated and ignorant that they cannot pronounce their own school's name without putting their own twang on it, changing the name in the process. This was my first real lesson in how Southern football represents much more than what we see on the field once a year. In effect, the schools have become symbols for long-standing differences and tensions within the state. Conflict between the upstate and the low country, farmers and wealthy planters, and agriculture and industry has been built into the core identities of the two schools. Those polarities serve as fuel to the fire.

While I was in town I also had the chance to talk to the aunt and sister of my friend Brittany from Chicago. Both attended South Carolina and bleed black and garnet. Susan graduated in 1977 and Holly in 2006. Even though they're from different generations, they still talk about Clempson the same way. Susan remembered a particularly heartbreaking loss when she was a senior, her vivid memories rolling back nearly 40 years later: "My dorm, Capstone, was painted with orange tiger paws, and I remember crying when Clempson won the game on a last-minute touchdown in '77. We camped outside the ticket office to ensure that we had tickets because legislators and other VIPs had to have tickets to that game." When I asked Holly about the rivalry, she touched on what it's looked like in recent years with the teams playing in different conferences: "The Carolina—Clempson rivalry is unlike any other. Carolina fans love taunting that the only reason Clempson has been seemingly good is because they are in such a weak conference. Clempson likes to make fun of Carolina and say we are the weak link in the SEC. The past few years we've proven otherwise."

⚑

On Wednesday morning, Brandon suggested taking a campus tour. I agreed because I still didn't know what experiences I would find useful along the way. It would take some weeks to train my senses. In the beginning, it was hard to recognize the meaningful and compelling things, and it took time to train myself to coldly discard things that held no value. During those first few weeks I picked up a lot of student newspapers and allowed what should have been two-minute exchanges to drag out into half-hour conversations.

We joined an 11 am tour with a half-dozen high school juniors and seniors and their parents. The guide took us around the main quad area of campus, the Horseshoe, a sprawling grassy area enclosed on three sides by various campus buildings. Included among them were a handful of original structures, still standing from the early 1800s, from when the school was South Carolina College. I spaced out for long portions of the tour, but tuned in when the guide recalled his favorite South Carolina memory. During his freshman year, in 2010, ESPN's *College Gameday* broadcast from Columbia before the school's matchup with Alabama, which was ranked number one. That Friday night, he and his buddies camped out in the Horseshoe to get inside the barricades and on TV for the broadcast the next morning. The campus was in a state of elation for days after Carolina knocked off the number one team in America. As he talked, his eyes glazed over and quickly drifted into a thousand-yard stare, like he was recalling his own on-field glory from years ago. My favorite part of the tour was near the end, when we stopped at a cafeteria to get lemonade and sweet tea. A student walked past Brandon and me with her lunch tray. She turned to us and gestured to the guide: "I've seen that guy passed out in a trash can on campus like three different times." Alright, alright. Welcome back to college.

Later that afternoon, we drove over to explore the Vista area of Columbia. While the college kids hang out in Five Points, Vista is for the post-collegiate crowd. Down Park St. and Lincoln St., one-and-two story red- and white-painted brick buildings populate either side as they intersect with US 1. We passed Pearlz Oyster Bar on the corner of Park, and Uncle Louie's farther down. Lincoln Street had that wonderful small town quality of cobblestoned streets and diagonal parking, and there was something subtly, almost indefinably cultured about this area of town. We ate dinner at Thirsty Fellow on Gadsden Street and then Brandon and I decided to check out the college bars near Five Points to see what was happening on a Wednesday night.

You wouldn't have known the season opener was less than twenty-four hours away at Jake's on Devine Street. In fact, you wouldn't have known it from any other night of the week. The back patio was packed by ten o'clock and a '90s cover band played Matchbox 20 and Train tunes while the crowd swayed and jumped their heels or talked over the noise. We walked around chatting up Carolina students and ended up at a table near the stage with a group of senior girls. Brandon told them I was writing a book on SEC football. Natalie, the girl to my left, raved about South Carolina and how it's the greatest school in the country and she wouldn't trade it for any other school. I kind of stopped listening, but think I remember how she decided to come to USC from Delaware or New Hampshire, some place in New England. She continued on in this ham-fisted way for a while. When she asked me if I was going to put what she was saying in my book, I made the decision right then to tell as few people as possible about my assignment. I wanted to interact with fans being themselves. Brandon, on the other hand, was loving this "writing a book" thing. Within an hour, he had talked to every good-looking girl on the patio telling them *he* was writing a book. I had to laugh. He struck out that night, but it wasn't for lack of effort.

A little after 11, we left Jake's and made our way to the state capitol building. Governor Nikki Haley had authorized the Texas A&M band leaders and fans to conduct their Midnight Yell Practice on the steps of the capitol. Midnight Yell Practice is a storied Texas A&M tradition, dating back nearly 100 years to a time when the school was a small, all-male military institution and freshmen would cheer for a losing football team. In time, however, the practice grew. At least a few thousand Aggie fans peopled the lawn in front of the State Capitol and the Yell

Leaders directed cheers from atop the front steps. According to one Aggie fan I met, the five yell leaders have full-on campus celebrity status for the year. "Oh, those guys get boy band ass for sure," he assured me.

When I asked Carolina fans, they suggested that Governor Haley would allow something like this because she's a Clempson grad. With fans, anything that goes against us must be orchestrated by some black hand and reinforces our sense of persecution. Look closely—you'll notice that sports fans are a conspiratorial bunch.

I noticed a thin beige statue just off the sidewalk on US 1, squared up dead center with the building it sat in front of. There was a palmetto in the front, and a man wearing a soldier's cap resting a musket on his right shoulder. Behind the statue, a Confederate flag lay still in the thick late-evening heat. I wondered how it was that a Confederate flag still flew on state capitol grounds.[6] Did I miss something? Some thirty yards in the distance stood the dull beige-grey capitol building. Vertical columns atop the staircase and a faded brownish-copper dome served as the backdrop for my introduction to one of the strangest traditions in American sports.

---

[6] This was all before the racially motivated shooting at the Emanuel African Methodist Episcopal Church in Charleston, South Carolina, in June 2015, and the subsequent outcry that led to the flags permanent removal from the capitol the next month. Also worth noting: the Confederate flag first went up at the capitol in April 1961 to mark the 100-year anniversary of the Civil War's beginning.

South Carolina fans turned out en masse as well and dueling chants battled throughout the Yell Practice. A large black pickup truck on oversized tires circled the block around the capitol every couple minutes, rolling by slowly and blaring the cheesy pop-electronica hit "Sandstorm" every time it passed. The Aggie fans mostly prevailed, but the back and forth was its own little college football-eve carnival.

"Game. Cocks. Game. Cocks."

The Texas A&M yell leaders shuffled in unison on the steps of the capitol with the choreographed precision of a Beyoncé music video, signaling the upcoming chant to the A&M fans amassed below.

"Beat The Hell Out Of South Carolina. Aaaaaa. Whoooo."

Not to be outdone, Carolina students clustered on the bottom left corner of the stairs, starting a new frenzied chant every time another well-executed Aggie chant ended.

"What's an Aggie? What's an Aggie?"

Just as fans were getting charged up, the energy of the chants echoing off the Capitol Building and into an otherwise quiet Wednesday night, it was over. Midnight Yell Practice had lasted less than half-an-hour and as I walked away, I scratched my head trying to figure out what the hell I had just witnessed. Two middle-aged Columbia cops stood on the fringes of the crowd. I passed them on my way out and asked "Do other teams have stuff like this when they come to play Carolina?" The officer with a mustache shook his head. "Son, I've never seen anything like that my entire life."

⚐

Despite their respective 100-plus-year histories, South Carolina and Texas A&M had never played each other in football. Texas A&M was a part of the Big XII for nearly two decades and before that they were charter members of the Southwest Conference. Meanwhile, South Carolina was independent in football for 20 years between 1971 and 1991, before joining the SEC in 1992. Prior to that, South Carolina was a founding member of the ACC.

While both Carolina and A&M joined the SEC as expansion members, their entrances couldn't have been more different, at least judging by on-field performance. Texas A&M's introduction to the conference was a proclamation shouted from the rooftops: they entered a bone-crushing SEC West in 2012 and nearly ran the gauntlet, beating No. 1-ranked Alabama in Tuscaloosa on their way to an 11-win season. Not so with Carolina, which took nine years to finish a season above .500 in conference play. The first years were hard. Susan remembered a Kentucky reporter talking about how South Carolina was an embarrassment to the conference, and she conceded the reporter was right. "I even remember when beating Kentucky and Vanderbilt were big wins," she said.

The most important thing to know about Carolina football—after the Clemson hatred—is that decades of defeat have made victory taste that much sweeter. The Gamecocks have only finished nine seasons in their history ranked in the top-25 in either the AP or Coaches Poll, and four of those finishes happened over the previous four seasons before my trip—all under coach Steve Spurrier. Think about it: the best season in the history of Carolina football happened in 2011, then again in 2012, and again in 2013.

It would make sense that a school with a history of losing might not know how to deal with sudden success. Old habits die hard, and having an defeatist mentality goes hand in hand with losing every fall. Perhaps, but I didn't encounter any fans who looked at the recent success with a sense of impending doom, as if the program Spurrier built up was a house of cards set to come crashing down at any moment. I also didn't encounter any fans obnoxiously flaunting that their team was finally good, acting like they'd never been to the end zone before. I was surprised by how Gamecock fans seemed to be taking it all in stride.

The old saying goes that success knows a thousand fathers,[7] but in Columbia the credit for Carolina's sudden rise is almost exclusively heaped on the shoulders of the Ol' Ball Coach. It's hard not to like Steve Spurrier. He's a quick-witted straight shooter who has no issue firing shots at anyone he thinks deserves one, whether it be an opposing coach, member of the media, his own player or even an opposing one. In an era where coach-speak is as constrained and evasive as any polished political speech, there's no way to look at Spurrier's cavalier attitude as anything but refreshing and funny. Unless, of course, you're the one being peppered by his quick jabs.[8]

As a college quarterback, Spurrier won the Heisman Trophy with Florida in 1966. Returning to his alma mater as head coach in 1990, he led the Gators to six SEC championships and a national championship in 1997. After a brief and unsuccessful stint with the Washington Redskins in the NFL, Spurrier came to Columbia in 2005 with the goal of

---

[7] The proverb, attributed to many throughout the course of history, is "Victory knows a thousand fathers, but failure is an orphan."

[8] After a fire at an Auburn dormitory destroyed some twenty books, Spurrier quipped: "But the real tragedy was that fifteen hadn't been colored yet."

raising the bottom-dwelling Gamecocks from the scrap heap. And though it took a few years, that's exactly what he did.

It was muggy with the temperature already in the low-90s by 10 am on game day. I stopped at the Starbucks in Vista, and while I was there, I met a woman in her mid-twenties named Jenny. She was all dolled up for the game in a white sleeveless top and garnet miniskirt. So it was easy to talk with her at the counter, even though I wasn't "writing a book." We made casual conversation for about twenty minutes. She shared a couple stories about memorable games she attended during undergrad and how being a fan changes after graduation. She explained that non-student tickets are more expensive, so she doesn't go to all the games anymore. Tailgating and watching the game on a big-screen in the parking lot apparently can be just as fun as passing through the turnstiles. We traded numbers and made plans to meet up later that night after the game.

Brandon explored campus while I went for coffee. When I returned to meet him, he was talking to a guy who hailed from Naperville, a suburb of Chicago. An affable fellow in his late forties, Jim was more than happy to talk Gamecock football and recount how he ended up moving to Columbia. Before we left, he gave us his parking pass for a lot right across from Williams-Brice Stadium and next to Gamecock Park. He said he'd be riding his bike to the game and didn't need the pass. I thought that was an insane idea in 97-degree heat, but I was also grateful for the prime parking spot. It'd only been two days, but I was already starting to believe in Southern hospitality.

Two things were clear to me by noon: the sleepy feel around campus Wednesday had been replaced by a palpable game day buzz, and I was sweating profusely. I needed a cold shower, change of clothes, Gatorade, and massive amounts of Gold Bond. We went back to Missy's house and while there, convinced her to come to the game with us. Missy was a USC grad student and undergrad alum. Somehow, though, she'd never been to a South Carolina football game. Never. I think we found the only USC student in the Spurrier era to never attend a game. So, the three of us headed over to Williams-Brice Stadium three hours before kickoff. Traffic was already bumper-to-bumper all throughout Columbia. Missy sent us zigzagging down back streets in hopes of beating the rush. After a half hour, we gave up and parked on a side street, handing off the parking pass to a car at the next stop sign and walking the rest of the way.

Brandon and I dropped Missy off at the fairgrounds to meet up with some of her family while we headed to Gamecock Park for the Gamecock Walk. Most schools have a similar game day ritual: as the team walks through to the stadium, adoring fans line both sides of a walkway stretching hundreds of yards. While I waited for the team with the masses, twin sisters in black dresses and pearls standing next to me told me they were texting their friends on the team, telling them to walk left when the opened gates form a little fork in the sidewalk. When I asked about their friends on the team, they rattled off a who's who: Gerald Dixon and Gerald Dixon Jr. (half-brothers with different mothers who both started on the defensive line), quarterback Dylan Thompson, and receiver and return man Pharoh Cooper. One of the twins offered: "They're cool. They're normal guys and, like, they don't try to hit on us all the time." Great story, ladies.

I didn't recognize any players by face, but I instantly recognized Coach Spurrier. The man struts with an easy swagger. Even if you knew nothing about South Carolina football, and saw all the middle-aged men walking by surrounded by the hulking twenty-year-olds in their coats and ties, you'd almost certainly point Spurrier out of the crowd and say to yourself, "That's the head coach. No doubt about it." As he walked past us, I let out a "Hey, Ball Coach!" He looked over and nodded at me. Steve Spurrier made me feel cool by just giving me the nod. A couple steps later, he saw someone he knew and gave the guy the wink and the gun. Ol' Ball Coach might be my favorite college football personality. Unless he's been making your team and coach look foolish for a couple decades—here's looking at you, Tennessee fans[9]—you can't help but respect the coach and be entertained by his personality.

After the team passed through and the crowd dispersed, still a good two hours before kickoff, I wandered through Gamecock Park. I looked halfheartedly for where the SEC Network crew set up their pregame show, but instead I found 1980 Heisman Trophy winner George Rogers doing a live segment on the Gamecock Radio Network. Right before commercial break, the host bragged on Rogers—the person, not the player—how he's always outgoing and kind, and never impatient or frustrated by fans seeking autographs, handshakes, or pictures. He's put his celebrity to good use, too, starting the George Rogers Foundation

---

[9] Conferences have various bowl game tie-ins. The SEC had ties to the Sugar and Citrus Bowls in the 1990s, when Spurrier coached at Florida. Essentially, the Sugar Bowl was the premier game for SEC schools and the Citrus Bowl was the consolation prize. In one legendary dig meant to point out Tennessee's notable lack of appearances in the top game, Spurrier famously quipped: "You can't spell Citrus without U-T."

of the Carolinas, which provides students in need with college scholarships. (He charges for autographs and directs the money to the foundation.) When he stepped off stage during a commercial, I introduced myself and asked if he'd take a picture with me. True to form, he was as gregarious a fellow as you'd want to meet.

Rogers remains a Gamecock legend for good reason. He's still the only Heisman winner in South Carolina history and his number 38 was retired at halftime during his last home game in 1980. I did a double take when he told me that. His number was retired while he was still an active player? Has that ever happened anywhere else in the history of college football? He let me try on his Heisman Trophy ring and his Super Bowl ring from the 1987 Washington Redskins. Short of having earned them myself, what more could I want as a football fan?

Back in the fairgrounds parking lots, grills and pop-up tents stretched across the asphalt in every direction. Half-devoured snacks and platters rested in the back of oversized pickup trucks. Grown men and women stood holding beers in one hand while throwing bags with the other.[10] They all had the same look fixed on their faces. Imagine the exuberance of a little kid waking up on Christmas morning, and the smile bursting forth from his or her lips. That's how everyone looked to me. Everyone.

The sun beat down and sweat dripped off my face as I moseyed through a blur of black and garnet. I stopped to talk with an older gentleman named John, a 67-year-old Columbia native. When I asked him what

---

[10] They were playing the outdoor drinking game known in other places as "cornhole." I guess.

it's like seeing Carolina win after living through decades of mediocrity, he said the recent surge of on-field success would have his father and his father's friends—all Columbia-born-and-raised, all life-long South Carolina supporters—spinning in their graves in disbelief: "No way would they believe it. A top-10 team? No way. I can hardly believe it." The program's newfound success has to be all the more rewarding for the older fans, the ones who remember twenty years of limbo as a football independent, and being kicked around in the ACC before that.

I found Missy and Brandon back at the tailgate with Missy's extended family. Everyone introduced themselves simultaneously and I promptly forgot almost all their names. Missy's stepbrother Garrett and I chatted for a while. He's been coming to games since he was a toddler, but hadn't been back in a few years because he moved out of state and started a family. He told me about how Gamecock Park and all the improved tailgating lots and condos around the stadium are relatively new. "All this industrial land was purchased to be razed so Williams-Brice could become the tailgate hub it is today." This development, incidentally, began around the same time the Gamecocks joined the SEC in the early '90s.

When I asked him about the decked-out rail cars I'd seen walking past the back side of the stadium, Garrett explained that I had come across a "Cockaboose." "[It's] the biggest thing in Carolina tailgating. There's no real equivalent anywhere else in college football." Sadly, I never made my way inside one of these converted party vessels, so I had to rely on word of mouth. The descriptions I heard from Gamecocks on my two trips to Columbia were as different as if I'd asked them about their favorite football memory. That's because each Cockaboose is individually owned and has it's own style and flair. The consensus, though, seems to be that no expense is spared in outfitting these lavish tailgating hubs for the "who's who" of the Gamecock Nation.

Brandon, Missy, and I headed toward the stadium about forty-five minutes before kickoff. Brandon picked up an upper-deck ticket for $40 from a middle-aged man who had an extra. A good rule of thumb is to look for a middle-aged man or woman standing by themselves near the stadium—they're either waiting for someone or they have an extra ticket. If they're holding, you won't pay more than face value for the ticket they're looking to get rid of. Missy and I picked up a pair from a scalper outside the stadium for $70 each. The tickets were five dollars over face value on the 40-yard line, fifth row.

I didn't buy tickets in advance for most of the games I attended for two reasons: First, as a matter of practicality, tickets tend to be more expensive before the season. Most fans convince themselves their team will have a banner year and all conference home games will be marquee events. (The secondary ticket markets on StubHub and Vivid Seats well reflect this reasoning/delusion.) Once the season starts rolling and teams fall out of the top-25, ticket prices fall, too. Second, I knew showing up without tickets and having to figure out the best way into each game would add to the thrill of my trip. Something about going with the flow appealed to me.

Upon entering Williams-Brice, stadium employees handed out little white towels. Though I didn't understand at the time, by kickoff I knew why. As "Sandstorm"[11] started playing. 85,000-plus fans stood up on their bleacher seats and most waved their towels overhead. There's a saying about Williams-Brice Stadium: "If it's a-swayin', they're playin'." The entire upper deck appeared to swing a half-foot in either direction in those last few seconds before kickoff. The building bubbled over with the anticipation of a new season and all the expectations that go with being a preseason top-10. Before I knew it, my whole body had goosebumps and I realized I'd been jumping up and down on the bleachers for a solid minute, ready for kickoff just as if I bled black and garnet, as if I'd been counting the days since last January.

The only way kill the pulse in a stadium like Williams-Brice is to quiet the crowd, and the only way to quiet the crowd is to beat up on the home team early. It'd been a few years since this last happened. In fact, South Carolina hadn't lost a home game since Auburn knocked off the Gamecocks 16-13 in 2011. (Since the loss, South Carolina had won 18 straight home games.) However, on this night the Aggies took the fight to the Gamecocks. From the first drive, Texas A&M Quarterback

---

[11] After witnessing this, my bizarre run in with the song at Yell Practice made much more sense. The 2001 techno song serves as Carolina's unofficial anthem. It all began in 2009, when the song accidentally played over the sound system late in the fourth quarter during an upset victory against No. 4 Ole Miss. The crowd went ballistic. And the rest, as they say, is history.

Kenny Hill[12] marched the Aggie offense down the field for score after score without much resistance. The result was a record-breaking night. South Carolina allowed the most yards they've ever allowed in a game. A&M's sophomore signal-caller seemed to answer all sorts of questions about filling Johnny Manziel's[13] shoes. Hill completed 40 passes for 511 yards, breaking Manziel's single-game record. The Aggies won 52–28.

Looking across the field early in the fourth quarter to the stands behind the Gamecock sidelines was, in a word, depressing. Small clusters of fans remained in the stands watching the end of a game that had long been decided. Nights like these are hard on fans, which is something most casual sports fans and almost all non-sports fans can't fully grasp. There's an emptiness, a pit in your stomach, that eats at you as a fan when your team endures two types of losses: heartbreaking last-second losses that leave you replaying crucial moments, wondering what might've been; and soul-crushing, over-by-halftime blowout losses that send you reeling, looking for either people to blame or shreds of positivity to help soften the blow and give you hope for the rest of the season. Tonight's game was clearly in the latter camp.

As the final seconds ticked away, Texas A&M played ball control and marched ever-so-slowly down to the South Carolina 2-yard-line where

---

[12] aka Kenny Trill, aka Trill Hill. Hill lost his starting job later in the season, and has since transferred to TCU.

[13] aka Johnny Football, aka Billy Vegas. He's a former Heisman Trophy winner whose life has begun to resemble a cautionary tale.

the game ended. I couldn't help but feel a sort of empathy for these Gamecock fans. I could relate. I've seen Notre Dame blown out of a National Championship game, looking like a high school team most of the night. I've seen Notre Dame lose to Michigan in the last thirty seconds three years in a row. Michigan![14] And I couldn't help but channel some of the Gamecock fans' anxieties as I watched in dismay from the stands: *Is the season screwed? Are they that good or are we that bad? Where in the hell were our running game and our defense? Where do we go from here?*

Early in the game, a mix of Aggie and Gamecock fans nearby sparred playfully about early pass interference calls and whose new freshmen receivers and defensive backs would be playmakers. By the end, Missy and I were surrounded by Ags. A pair of brothers from Dallas raved about how bright the A&M future looked with a sophomore quarterback who just threw for 500 yards, and two freshmen wide receivers in Ricky Seals-Jones and Speedy Noil, who are "only going to get better."

Listening to these Ags talk, it occurred to me that they were high on potential. The game hadn't even ended and they were already dreaming bigger dreams. It was in the way their eyes lit up. I'd never noticed it before, but looking back through my interactions with sports fans over the course of my life, I realized this kind of fantasizing is *always there*. As fans, we allow ourselves to become intoxicated on the promise and hope of better things to come. Win a big game, and all of a sudden we're thinking about a national championship. Quarterback has a big game,

---

[14] There are few things in the world I hate more than Michigan football. I know it's irrational. They never did anything to me personally. But still…

and all of a sudden we're thinking about two Heisman Trophies in three years. Team wins a national championship, and all of a sudden we're disappointed if the coach doesn't deliver one every year.

After a big win, the Five Points area is swamped with college kids out partying and Vista is swarmed with overserved grown-ups. But after a loss? I didn't want to wade through the gloomy atmosphere and midnight laments. Jenny, the girl I'd met at Starbucks, texted me that she was too bummed to go out. Somehow, I didn't think she was the only one.

Missy and I found Brandon sitting on a golf cart with an elderly couple. They were well into their 80s and had driven all the way from El Paso to see their Aggies win. (In a different vehicle, presumably.) If nothing else, I was happy that old couple didn't have to drive eighteen hours home after a loss. Missy, Brandon and I went out for BBQ—pulled pork sandwiches with the Carolina-style vinegar-based BBQ sauce—and headed home.

Home that night was the guest bedroom in Missy's one-story Columbia house. The next night it would be another guest bedroom in another stranger's home, this time in Athens. A week before it had been a comfortable queen-size pillow-top on the South Side of Chicago. My concept of home had already changed.

#16 Clemson vs. #12 Georgia

August 30th, 2014

Athens, Georgia

In the morning, before Brandon and I headed for Athens, we grabbed coffee with Missy. The three of us traded opinions about the game. The crazy fans stuck out to all of us, and Brandon and I noted how there really did seem to be a different energy—another level of excitement and buzz around the game—than either of us was accustomed to up north. For her part, Missy said she finally understood what all the hype was about. And even though she didn't plan on becoming a fan, she was happy she finally attended a football game. After thanking our hostess for her hospitality, we set off for Athens. Neither of us had any cell phone reception through miles of two-lane highway and no real way of knowing if we'd missed our next turn. We crept slowly through kitschy small towns along the way, like Washington-Wilkes, Georgia. The excursion made small-town living look pleasant. I pictured myself resting easy in a wicker-backed rocking chair, sipping homemade tea and waiting for the Braves game to come on TV. I found myself drifting off and imagining a simpler way of life as we rolled past a baseball diamond, the town square and City Hall. But I was still anxious about that missed turn.

When we rolled into downtown Athens around 5 pm, we found parking and started walking. Across Hancock and down College Avenue, back down Broad and up Lumpkin Street, we wandered aimlessly, people watching. Alumni were back to see their old stomping grounds and reminisce with friends, and families ate dinner on patios. It's a different, more laid-back atmosphere than after 10 pm when the UGA student body takes over downtown.

As we passed the Georgia Theatre on Lumpkin, the marquee read: **KENNY CHESNEY SOLD OUT.** I had no idea Kenny Chesney was going to be in town, and no idea why he'd be playing such a tiny venue. But sometimes it's better to not ask questions. I stood outside drinking an iced coffee, making small talk with the door man while he checked IDs and put 21-and-over wristbands on concert goers. I noticed he didn't seem to be checking the wristband tickets nearly as carefully as he was checking IDs and applying separate wristbands for drinkers. So when I finished my coffee, I walked around the barricade, said "I'm not drinking tonight, buddy," and he waved me in.

Brandon followed my lead and we stood there trying to figure out what had just happened. I half-convinced myself we would see a live video feed of his concert somewhere else, or someone would discover that we weren't wearing wristbands and make us leave. But instead, we found a corner spot less than thirty feet from the stage. The Georgia Theatre is a standing-room only venue on the bottom floor with an upper balcony that holds half a dozen high-top bar tables. The official capacity is 859, so for an artist who sells out arenas, this was a notably intimate setting. As we waited for the show to start, I pieced together the scene from a couple of Georgia undergrads. At 11 am, the theatre announced that a private show was going to be filmed for Country Music Television (CMT). Free wristbands were handed out to the first 600 people in line at 1 pm. The crowd was packed with students.

If you've ever seen *The Color Orange: The Condredge Holloway Story* or *Boys of Fall*, the ESPN documentaries Chesney produced, it's clear he has a great love and reverence for college football. So it was probably no coincidence Chesney chose the eve of the first college football Saturday of the season to put on the show. Between songs, the crowd began to chant:

> *"I said it's great—to be—a Georgia Bulldog*
>
> *I said it's great—to be—a Georgia Bulldog"*

and

> *"U-G-A, U-G-A, U-G-A, U-G-A, U-G-A, U-G-A"*

"Ain't no doubt where we are tonight," Chesney quipped when the cheers finally died down. And—just to be sure you got the message—he closed out the roaring two-hour set with "The Boys of Fall." What you've heard on the radio doesn't compare to what Chesney belted out in the Georgia Theatre. Nobody in that room happened upon downtown Athens Friday night by accident. They descended upon Athens for the start of another college football season carrying with them all the hopes and dreams that go along with it. Officially, this show may have been filmed for a CMT special that Chesney was probably paid a lot of money to do, but for everyone there, including ESPN commentators Brad Nessler and Todd Blackledge, (who got their own shout outs during the set), this show was meant to ring in the return of football.

By the time we stepped back into the Athens night, it was a completely different place than the one we'd left a few hours earlier. We wandered through downtown, stopping in various bars and talking to gorgeous Georgia girls showing off their pearly-white smiles and suntanned legs in miniskirts. I tried to pretend those soft breathy Georgia accents weren't the sexiest things I'd ever heard, but they could've been quoting the book of Leviticus or reading me my Miranda rights and I still would've been into it. But as the night wore on toward eleven, toward midnight, it started to feel like my elbows were pinned to my ribs everywhere I walked. Most Athens bars are jam-packed on a game weekend, with lines out the door and around the corner. At one bar, Bourbon Street, girls were standing on tables as if waiting for a song they liked so they could dance, and a guy was so drunk his buddies were taking turns slapping him in the face. He had no idea who was slapping him and didn't seem to care much. After wading through human traffic for ten minutes to get to the back of the bar, we turned around and shuffled out.

❧

A secluded back-road farmhouse some five miles from campus would be our Airbnb rental this time. The drive to the house took us down a quarter mile of hilly red dirt and gravel road with wild, knee-high grass and weeds growing on both sides. The family that hosted us had this wonderful quality of being both outgoing and friendly, and unobtrusive at the same time. They showed Brandon and me to our beds, pointed out the coffeemaker, offered us sweet tea, and then carried on with their day. Saturday morning found me in the living room playing Kenny Chesney's "Summertime" over and over again on one of the guitars the family had lying around. After breakfast, I put on my loud green Notre Dame t-shirt and we returned to campus.

Stepping through packed parking lots a mile away from Sanford Stadium, we experienced our first true all-out SEC tailgate. Trucks with small hitched trailers lined the lots, and pop-up tents provided shade on another mid-90s day. From the very start, people were poking fun at my shirt. Typical greetings included: "Hey buddy, I think you're at the wrong game," "You're in the wrong state, feller," and "Gonna see some real football today, son." I think the thing I liked best about Georgia was that nobody was mean or malicious in heckling me for wearing an ND shirt. It all seemed playful in the same way that we'd see an stuffed orange tiger hanging from the awning of somebody's tent or a stuffed bulldog standing with it's leg lifted to piss on a Clemson helmet and laugh. Granted, wearing the wrong colors makes people a little leery when you walk up to their tailgate with a smile. But at the same time, it was an easy way to strike up a conversation and let people know I was a man without a country down here.

An enthusiastic older guy named Bill flagged me down when he saw an ND shirt passing by. Bill spoke in a measured cadence, and his left hand would knife-edge the open palm of his right whenever he wanted to make a point. Though I never asked what he did, I pictured him sporting a black robe and carrying a gavel. He hailed from Georgia but went to school at Notre Dame in the early '70s during the Ara Parseghian era. He told me about being both a Georgia fan and a Notre Dame fan and about his experience living up north: "I wouldn't trade it for anything. But I moved back after graduation. Haven't left since. Never saw another South Bend winter." I asked him about the 1980 Sugar Bowl where Georgia defeated Notre Dame 17–10 to win the national championship: "That one was tough, pulled at my heart strings a bit, but I was for Georgia because they had a chance to be national champs," he said. "Notre Dame still wouldn't have won it all if they won that game."

Bill tossed a mini-football in Georgia colors with his seven- or eight-year-old grandson outside their family tailgate as we chatted about Notre Dame and Georgia's upcoming home and home.[15] But I felt uncomfortable, though, interrupting that family moment, so I excused myself and found Brandon a couple tailgates over with some recent Georgia grads. It wasn't quite a scratch-and-stop-the-turntable-everybody-turn-and-look moment when I walked up, but it wasn't far off either. I don't remember exactly what was said, but the group didn't utter more than a few words, something to the effect of "Explain yourself, Notre Dame." On cue, I gave my elevator pitch: "I'm from Chicago. Grew up a big ND fan, but I want to see what all the SEC hype is about." And that was all it took for them to take me in. "Oh. Nice, dude. Welcome. It's everything you heard, and then some."

Throughout the season I found that time and again my standard "I wanted to see what it's all about" line was the only explanation necessary. Sometimes I thought Southern hospitality impelled people to warm up

---

[15] A two-game series between schools who don't normally play each other. In 2017, Notre Dame will host the Bulldogs. Georgia plays host to the Irish in 2019.

to me. Other times I thought my out-of-place T-shirt gave them an opportunity to brag on their team, school and town to someone who didn't know about them, like it was an opening to be a teacher on a subject matter they were an expert on. Looking back, it was probably both.

What impressed me about this group was that they had their tailgate game locked down despite being only twenty-four or twenty-five. Most were only two years out of school yet they'd held the same pregame spot since the 2012 opener. Graduation becomes a rite of passage that allows an alum to start claiming their own turf away from the residence halls and frat tailgates. Just like a toddler in a plastic Georgia helmet and jersey or mini-cheerleading outfit is the seedling that inevitably becomes a fanatical Bulldog as a grown-up, the young alumni tailgaters who claim a spot in their mid-twenties are the seedlings that grow a tailgating tradition for new families as the grads get married and have little Bulldog babies of their own. Surely, the Bulldog babies will be outfitted in plastic Georgia helmets and jerseys and cheerleading outfits. The cycle will have begun anew, the circle of life spinning around a black and red G-shaped sun. I'm not sure why all this occurred to me while we stood around chit-chatting. Sometimes I'm glad people don't know what I'm thinking about while I talk to them.

After wandering on, Brandon and I and found ourselves atop a small hill at another tailgate. Maureen, a mother in her fifties, and her daughter Caroline (mid-twenties) greeted us and invited us into the shade of their red Bulldog tent. Like the tailgaters down the hill, the family claims the same spot for every home game. Maureen explained that "there are no reserved spots—you get the same tailgate spot you've always had because you can get here early enough." She attended grad school at Georgia from 1980 to 1982, which means that she was around to witness the Great One.[16] Herschel Walker represents the peak of Georgia football: he was both a 1980 national champion as a freshman and the 1982 Heisman Trophy winner. Georgia Bulldog football fans have waited patiently for the Second Coming of Herschel ever since.

Maureen recalled Walker's first game and spared no details in explaining that it only took one play to realize Georgia had a once-in-a-generation talent in their backfield. I didn't know the particulars, but I knew the moment she was referring to; I'd seen the highlight over the years.[17] Georgia won the game by a point and, more importantly, Maureen was hooked on Georgia football from that day forward.

Caroline graduated from Georgia, too, in 2011. As she fixed plates of breakfast biscuits with sausage, hot dogs, baked beans, and boiled peanuts for Brandon and me, she explained that she lived in Washington, DC, but still had Georgia season tickets. Apparently, boiled peanuts are a big thing in the South, Georgia in particular. They were mushy and a little warm but I enjoyed them. My attention fixed on the interactions between mother and daughter, the two generations of Georgia fan, as they shared various Georgia football anecdotes. Caroline would start

---

[16] A subjective sports term, admittedly, whose definition changes depending on the speaker's preferences and biases.

[17] September 6, 1980: Georgia trails Tennessee 15–2 at halftime. Herschel Walker enters in the 2nd half and tramples All-SEC safety Bill Bates on his way to the end zone to spark a 16–15 comeback victory. Welcome to college.

into a story about her time as an undergrad, and halfway through Maureen would fill in missing details with her own exclamatory gestures. It was touching in a way that I couldn't quite comprehend.

We met a few other people around the tailgate, including a boy who was still in high school. When I asked him where he was thinking about going to college, everybody within earshot laughed. Dumb question, I guess. When it was time to head over for the Dawg Walk, we thanked them for their hospitality and took off through asphalt-topped lots and down railroad tracks lined with beer pong tables and other bric-a-brac native to the makeshift collegiate tailgate. There was no need for directions with Sanford Stadium in the distance as our North Star.

Brandon and I split up. I walked across the Sanford Drive bridge and down the stairs toward the cleared path for the Dawg Walk. People scurried to find spots, and I found a place without anybody in front of me. To my right stood two women in their late fifties or early sixties. Bev and Jackie were the type of ladies who'd been saying "It's five o'clock somewhere" before the expression became popular. The three of us talked for the whole hour as we waited for the football team's procession into the stadium. All the while, I kept thinking that their natural habitat was lounging poolside on some cruise ship sipping tropical drinks. For all the party girl in their DNA, they proved quite knowledgeable and provided historical background on the Georgia Redcoat Band as the tubas and drums lined up in front of us and began to play. When the players walked through in sport coats and ties carrying their helmets and shoulder pads, the ladies pointed out their favorites and informed me who was primed for a breakout season.

Despite both being married, Bev and Jackie shared a pair of season tickets on the 30-yard line, 30 rows up. They'd been buying tickets together for over a decade, and unless one of them can't make it, they leave their husbands home on Saturdays. When I asked why their husbands don't come to the games and what they do on Saturdays instead, one of the ladies offered: "My husband's not from Georgia. He doesn't get it. He's probably doing yard work, or out golfing, or out drinking. I don't know. Who cares?" Marriage is all about compromise, they assured me, but they're unwilling to compromise their fall Saturdays under any circumstances. I got a good chuckle from their candid responses. Having left their men at home, the women felt free to share their love for wide receiver Malcolm Mitchell. They asked me if I'd seen the video where Mitchell joined a book club with a bunch of middle-aged white ladies—that could easily have been either of them—so he could better himself as a reader. I had seen it. It's definitely one of those feel-good stories where a student-athlete makes an extra effort to improve themselves off the field. Bev and Jackie mooned over Mitchell as he passed by; they might as well have been 12-year-old girls giddy over the Beatles first setting foot in America in 1964. Then they told me about wide receiver Chris Conley and how he's on the student-athlete advisory committee that works with the NCAA, and that he's an honor student, and this and that. The duo loved who their Georgia Bulldogs were just as much off the field as on it. I suppose a community doesn't rally around a college football team if it's only about football.

Sure, for the average fan the passion revolves around the game itself, but the die-hards are always looking for additional reasons to be proud of their squad. The clearest and most frequent example is when fans talk up the "great player, better person" type. Fans revel in bragging on the star athlete who's also a good ambassador for the school both during and after their playing days. It's like the pride a parent has for their own kids' accolades: they don't see any accomplishments as quite their own, but they sure are pleased.

Forty-five minutes before kickoff, I found a middle-aged man standing by himself holding a single ticket inconspicuously at his right shoulder. When I approached him, he only wanted face value for the ticket. $40.[18] I have no idea how Georgia's ticket prices can possibly stay so low, but that's another matter altogether. Mine was a lower bowl seat, two over from the aisle that separated season ticket holders from the student section, starting on the visitors' 25-yard line. The man had two extra tickets and told me he preferred to find fans and sell them for face value rather than making twenty bucks' profit selling to scalpers who would turn around and make an additional sixty. I recognized that there was something symbolic couched in this gesture, even though I never found the words to explain exactly what it was. I wish I'd stayed and talked to the man for a while.

When I arrived at my seat, I found the holder of the other extra ticket. I didn't learn Roger's name until after the game. And it took a while for him to warm up to me, a green shirt in a sea of red. The Georgia band finished their pregame performance and cleared the way for the players to come out of the tunnel four minutes before kickoff. The hook from Elton John's "Saturday Night's Alright (For Fighting)" blared over the loudspeakers and the crowd went ballistic.

"Saturday, Saturday, Saturday, Saturday, Saturday, Saturday, Saturday, Saturday, Saturday night's alright."

---

[18] Easily the cheapest face-value ticket in the SEC.

Something happened to me in that moment. Something very much like what I experienced at kickoff inside Williams-Brice Stadium, yet somehow different. I think I became a Georgia Bulldog fan right then and there. At the very least, I knew I was a Bulldog fan that day.[19] My eyes scanned the stadium, tens of thousands of red pom-poms hurtling forward and back and forward again as one. I made eye contact with Roger and said, "Man, this is somethin'." He didn't say a word, just nodded his head forward and back and forward again. And he smiled.

As the team took the field for the first time in 2014, questions seemed to linger in the air: Will Todd Gurley II bring a Heisman back to Athens for the first time in 32 years? Will this finally be the year that Head Coach Mark Richt gets over the hump and wins a national championship? Or will another supremely talented Georgia team underperform and finish 9–3 when they should've finished 11–1?

A minute before kickoff, the Who's "Baba O'Riley" blared through the stadium, each note on the piano sharp and clear. I felt that song in my bones, like the first time I heard it when I was 13. My eyes scanned the stadium again. This was the precise moment football fans live for: right before kickoff, when anything is possible. A division championship, an SEC Championship, a national championship, it's all attainable. The reality of losing hasn't stamped out anyone's dreams of perfection. You can't be in that moment and not be affected by it.

---

[19] Two years later, I still have the same response to hearing this song on the radio. I turn it to full blast and I'm transported back to Sanford Stadium. Before I know it my whole body is covered in goose bumps. Every. Single. Time.

After the game started, Roger and I began to turn to each other and discuss what was happening or fist-bump after a big play. Roger was an inherently likable individual. He was a fifty-something, barrel-shaped gruff biker type with a tight goatee, and his eyes bulged whenever he got excited. He made both painfully obvious observations about the game and comments that demonstrated a fair amount of situational awareness, such as "They need to give Gurley the ball" and "If they stop 'em here, they'll get that punt about the 40-yard line and they're in business." The thing I'll always remember about Roger was the glee he expressed after Todd Gurley's kickoff return for a touchdown. His jowls stretched back to reveal an irrepressible yellow-toothed smile; his glee was positively child-like. Not thirty seconds before Clemson kicked off to Gurley, Roger turned to me, his eyes widening as he prophesied. "Gurley's gonna be able to take this one out. Just watch, it's gonna go to the house."

I'd heard all the hype about Todd Gurley and watched enough Georgia games over the past couple seasons to know he's the real deal. Everywhere I went I heard about Gurley. Everybody suspected he had Heisman potential after his freshman season, when he rushed for 1,385 yards and 17 touchdowns. The Bulldog faithful were forced into wait-and-see mode his sophomore year, however, after he was hampered by injuries and managed just 989 rushing yards and 10 touchdowns. With all the hype heading into 2014, it seemed most people were convinced of his greatness and simply waiting on the proof to emerge. And it's only in hindsight that I realize what I witnessed during the Clemson–Georgia game.

Seconds after Roger told me Gurley was about to break a big one, he did. He returned a kickoff 100 yards for a touchdown, his second score of the day. After the play, Lil John's "Turn Down for What" came on over the stadium speakers and a roar boomed from the crowd that was louder, longer, and more reckless than anything I heard the rest of the season. It was the single greatest in-game moment of my entire trip.

By halftime the score was tied. A Morgan Mitchell field goal put Georgia ahead 24–21 early in the third quarter, but after that nobody scored until early in the fourth quarter. There was a lot of sparring back and forth for the first twenty minutes of the second half—and then Georgia exploded. The beating afternoon sun gave way to early evening dusk as the Bulldogs landed a three-score combo that knocked Clemson out in under three minutes. Sometimes, it all happens faster than you can flag down the hot dog vendor. This was one of those times. With 10:26 remaining in the fourth quarter, Gurley scored his third touchdown of the day on an 18-yard run. *Georgia 31, Clemson 21.* Less than ninety seconds later, true freshman Nick Chubb broke for a 47-yard touchdown run. *Georgia 38, Clemson 21.* And less than ninety seconds after *that*, Gurley scampered to the end zone for his 4th touchdown of the day on a 51-yard run. *Georgia 45, Clemson 21.* That ended up being the final score, and although the Bulldogs ran away with the game late, the contest was much closer than the score would suggest. It's funny how that works; both of the opening-weekend games I watched posted a 24-point margin of victory, but each win seemed so different. Texas A&M beat South Carolina by 24 but it felt like 50. Georgia beat Clemson by 24 and it felt like a 10-point victory.

Todd Gurley totaled 297 all-purpose yards and 4 touchdowns against a ranked Clemson team. The highs don't get much higher on opening weekend. When the clock read 00:00, Georgia players rushed the student section and jumped up on the concrete slab behind the hedges and in front of the first row. The players danced and celebrated the moment with the rest of the student population, who seemed to be their peers in name only. After all, someone who worships you can't be your peer.

Curiously, while the sidewalks and bars of downtown Athens were a free-for-all after the game the streets and crosswalks remained orderly. I discovered that's because Athens police are notorious for ticketing jaywalkers. Brandon and I met up at the only restaurant downtown that wasn't jam-packed: the Utage Sushi Bar on Clayton Street. We watched the LSU–Wisconsin game, and he explained how he snuck into the stadium. Brandon, ever the writer, shared his experience with dramatic flourish: "Jim, it was crazy. When I got in, I ran into these kids unloading concessions and I was like, 'Hey, I just hopped a fence in here. Can I help you guys out till people start coming in?' They were pretty cool. I even sat with three of the guys in the student section." As we sat laughing about a wild opening weekend in the South, I bounced a couple ideas off Brandon. I noted a big difference between the more structured interview-style conversations I had with people like Nancy at South Carolina and the casual chitchatting I did with people like Maureen and Caroline at Georgia. While the former yielded more information, the latter felt more organic and in line with the spirit of what I was looking for. In the same way that I decided to tell as few people as possible I was writing a book when the Carolina girl accosted me with platitudes at Jake's, the bar in Columbia, I decided in that sushi bar that I would enter conversations and roll onto these campuses with as little agenda as possible. I wouldn't have a list of questions and topics in mind beforehand; I'd simply let the stories come to me.

#15 Ole Miss vs. Vanderbilt

September 6, 2014

Nashville, Tennessee

I bought a coffee and a cinnamon roll, sat down at a two-seater table near the door, and began to write. An hour later, a scream erupted from behind the counter. What happened next moved through my senses in slow motion, and I say that because the entire scene sticks in my mind with a frame-by-frame clarity. I jerked my head up and to the right toward where the scream came from but didn't see anybody. (As I would find out later, the employees and the owner had run out the back of the store.) Turning left, I watched as two men rushed through the front door about ten feet from my table. I looked up, saw a mask; looked down, saw a black metallic glimmer. I rolled out of my seat facedown onto the ground before the men could shout "Everybody on the ground!" I didn't feel any fear as I processed what was happening. In all honesty, the only thought that went through my head was "Sonofabitch. It's gonna be a pain in the ass to get a new driver's license."

The last thing I expected on the Tuesday morning after Labor Day was to be robbed at gunpoint while I sat scribbling notes inside an Atlanta coffee shop. Brandon and I had made the hour drive to Atlanta after attending a Presbyterian church service in Athens Sunday morning. (I'm far more spiritual than religious, but I dragged myself out of bed early because I thought attending various churches across the south might benefit the book—it didn't; at least, not directly—and because an hour of quiet reflection never hurt anyone.) I was staying at my friend Alex's apartment in Atlanta for the week. We became friends when he moved to Chicago for art school a few years back. Brandon and Alex knew each other, too, so Brandon hung around for a couple days before flying back to Chicago.

Anyways, after some random Internet searching for caffeine Tuesday morning, I had settled on Mae's Bakery in the ritzy Buckhead neighborhood, a quaint little coffee and pastry joint with wicker-backed chairs and various fresh-baked cookies, muffins, and scones. It was, one reviewer noted, a "rare find in Atlanta…an old-fashioned bakery who actually uses family recipes."[20]

Since my face was down (TV and movies had taught me the drill in these situations), I didn't watch most of the robbery take place. I gathered after the fact that a young blonde girl had frozen standing up when the robbers rushed the store. They called for her wallet and she couldn't

---

[20] Thanks, Google reviews.

move; all she could do was scream "Take whatever you want! I don't know what you want!" After snatching her purse, they proceeded to the cash register behind the counter. A young Chinese man lay in the corner across the room from me, but for whatever reason the robbers didn't take any of his belongings, nor did they take anything from the elderly Indian woman they forced inside from her patio seat outside the front door. They also didn't take any of our laptops or cell phones, which makes sense because of GPS and tracking technology. As they headed out, I heard a voice very close to me say, "The wallet, big man." I reached into my shorts pocket and flipped my wallet in the voice's general direction. Seconds later, I heard tires screeching and knew it was okay to stand up.

I comforted the girl while calling 911, checked to see if everyone was alright, and told the girl to call and cancel her credit card. Then I cancelled mine, and called the Illinois DMV to get a temporary license sent to Alex's apartment. Next I called a friend in Chicago and asked him to pick up my passport from my dad's house without telling my dad why. Who wants to worry their parents about something like this? I was safe, so why make my mom and dad toss and turn in their sleep? As we all waited for police to arrive, I thought to myself, "Since when am I the guy who reacts calmly in this situation? That's cool."

The owner of the store was a woman in her thirties named Beth. She named the bakery after her daughter, and she was one of the four women to run out the back as the robbers exited their getaway vehicle and rushed the front door. When she finally came back around the front, I was standing outside getting an address for the 911 dispatcher. Beth walked up to me, asked if I was okay, and squeezed my hand as we walked back inside together. After finding out I had a hundred dollars cash in my wallet and a Visa gift card with between three and four hundred dollars on it, she handed me a hundred-dollar bill. When I refused, she insisted. And on my way out after talking with police, she handed me a box of pastries to take home with me. I messaged Beth later that night on Facebook, thanking her for her kindness. Her response was touching. She wrote: "I wish you much success and joy on your journey of following your dreams. That is how Mae's started." Such kindness was incredibly moving. When you're confronted with the best in people, it forces out your cynicism and guardedness, even more so if they are complete strangers reacting to a bad situation.

I didn't leave for Nashville until after rush hour Thursday night because I had to wait for my new debit card and my passport. I arrived at my Airbnb rental a little after 10 pm and met the other guests. It was an odd place. A house and barn sat on the three-acre property located roughly ten miles outside of Nashville. After poking around, I decided I must have stumbled onto a modern little hippie commune.[21] Some of the people staying there—I believe I counted six or seven guests in total—were long-term residents, and two of them had lived there for multiple stretches of time. I had no idea where all these people slept, since I only counted four bedrooms. The guy who ran the place, Ed, was certainly the hippie ringleader. When I came home from downtown Friday night, half a dozen people sat on the front porch sharing drinks. Soon after I arrived, Ed said, "I think we should have a drum circle." Like automatons, two men with glazed-over eyes stepped inside and retrieved

---

[21] Remember, I was working on a tight budget.

a pair of bongos and another returned with a tambourine. Ed's vibe radiated a bit more Jim Jones[22] than Ken Kesey[23] to me, so I mostly kept to myself. I doubt these were anything but decent people, but being open-minded doesn't preclude trusting your gut. After witnessing the drum circle, I walked downstairs to my room and went to sleep. I didn't want to drink any more Kool-Aid than I had to.

ಶ

Downtown Nashville. The smell of leather crept out from the countless cowboy boot stores lining the streets Friday morning, filling my nostrils. It was a pleasant smell. Valets in powder-blue shirts picked up and dropped off cars all around 2nd Avenue, the clip-clop of their shoes echoing and pinging off buildings on either side of the street as they hustled back and forth. I walked down 2nd and then Broadway Street, where the twangy sounds of country were already spilling out into the street and bouncers tried steering passersby inside. I showed one bouncer the coffee in my left hand and he said, "C'mon in and throw some Bailey's in that, brother. It's almost noon."

I wandered inside the Tennessee State Museum on Deaderick Street. It reminded me of a grade school field trip, and as I walked through I wondered who goes to places like this unless they're on a school trip or

---

[22] American cult leader responsible for the mass suicide of more than 900 of his followers in 1978.

[23] American author and leader of the Merry Pranksters, a group in the mid-'60s that promoted LSD—which was legal at the time—as a form of consciousness-raising. The Grateful Dead played at a lot of their acid parties.

trying to escape the nursing home. Daniel Boone's pocketknife and a tuft of Andrew Jackson's hair grabbed my attention. Still, as I planted myself on the bench in front of a video screen, I asked myself how I ended up in a state museum. All the things to do and see in Nashville, and I veer off into a dusty museum? But, I've always been a bit of a history buff, so I suppose it made sense. I watched a film on the Civil War in Tennessee and began thinking about the idea that Southern football culture has its roots in the Reconstruction era. I've had conversations with amateur football historians who argued that college football became what it is in the South because of a need for identity, community, and a source of pride in the wake of the Civil War. The destruction to the land and collective psyche of Southern people demanded a constructive outlet, the reasoning goes. Southerners needed something to rally around and believe in.

Two of the more prevalent escapes to rise up from the ashes of the Civil War were, first, a religious revival, and then later, a college football-centric culture. Both fit perfectly. If people can't make sense of the things happening around them—in this case: how and why did we lose this war, and what happens to us now?—their world becomes incomprehensible and they experience a feeling of helplessness from the lack of control. A person who feels powerless to determine their own fate often seeks solace in a religious community; it's either that or the bottom of a bottle. Similarly, if people felt emasculated, it would serve to reason that they would look for a way to assert themselves through physicality and force to recapture some piece of their lost pride and manhood.[24] Contemplating the game in such a light, I suppose, makes it easier to understand the intensity with which Southern communities rallied around football, at least during the outset.

I sat quietly, taking in a few more Civil War videos, and had another thought: even if the ripple effect of the Civil War explains why college football overtook the South, there's nobody talking about it on fall Saturdays now. If a Civil War connection accounts for why the South houses the highest concentration of college football crazy, does it really affect what the SEC is today?

After the museum, I dropped into Rippy's on Broadway for lunch. From a high-top table, I watched a blonde-haired girl in her early twenties belt out soulful renditions of pop and country standards while salt-and-pepper-haired journeymen guitarists flanked her on either side and seasoned her raw, powerful voice with smooth guitar fills and soothing backup vocals. Danielle, my waitress, was quick to recommend the BBQ pulled pork sandwich—which was outstanding—but had a much harder time making recommendations for things to do and see on Vandy's

---

[24] It should be noted that while some of the religious fervor at the time proved beneficial to many individuals and communities, there were certainly darker elements at play as well. Religion was often used as a means of social control that aimed to subvert and circumvent the freedom afforded black people in the wake of the Civil War. The Reconstruction era also gave rise to terror organizations like the Ku Klux Klan, which was founded by former Confederate army officers purporting to defend white Protestant honor. The Klan's influence quickly spread throughout the South, giving rise to similar groups like the White League in Louisiana and the Red Shirts in Mississippi.

campus: "I don't know. I go there but I've never really hung out around campus." She gestured out the window, toward Broadway, already buzzing with life at 1:30 pm on a Friday, "Why would I hang out there when all this is right down the street?" I looked out the window. What else did she have to say?

I drove to Vanderbilt's main campus anyway, passing what felt like a dozen churches and a few dozen bars. Before arriving, I was aware that Vanderbilt is the conference outlier in a number of ways. The two obvious differences are that it's the only SEC school in a major American city, and that the university is the only true academic powerhouse in the conference. A handful of Division-I FBS schools across the country try to balance high achievement in both academics and athletics. Stanford, Duke, Northwestern, Vanderbilt, and Notre Dame immediately come to mind.[25] The alchemy has its challenges, though. In a conference where the premium on winning football games is higher than anywhere else in the country, it makes sense that Vanderbilt would become a doormat. Finding elite athletes and convincing them to play football at your school is a challenging enough task on it's own, but when higher admissions standards automatically disqualify a not-insignificant percentage of prospective Division I players, the challenge intensifies. And when those athletes who do qualify realize that it will likely be a much tougher road academically than at a less challenging school—the phrase "football factory" comes to mind—many student-athletes choose a path of less

---

[25] My editor, Adam, is a Michigan grad. (Gross, right?) He made the following comment: "Ahem, I think you're missing a certain school in the Big Ten. It's just outside of Detroit…" I stand by my original list.

resistance. Vanderbilt competes at a disadvantage well before their team even takes the field.

How many student athletes want to put in the work it takes to be successful at college football's top level *and* shoulder the course demands of a top-25 university? I'm no recruiter, but selling that to a seventeen-year-old kid seems like an uphill battle. A coach can make the pitch that a degree from Vanderbilt will take care of life after football and point out the statistical improbability of making an NFL roster. He might also point out the percentage of players who go bankrupt within five years of being out of professional football. But again, he's talking to a teenager full of dreams and delusions.

That pitch also doesn't account for the fact that most top-tier athletes being recruited by SEC schools have been the best at what they do from the moment they started playing sports. And more often than not, the community surrounding star athletes gives them some level of exalted status and privilege. This may range from being given their own press coverage in the local paper every week from the time they're thirteen or fourteen to having test scores changed to maintain their eligibility, but however it works out, the message is clear: star athletes are treated differently than other teenagers.

As well, given their history of success and positive reinforcement from their community, most of these young men have a level of self-confidence that leads them to believe *they* won't become a statistic. They won't be the guy who blows out his knee, the guy who doesn't crack the two deep[26] and walks away with no degree, or the guy who, after four years, ends up with a general studies degree with no real-world value and no NFL contract. These scenarios play out way more often than anyone involved cares to admit at the so-called football factories. But, "it won't happen to me" is still the prevailing mentality of recruits.

All things considered then, Coach James Franklin's recent accomplishments at Vanderbilt are all the more remarkable. Imagine this: the last time your school finished a season ranked in the top-25 was 1948. Then, out of nowhere, a young upstart coach leads your team to back-to-back 9-win seasons with top-25 finishes. That's exactly what James Franklin delivered in 2012 and 2013. Franklin infused life into a floundering program and pulled a perennial cellar-dweller up from the depths of the SEC standings. Vanderbilt fans started to believe things might be different; that maybe—just maybe—Commodore Nation could aspire to greater heights than six wins and a bottom-of-the-barrel bowl game. The problem with being a doormat, though, is that if they ever rise up, it draws the attention of traditionally successful programs. When bigger programs take notice of a bottom-feeder's coach, it's usually only a matter of time before the coach leaves for a bigger payday and the promise of an environment where winning is more sustainable. Schools like Vanderbilt serve as stepping-stones for coaches with championship aspirations. When Penn State came calling after the 2013 season, James Franklin cashed in his Vanderbilt success for the head job in Happy Valley.

---

[26] Football slang for first- and second-string players; players likely to see the field on a regular basis.

At a school like without a winning tradition (like Vanderbilt), it's easy to credit any hint of success to the coach rather than the school, or even the players. Whenever the media and fans talk about Vanderbilt's 2012 and 2013 seasons, they usually point to what Franklin did, not what the team accomplished. Vanderbilt hitched its wagon to a rising star. With Franklin gone, however, the Commodore wagon was set to come crashing back down to Earth. (And crash it did. In 2014 the Commodores went 3–9; in 2015, 4–8.) When a more successful program like Penn State poaches a newly ascending program's coach, fear and anxiety spread through the fan base like wildfire. Many supporters will try to downplay the departure's significance, but it's a crushing reminder that the school is still second-rate.

Sleepy is the best way to describe Vandy's campus on late Friday afternoon. The low-hanging magnolia trees interspersed throughout the quad and students beneath them lost in heavy textbooks intimated that higher learning was the priority, not day drinking or rowdy pep rallies—or producing first-round draft picks. A walk through Frat Row early Friday evening revealed absolutely no signs of life. An eerie silence filled the air, interrupted only occasionally by the swishing of backpacks hanging loose off students' shoulders and the muted clop of boat shoes and sandals as they sauntered down angled sidewalks. I don't know why—probably because downtown Nashville is less than three miles away—but I'd never seen a college campus so dead on a Friday night in early September. Since there was nothing to see, I doubled back to Broadway for another round of BBQ and live country.

⚑

I sought out the Vandy faithful Saturday morning downtown and had a strange experience: the only fans I spotted were in small clusters—twos and threes—walking down 2nd or down Broadway. However, the streets were painted Yale blue and Harvard crimson,[27] the colors of all of the Ole Miss fans packing downtown. Through a friend on one of the Notre Dame football message boards I frequented,[28] I had arranged to meet up with an Ole Miss grad around my age, Russ, his wife, and their friends at Acme Restaurant on 1st and Broadway. They were a lively bunch. According to the group, Ole Miss simply takes over the city and turns it into a de facto home game whenever they come up to play Vanderbilt. It serves as a reunion weekend for Ole Miss alums who live in different cities.

Russ's friend Seth proclaimed his lineage ran through Mississippi State. His parents, all his siblings, etc.—they all wave the Bulldog banner. Seth, however, decided to attend Ole Miss. His father, a former State tennis player, is an otherwise reasonable, well-adjusted adult. But he refused to talk to his son for two weeks after Seth's decision. Thereafter, he refused to sign the checks to Ole Miss for his son's tuition; he had his wife do it for him. The house divided by SEC football allegiances is more than a cute license plate holder: it's a real thing that goes deep enough to affect family dynamics. I'd heard these types of stories for years through secondhand anecdotes. On some level I didn't believe they were true, or at the very least thought they were exaggerated. But

---

[27] According to the school's website, the colors were chosen in 1893 because "it was well to have the spirit of both these good colleges." Some refer to Ole Miss as the Harvard of the South; as far as I can tell, this is meant as a joke.

[28] Jack Shugg. Jack has since passed away, and I regret that we couldn't meet for lunch the two times I passed through Louisiana.

when multiple generations attend the same university it becomes a central part of the family identity and provides a deep sense of bonding. On the other hand, for as long as the nuclear family unit has existed, children have done the exact opposite of the plans their parents laid out for them. In SEC football families, the recipe for becoming the black sheep is mac 'n cheese-simple: attend a rival school.

I did find a small group of Vanderbilt fans moping upstairs at Acme. One of their crew had played offensive tackle for Vandy in the mid-2000s. We rapped briefly about the Chicago Bears' love for former Vandy players—Jay Cutler, Hunter Hillenmeyer, Earl Bennett, and D. J. Moore. But inevitably the conversation turned to their disgust in realizing Ole Miss fans had overtaken *their* bar. Overtaken is an understatement, actually: the ratio had to be twenty-five to one. The lonely Vandy grads and grad students masked their apprehension about the season, and the shellacking they took at the hands of Temple the week before, by looking down at their shoes and sipping at their drinks in steady succession. "I'm kinda hoping once they figure out this QB situation and [new head coach Derek] Mason gets settled into the job, it'll get better," one of the guys offered sheepishly. Though they were an affable bunch, they didn't have much to say about their hopes for the season or why their fellow fans declined to show up in any meaningful way. Later on, outside the stadium, one of their crew saw me walking through the crowd with one finger up, a universal signal that a person is looking for a single ticket. He said, "Hey I remember you from earlier. We've got an extra. Enjoy the game, brother." Like I said, friendly enough guys. After a few enjoyable hours at Acme, I decided that I needed to find the rest of the Vandy fans. They had to be somewhere.

This week's game was being played at LP Field, the home of the Tennessee Titans. The stadium is across the river from downtown Nashville. Had the game been held at Vanderbilt's home stadium, I suspect, Vandy fans would have been easier to locate and the scene would've been a more traditional parking lot tailgate. On this day, however, most of the tailgating took place at bars around the downtown area. Throughout the pregame, I wondered if maybe Vanderbilt's biggest contribution to SEC football—with the exception of the Franklin years—is that it provides a welcome vacation weekend getaway to a bigger city for SEC fans from other schools.

I did find Vanderbilt fans, though. There were two decent-sized tailgates in various parking lots around the stadium. The first I walked up to with a Vanderbilt student and two Georgia students I chatted up as we crossed the bridge toward the stadium. All of them were flowing in black Vandy dresses, because "it's just easier to dress the part and fit in, ya know?" I looked down at my green Irish shirt and chuckled. "Sure." It didn't take much convincing to follow them over to the Beta Theta Pi frat tailgate. Once there, a spray-tanned girl with temporary tattoos of Commodores on her cheeks started talking to me about Notre Dame and how she was from South Bend. Then she asked me if I was a Beta at my school. I didn't know how to respond. I was almost thirty. Not that thirty is old, but I didn't know people visited other chapters of their fraternity at other schools. Everybody I talked with was more than happy to discuss Notre Dame, or the Notre Dame–Michigan game later that night, or the city of Nashville. Hell, I think they would've rather talked about the weather than the game we were all attending that afternoon. Nobody wanted to talk Vanderbilt football. Nobody was excited for the game. They'd all seen the same things I did in their week one game against Temple. For all the magic that James Franklin brought to this school, it all seemed to vanish with him when he left for State College.

I wandered away from the girls in the black dresses to another oversized tailgate with multiple tents and an '80s cover band playing Whitesnake and Lionel Richie. I fueled up with a hot dog and a water and made small talk with a few more Vandy girls. Becky, a senior with freckles and slurred speech, informed me that "this chick is gonna be blacked out by halftime," nodding to her roommate, who was mumbling through some story to a pair of frat brothers. Despite their lack of interest in discussing anything other than their day drinking feats, I headed for the stadium with them. As we stood in line, I watched in awe as they polished off the better part of a fifth of Jack Daniel's Tennessee Fire, the storied distiller's answer to Fireball. A strong smell of cinnamon filled the air as the ladies belted out a couple uninspired "Anchor Down" and "Fuck Ole Miss" chants. Still, nobody wanted to talk Vandy football. I wondered if they knew how badly they were about to get beat. I had no doubt about the outcome.

I found a seat in the second row of the student section, in the corner of the end zone next to the band. The seat had a perfect view, and was just a few feet away from the dance team, who were doing their bit on the field. Before kickoff the word that kept running through my head was *disjointed*. I nearly wrote it on my hand to remind me because it perfectly described everything I saw. The student section couldn't seem to get their pregame chants in sync. The stadium loudspeaker started playing the White Stripes' stadium anthem "Seven Nation Army" about four and a half minutes before kickoff, threatening to whip the crowd into a frenzy way too early; the teams hadn't even taken the field yet, and there was no hope of maintaining that energy level for another five minutes.

Vanderbilt's entrance drew very little attention, too—it seemed like they had already taken the field before the student section even noticed their presence. Seconds later, the Ole Miss entrance had an entirely different effect, as everyone fixed their attention on the Rebs. Without question, the ovation for Ole Miss was louder and more spirited than Vanderbilt's. The final pregame flub occurred about thirty seconds before the kick. Ozzy Osbourne's "Crazy Train" boomed over the loudspeakers, injecting a hint of life in the air, a glimmer of spirit. But at that exact moment the band broke into song, their din cancelling out any possible energy for the team to feed off of.

⚑

Ole Miss received the opening kick. They drove straight downfield and put the ball in the end zone for a (very) early 7–0 lead. Vanderbilt looked good on their first few snaps, rushing for 30 yards and two first downs on their first three plays before stalling out and punting the ball away. When Ole Miss had the ball, I would hear strange one-word cries directed at the defense such as "tackle" and "block." You have to give it to the "smart" kids at Vandy: they really understand the fundamentals of the game. (To be fair, one fan behind me seemed to have a firm grasp on what he was watching.)

With 2:30 left in the first half and the score now 20–0, Vanderbilt got the ball back. They ran on first and second downs, then threw a short pass on third to pick up a first down. With no particular sense of urgency, the offense repeated the process on their next three plays. The ball was near midfield but Vanderbilt was bleeding their own clock so Ole Miss didn't have a chance to make it a four-score game. Yawn. Listless, indeed. I couldn't fault Vanderbilt fans for being unenthused about the game. What was there to be excited about? A perennial doormat was finding its expected, familiar place back at the bottom of the SEC for the 2014 season. As I watched the final seconds tick off the first half, I wished I'd seen Vanderbilt sometime in the last two years. I remember watching them on TV a few times during their 9-win seasons and being psyched for them. It's fun to see the lovable loser come out on top once in a while.

In the closing seconds of the second quarter some fans behind me started making disparaging remarks about Ole Miss fans being dumb hillbillies: "They can't even read"; "That jumbotron is the first TV screen they've ever seen"; "We might suck at football, but at least we're not gonna marry our cousin"; and so on. Something about their tone bothered me. I guess people need to find comfort somehow when they're hurt. Taking digs at others is an easy way to do this, but who really feels good about themselves for taking the easy way out? I think the real idiot is the guy who needs to hurl insults like a butthurt[29] nine-year-old. I also understand from being a sports fan, and human being, that attacking others when our pain consumes us is a normal—if unproductive—coping mechanism. Most of the fans I met at Vanderbilt didn't fall into this category. I don't think the majority cared enough to be affected or bother with insults. But, as is often the case, an outspoken minority made the strongest impression.

While the tired "Mississippians are stupid" insults rolled over my shoulder, I drew my attention back to the dance team in front of me. They lined up between the 5- and 15-yard lines, and the dancer closest to the

---

[29] Millennial-speak for acting in a petulant manner when something doesn't go your way.

student section was facing us while the rest of her squad looked out toward the field. The whole time she had a big smile on her face, jumping up and down, doing leg kicks, and yelling "C'mon 'dores!" and "Let's Go Vandy!" In the face of such a dead-fish crowd, a crowd that slumped into their seats by the start of the second quarter, she kept smiling and doing her thing with as much enthusiasm as she could muster. Given the black hole of positivity, she might've been the bravest person in the stadium.

I spent half of the third quarter on the 50-yard line, about fifteen rows from the field. The stadium was starting to empty, and did the ushers really care? I chatted with a husband and wife in their early sixties sitting behind me. As it turned out, Frank and Cathy were season ticket holders and die-hards. "You're gonna be here for it all?" I asked, "You're looking at a 3–9, 2–10 type season." Frank sighed. "Yeah, I think you're right. But we'll be here either way."

They represented the kind of fans that make college football special. Frank spoke wistfully about the Franklin era. It seemed sad that an era not a year gone could be reflected upon with such longing and melancholy. As Ole Miss was about to punch it in, putting them up 34–0 halfway through the third quarter, I said goodbye to the true believers and exited the stadium. I found a phone charger and had a quick bite to eat before making my way to Honky Tonk Saloon on 4th and Broadway for the Notre Dame–Michigan game.

Notre Dame–Michigan games do something strange to me. Maybe it was enduring three consecutive Michigan wins in the last thirty seconds of regulation (which is what happened at every game between 2009 and 2011). I can't tell you why exactly, but I hate Michigan. I can't stand that school. I hate everything about them. I hate their stupid winged helmets and their obnoxious fight song. I hate watching Desmond Howard hype the Wolverines on ESPN every fall. I hate seeing Notre Dame lose to Michigan far more than Southern Cal. So when the Irish square off with Big Blue, I'm on edge. I'm anxious and I'm locked in on the game. I'm nearly incapable of conversation or even a general awareness of my surroundings.

Some time during the first quarter, a gorgeous girl in a white dress came up to me and started talking about Notre Dame. Very few things can pull my razor focus from a Notre Dame–Michigan game, but she did. Everything about her grabbed my attention, from her smile, to the way she rubbed her suntanned legs against mine as she leaned in to talk to me, to the picture she showed me of herself in an ND tank top earlier that day. She's from Indiana, but attended Ole Miss. I should've followed her and her "guy friend" when he pulled her away, but I didn't. I decided I'd wait until halftime, and then I'd go find her and make my move. Every once in a while, I get a reminder that I care way more about college football than I should. This was one of those reminders.

I watched Notre Dame rush out to a 21–0 halftime lead. And at halftime I set out to find my destiny[30] in the white dress. I headed up to the third floor and took a lap around the bar, but she was nowhere in sight. I walked out onto the balcony overlooking 4th and Broadway and started talking to a different pair of ladies. They were a little drunk, in town for a girls' weekend from Indiana. Is everyone in Nashville from Indiana? When I told them we were up 21–0, they hugged me and we joked about

---

[30] "I'm George, George McFly. I'm your density. I mean…your destiny."

Michigan being terrible. The whole time one of the ladies radiated sexual energy toward me, inching in closer and closer. I didn't even have to drop the "I'm a writer" line.

When I told them I was a teacher back in Chicago, the other lady said she had a son going into seventh grade. I thought for sure these girls were my age, in their late twenties. Turns out these women were forty. And the vibe I picked up, I realized later, was the vibe of a woman who's been with the same man far too long.

They said they had to go find their friends. The one who had been all over me kissed me on the cheek, and then on the lips. I leaned in and started kissing her neck. She breathed heavily in my ear and down my neck. And as her friend pulled us apart, she leaned back in and said, "The things I would do to you if I wasn't married." I looked down and saw the glimmer on her ring finger. I stepped back. And like that, they were gone; her friend escorted the two of them off the balcony and out of Honky Tonk Saloon. What happens in Nashvegas…

I wasn't far behind, having decided that a change of venue might be good for the second half. A block down the street I walked back into Rippy's and found a TV on the second floor with the game on. I made small talk with some Ole Miss fans around me. Again, there were no Vanderbilt colors to be found. One Ole Miss fan recognized me from earlier in the day; apparently he and his buddies were chanting "Rudy" at me from some bar balcony. I had a brief flashback to fellow students chanting "Rudy" at me ten years earlier at Marquette, where I wore a Notre Dame jacket around campus every winter. I shuddered. He said they all laughed at however I responded, but I couldn't remember the exchange. They offered to include me in their round of Fireball shots and then one of the frat brothers in the group expounded on the importance of frats at Ole Miss: "Pretty much, if you're white and you don't have a sport or activity that takes up a ton of your time, you join a frat. And they're great, man." Another guy shook his head and laughed at his buddy's tone-deaf explanation. The final seconds ticked off in the first shutout in the history of the Notre Dame–Michigan rivalry, and I couldn't have been happier. The Ole Miss guys high-fived me and shared in my celebration. Victories make it so much easier to be friendly...even with racist rich kids decked out in Vineyard Vines shirts and those stupid sunglass neck straps.

That's one thing I do understand about college football in the South: when you win a rivalry game, there are few better highs in the world. All is well with the world the night of a big rivalry win. When your team beats the hell out of the team you hate most down to the last play of the game, you swell up with a sense of personal accomplishment. Now I know I didn't strap on pads and play in South Bend, and it defies logic, but we fans feel like a contributing part of the victory even though we played no actual part. No matter how intense college football down South is, there's some irrational, die-hard fandom that cuts across all sports and conferences. However, there are definitely experiences down here that I would never have back home. As I was leaving Rippy's around midnight, the bar was jam-packed with Ole Miss fans. Someone screamed, "Arrrrrree Youuuu Readyyyyyyy?" at the top of their lungs. The whole bar joined in to answer:

"Hell Yeah / Damn Right / Hotty Toddy Gosh Almighty / Who the Hell are We? Hey! / Flim Flam, Bim Bam / Ole Miss By Damn!"

On the way back to my car, I spotted a defeated-looking man in a Michigan T-shirt standing just inside one of the bars with its retractable front windows open. I stopped and waited to make eye contact. His buddies, all Ole Miss fans, noticed me first.

When the Wolverine backer finally noticed me standing there, his buddies all started to laugh. His face turned to a scowl. "Don't say shit to me, guy." My smile beamed from ear to ear. I didn't have to say a thing.

Kentucky vs. Florida

September 13, 2014

Gainesville, Florida

As I walked around Florida's campus Thursday morning and afternoon, I didn't talk to anybody at all. Instead I wandered around for a few hours, taking mental note of the uniform red brick buildings that colored the campus, the Spanish-tiled roofs, the tree-lined streets of Gainesville, and the ever present Spanish moss. I felt like a tourist on these solitary walks around the university and town. There's a newness to each place that I prefer quietly taking in with my eyes, if possible, before talking to the locals.

I lapped Ben Hill Griffin Stadium as students were picking up their game tickets for Saturday. The stadium is open to the public Monday through Friday, so I went inside and climbed some stairs. Guys in T-shirts and shorts, and girls in tank tops and shorter shorts, ran bleachers all throughout. The grounds crew was painting the yard lines and the patented Gator at midfield. Back outside the stadium, I took pictures of the Gator statue erected in honor of the 2006 National Championship team, and inside the football complex, I snapped photos of the 1996, 2006, and 2008 National Championship trophies, the Heisman trophies won by Steve Spurrier, Danny Wuerrfel, and Tim Tebow, and a handful of SEC Championship trophies.

Seeing how recent most of the Florida hardware was made me realize that the Gators have only ascended to the upper echelon of college football within the past twenty-five years. Because I grew up in the Spurrier era and was in my early twenties through the Meyer era, I've only ever seen Florida be successful. It wasn't until I visited campus and talked to people that I discovered that for decades the program was, as Bear Bryant described it, "a sleeping giant." It's only natural then that Steve Spurrier was the coach who awakened the Florida program from its prolonged slumber and led the Gators to unprecedented heights. In twelve years at Florida, the "Ol' Ball Coach" amassed a 122–27–1 record, eight top-10 seasons, six SEC championships, and a national championship in 1996. (They would have won seven SEC titles, but Florida was still on probation during Spurrier's first season.) Under Spurrier, Florida never won fewer than nine games in a season.

Back outside the stadium I found Florida football's legends in bronze: Tim Tebow, Spurrier, and Danny Wuerffel. All three were part of national championship teams—Spurrier as a coach, not a player—and all three are held in the highest regard in Gainesville. As I stood there in front of the statues, which were unveiled in 2011, I thought back to two separate conversations I had with Florida fans over the summer. Both told me about Spurrier, Wuerrfel, and Tebow, and how Florida views them as the gods of Gator Nation. Their explanations for Gator fans' unique strain of football-worship, though, spurred me to look beneath the surface of what separates a great college player from a legend.

One of the fans I talked to, Dale, was a neuropsychologist and former college professor. According to him, there's a religious element to the relationship between Florida fans and these three heroes. He emphasized the fact that all three of them are preachers' sons, and that this is one of the most significant aspects of their legacies. Florida fans love being able to point to the fact that all three were phenomenal football players, but better human beings.[31]

Chris was a Florida grad and contributing writer to one of the Florida football websites. He saw the religious aspect of the Florida triumvirate differently. In his view, confirmation bias is built into both how and why fans choose their heroes: "Fans in the SEC—and in general—love a winner. Spurrier, Wuerffel, and Tebow could just flat-out play football. The narrative that came along with them was nice to embellish, but that's not why people love them. They loved them and they became mythical because of their Christian narratives. To me it's all about confirmation bias: people want a hero to worship, and these guys were all clean-cut, decent-looking white guys that were decent athletes. You can contrast how revered they are against Chris Leak, who actually quarterbacked the 2006 National Championship team, Rex Grossman, who had one of the all time great seasons for a quarterback in college football

---

[31] The "good player, better person" archetype. We've seen this before.

in 2001 (seriously, look at his stats), and Percy Harvin, who was the best Gator football player I have seen in person."

As I stood there weighing these opinions on what turns Florida football stars into deities, a strange thought occurred to me. I thought of Jesus in the middle of the penitent and impenitent thieves being hanged on crosses. Spurrier, the gold standard of Florida football, stood in the middle.[32] With all the football-as-gospel talk I'd been hearing, this religious image presented itself to me. Gator football's savior stood tall with his right arm cocked and ready to throw. The image wasn't sacrilegious to me. In that moment, I felt certain I wasn't the first person to see the three quarterbacks in this light.

A mile down University Avenue, most of the bars and restaurants downtown were neither chains nor so fancy that they looked or felt cold and uninviting. I sat on a park bench Friday night at the Bo Diddley Community Plaza, which has an outdoor open-air music venue. It was peaceful. There's something about cobblestoned streets and diagonal parking spots in a small town. Likewise, I'll look down a row of incandescent lanterns and glamorize a sleepy existence I know nothing about. I always feel like I want to set down roots and become part of that community

---

[32] Steve Spurrier on the difference between himself and Danny Wuerffel: "He's like a New Testament person. He gets slapped upside the face and turns the other cheek and says, 'Lord, forgive them for they know not what they're doing.' I'm probably more of an Old Testament guy. You spear our guy in the earhole, we think we're supposed to spear you in the earhole."

immediately. The feeling is fleeting and lost when the moment is past, but I always feel it strongest at night under the streetlamps.

At the plaza, I struck up a conversation with a pair of guys in their forties as a bluegrass band finished their set. Mike and John, who could've easily passed for siblings, stood arguing about Florida's coach, Will Muschamp. I quickly discovered that Mike loved Muschamp while John couldn't stand him and wished he had been fired after the 2013 season. When the show ended, they headed to IHOP and invited me to join them. Once we arrived, I realized there was an Alabama fan in the group, Robert. He smiled and said, "I didn't choose to move here." He came from a split Alabama family; Mom went to Auburn and Dad attended Alabama, but football wasn't a big deal in their household. Just because I'm in the South doesn't mean that everyone I meet will have their lives dictated by their allegiance to a set of colors and the wins and losses of their football team, I realized. Graham was a straitlaced accountant type who hinted at a past life as a collegiate party animal before a career, wife, and children rendered him docile. His family hailed from Gainesville but he attended Florida State, and his was another split family: he and a sister attended FSU, and their other sister went to Florida. Graham and his sisters were in college when Spurrier and Bowden[33] were atop the college football world and those rivalry games often

---

[33] Bobby Bowden, Florida State University's coach from 1976–2009. FSU finished in the top-5 nationally every year from 1987–2000, with national championship wins in 1993 and 1999. Bowden only had one losing season (his first, in 1976) in thirty-four years.

helped decide the balance of power in the college football world.[34] Graham's sister at Florida used to cut out press clippings about the UF–FSU games, laminate them, and mail them to Graham and his other sister in Tallahassee. He mentioned that though they didn't fight growing up, this act caused the siblings not to speak to each other—sometimes for months at a time—throughout college.

While we were combing through college football at large over undercooked hash browns and runny eggs at the IHOP, someone mentioned the Big Ten and their rough week the previous Saturday. Notre Dame throttled Michigan, 31–0 (notice how I listed that one first), Michigan State fell to Oregon, and Virginia Tech upset Ohio State. When Ohio State came up, Mike, the most outspoken of the bunch, seemed very pleased by the news: "Oh, that's great. And not just because of the way that piece of shit left us." "That piece of shit" was former Florida and current Ohio State Head Coach Urban Meyer. Meyer led the Gators to national championships in 2006 and 2008 before leaving after the 2010 season. Somehow I sensed this wasn't the last time I'd hear about Urban Meyer on my trip through Gainesville.

The second Saturday in September marked the first true night game on my schedule, as well as my first and only visit to the Swamp (as Ben Hill Griffin Stadium is affectionately known). When I finally arrived to the stadium, I navigated through dozens of fans decked out in orange and

---

[34] 1996: Florida State beat Florida 24–21 in the regular season—and then Florida routed Florida State 52–20 in the Sugar Bowl for the national championship.

blue lining up to taking pictures at the Holy Trinity of Florida football statues. Farther on, kids stood on and around the Gator statue outside the stadium complex. Much like a religious pilgrimage, paying respects to these statues is a rite of passage for young fans, who have come to see and behold Florida history as their proud parents take pictures of future Gators. As I turned the corner from Lemerand Drive toward Stadium Road and the student section entrance, I saw a car trying to pass through a blocked-off street. The car's passenger was showing a reflective pass to the security guards enforcing the closure. I looked closer and realized the man holding the pass was none other than Brent Musburger, one of the best-known play-by-play announcers in college football. Without thinking, I barged in. "What's up Brent Musburger?" I inquired, and walked over to shake his hand. He smiled and greeted me between his back-and-forth with the security guard, who refused to move the sawhorse blocking the way.

When Musburger's car drove off frustrated, I asked the guard if he knew who that was. "I don't care who that was." I shrugged and turned to leave. "Wait, who was it?" "The guy who's announcing the game on TV tonight," I said. He shrugged and I moved along, totally satisfied.

⛳

Florida was one of the schools where I'd arranged to meet people at tailgates in advance. Before embarking on my Southern adventure, I spent chunks of time throughout the spring and summer on various fan message boards for each school. One of the fellows I started talking with on the Florida message boards was the former professor I mentioned earlier, Dale. He offered his support as a well-informed sounding board on the logistical planning of my trip—which rivalry games held the greatest historical significance, which Southern landmarks I'd want to see on my travels, and so on. In time, our exchange turned into a more general conversation about which themes and ideas were worth exploring while I spent an entire college football season in the South.

I met Dale outside The Swamp, a restaurant on University Avenue in the midtown hub on campus. We walked across the street to the tailgate spot he and his friends held down every week, and I spent the next three hours there meeting some well-informed, friendly, and well-connected fans. Dale and his wife Sue are both Florida natives and have been UF season ticket holders for the past 25 years. Neither actually attended the school, but both have been fans as far back as they can remember.

Most eyes were glued to the South Carolina–Georgia game when Dale and I arrived. I was surprised to see everyone at the tailgate actively rooting for South Carolina. Then I remembered: Steve Spurrier, the gold standard for Florida football. Player. Coach. Messianic figure. Spurrier is Florida football. With the lone exception of legendary Alabama coach Bear Bryant, I don't believe that another individual means more to their school's legacy and tradition than Steve Spurrier. It's probably no coincidence then that the two winningest coaches in SEC football history are Bear Bryant (number one) and Steve Spurrier (number two).

These Gators had many reasons to root for South Carolina and against Georgia. The SEC East division standings played a part: USC already had a conference loss, but UGA didn't. Georgia also stands as one of Florida's biggest rivals and most hated schools. But it all boiled down to Coach Spurrier. Everyone there roots for South Carolina unless they're playing Florida, or unless South Carolina needs to lose for Florida to benefit in the standings. This sentiment, however, will undoubtedly change the day Spurrier steps down as head coach in Columbia.

Watching the USC–UGA game and observing Florida fans' reactions to it made me start to consider the layered nature of allegiance for college football fans in the South. First and foremost, you root for your team. This is a given. Beyond that, things get murky. People have different reasons for rooting for and against other teams, and these reasons may make varying degrees of sense. In contrast, this sort of nuanced thinking and conditional fandom doesn't exist to nearly the same extent in the North. If you're a Michigan fan, you probably want Ohio State and Michigan State to lose every game on their schedule. It makes no difference if they're playing a non-Big Ten team. Conference affiliation plays no part.

Grant was the first person I met at the tailgate Saturday. Mid-thirties, personable, outgoing and clearly well versed in all things Florida football. He knew plenty about the rest of the college football world, too. Of all the college football fan types, Grant is my favorite to talk to and the one that reminds me most of myself. He's quick to acknowledge his own team's shortcomings and acknowledge what other teams are doing well. It's not all black and white for Grant. "Florida good, other teams bad" isn't the way he sees the game.

So Grant and I toured the SEC, bouncing around various topics along the way. He believed South Carolina and Auburn don't belong in the SEC, but I don't think he ever explained why. He told me about how Arkansas's coordinators found themselves stuck in the elevator at Jordan-Hare Stadium, Auburn's home field, during the teams' opening week game. It was halftime, and they were on their way down to talk with their team, which was tied with Auburn 21–21. "[Auburn starting quarterback] Nick Marshall's coming back for the second half,[35] the game is much closer than Auburn expected, and whoops, Arkansas's coordinators can't get down to make halftime adjustments. Yeah, they said it was some malfunction and power went out but c'mon," Grant fumed. This initiated a list of all the horrible things Auburn supposedly does to keep up with all the other schools in the SEC, with Grant making the point that the Tigers would, in fact, eat their young in order to beat Alabama. I never understood how this differed from the mentality of every other big football school in the South.

Discussion shifted to Alabama and how they *really* run the SEC despite the even revenue share the conference employs. "How else could Missouri have ended up in the East?" Grant asked rhetorically. "Alabama had them put in the East because they didn't want to end their [cross-divisional] rivalry with Tennessee, even though we [Florida] had to end ours with Auburn, which had gone on longer than any in the SEC except for Auburn–Georgia." I understood what he was saying, but still couldn't see the connection. What I did comprehend was how a college football mind like Grant's works. There were a couple of steps in the equation he omitted because, to his mind, they were so basic and universally understood that saying them out loud would be redundant and border on insulting to a fellow college football fan. And our conversation spun around and around, bouncing from team to team, theme to theme, faster and faster because we're all—Grant, Dale, Dale's brother Ken, and me—college football intellectuals. We're not condescending or uppity about it; we all just love and know a ton about college football. So

---

[35] Marshall was suspended for the first half of the game.

we moved at lightning speed. For a good ten minutes the topics bounced around. Most boomeranged back to "Fuck Alabama."

Grant was driving at some point, something about how lousy Alabama was. Maybe they were the driving force behind the Jameis Winston sexual assault investigation, had been keeping it alive as long as possible? Grant's theory felt conspiratorial, but it's fun to kick around theories about how well-connected fans will use their influence to not only help their own school win, but also to sabotage other schools' chances of winning. How "true" the theories are is almost irrelevant. Plausibility is far more entertaining.

At some point I brought up the Kick Six game, the 2013 Iron Bowl between Alabama and Auburn. Auburn won the game on a missed field goal that they returned for a 109-yard touchdown. "I really wanted Bama to win that because I knew there was no way Florida State could beat them,"[36] said Grant. And like that, I further understood the intricacy of fan loyalties down South.

---

[36] Florida State is an archrival of Florida and an ACC opponent that had already secured a spot in the 2013 National Championship game. The winner of the 2013 Iron Bowl would represent the SEC West against the East division champion, Missouri. Most people understood that Missouri couldn't beat either Auburn or Alabama. Grant's point—which was indirect but instantly comprehended by me—was that Florida State couldn't beat Alabama, either, but they could beat Auburn. Thus, despite his hatred for the Crimson Tide, Grant wanted them to win the Iron Bowl. In his mind, an Alabama win would have guaranteed an SEC national champion. And that was preferable to Florida State winning a title.

To me, this entire exchange encapsulated the layers of being an SEC football fan. We talked at length about Alabama football: how dirty it is, how corrupt it is, how much Grant can't stand the Crimson Tide. But as soon as the issue became the SEC winning a national championship or a team from another conference winning it, all the Bama hate was set aside in an instant. For most fans, the SEC seems to be rung number two in the hierarchy of Southern college football allegiance. Beyond these two rungs, preferences depend on the individual. For instance, generational differences shape fans' rooting interests, especially when it comes to rivalries. I asked the guys the following hypothetical question: If Florida went 1–11 on the season, God forbid, what team would you want to beat more than anyone? For Dale and Ken, it was Georgia. But for Grant, it was Florida State. Dale and Ken are in their late fifties and Grant's in his mid-thirties. A brief history lesson shows that in the '70s and '80s there was no bigger rivalry for Florida than Georgia. However, in the 90s, the era when Steve Spurrier and Bobby Bowden were the premier coaches in all the land, Florida State was Florida's arch-nemesis.

⚑

Steve Spurrier is universally loved at Florida despite leaving and eventually coaching another school within the same SEC division. As confusing as this is to an outsider, equally confusing are Gator fans' thoughts on Urban Meyer. To put it succinctly, most Florida fans despise Meyer. Why is that confusing? Plenty of schools hate former coaches who leave for another school.[37] It's confusing at first glance because Meyer stepped onto the scene in Gainesville, won two national championships, and then left, taking a year off before returning home to coach Ohio State, a school that doesn't play Florida outside of bowl games. Still, the disdain for Meyer rings loud and clear among Gator fans. They explained it to me like this: First and foremost, Meyer left the team in disarray. There were at least twenty-five players arrested during his tenure, some multiple times. To Gator supporters, Ron Zook—the coach between Spurrier and Meyer—may not have been a good football manager, but he recruited talent to UF and maintained some semblance of discipline on his teams. It was the worst kept secret in Gainesville that the players walked all over Meyer. Two stories, the stuff of tailgate fodder, seem to illustrate the point.

For the record, these "real dish" conversations are bar none my favorite part of tailgates. The game is still my favorite piece of the puzzle, and rightly so. But outside of that, these juicy bits of insider info are the best for a simple reason: There's a sense of importance that comes with being "in the know" when it comes to a college football team, a feeling that you are a special member of a community, privy to information not handed out to every card-carrying member of the tribe. Everybody wants to feel welcomed, loved and accepted, a part of something greater than him or herself. This is a given. Once this human want—or need—is satisfied, the next step in the progression is to be somebody within

---

[37] See: LSU fans on Alabama Head Coach Nick Saban. In college basketball, there's former Kansas coach Roy Williams, who after his team's 2004 national championship loss to Syracuse told the press he "could give a shit about North Carolina right now." By the end of the year he was the coach of North Carolina.

that community. People want to feel special, and nothing makes an average guy feel more special at a tailgate than taking part in conversations containing classified information.

Both stories use former Florida wide receiver standout Percy Harvin to illustrate the point that Meyer had no control over the team. The first comes from a practice where Meyer was unhappy with some aspect of his players' performance. The story goes that Urban walked up to his players and told them to run bleachers to make up for whatever transgression Meyer observed. Allegedly, Percy Harvin told Meyer to "fuck himself" and that he wasn't running stairs. Sensing that he had no power to do anything in the situation, Meyer simply walked away. The second story took place during the 2008 National Championship game against Oklahoma, and it seems to be much more verifiable. With a little over two minutes left in the game, supposedly Harvin walked up behind Meyer, wound up, and slapped him hard on the butt. Meyer's head snapped around, startled, and the two had a brief stare down. You don't need to be a body language expert to see that this was no playful exchange between player and coach. Harvin disrespected his boss on national television well knowing no repercussions would come of it. The event is undeniable. The conclusion drawn by Florida fans, that the players ran Meyer, is plausible.

After hearing these stories, two thoughts rippled around my mind. One: Even now at Ohio State, Meyer's key recruiting pitch to offensive skill players is that he'll use them like Percy Harvin, that they're going to be the next all-purpose game-breaker in his Buckeye offense. It's a running joke on Notre Dame fan message boards that Meyer could offer a 300-pound defensive tackle a scholarship and tell him he's going to be the next Harvin up in Columbus, Ohio. But the logical conclusion to draw is that beyond being a great game-day coach, Meyer is an exceptionally good recruiter. And, he realizes that putting aside his own ego in order to stroke the ego of a seventeen-year-old is the smart thing to do. What better pitch is there than telling a kid he's going to be the next Percy Harvin? The kid doesn't need to know that Harvin (again, allegedly) had no respect for Meyer.

My second thought was that, traditionally speaking, there are two types of effective coaches in football: disciplinarians and "players' coaches." Either can work well with a team. Yet when a players' coach loses control of his team and doesn't have the ability to enforce discipline, it seems likely that fans will use this as proof that you need a disciplinarian. The converse is true also when a tough-as-nails coach loses his team by being a drill sergeant barking orders, and not acting as a mentor molding and shaping young players. The fan base calls for a coach who's better attuned to his players' wants and needs. The grass is always greener when you're not winning.

So between the Harvin stories, which I hadn't heard, and the arrest stats, which I had, I began to grasp what these Florida fans meant when they claimed Meyer left Florida worse than he found it despite winning two national championships.

After more chatting, I discovered that the tailgate I was lucky enough to squirm into is attended by movers and shakers within the Florida football community. Shelley Meyer, Urban's wife, was a regular attendee in the past, as was Tim Tebow's father Robbie. The wives of former defensive coordinators Charlie Strong[38] and Dan Mullen[39] were also regular attendees. In fact, one of the guests at the tailgate told me that Mullen's wife always talked about how her husband plans to write a book on his insider experiences with SEC football when he's done coaching. I know I'll buy a copy.

While South Carolina beat Georgia (to the approval of everyone around me), Fred Taylor walked up. Taylor is one of the best running backs in Florida history and a longtime NFL running back (since retired), and his son is current Florida running back Kelvin Taylor. As people swarmed, Taylor shook hands and took pictures. Meanwhile, the man next to me explained that Taylor stops by on a regular basis and that he's one of the best ambassadors Florida football has. When I went to introduce myself, before I even got within five feet, he noticed the leprechaun on my navy-blue polo and half-shouted "Hey! Who let Notre Dame into the tailgate?" He stared stone-faced for about a half second before cracking a smile and extending his hand. "I'm just playin' man, what's up?" I got a picture, a story, and some juicy intel. I chalked the Florida tailgate up as a W, and then made my way into the stadium.

The score was tied 3–3 at halftime. I was bored. Even Grant, a die-hard Gator, had to stifle a couple first-half yawns. In the second half, though, the Swamp came to life as both offenses began picking apart the oppo-

---

[38] University of Texas's football coach from 2014 to 2016.

[39] Mississippi State University's football coach from 2009 to present.

sition. The Wildcats and Gators were tied at twenty at the end of regulation, which left a sense of foreboding in the air since Florida, an eighteen-and-half-point favorite going into the game, appeared on the verge of letting Kentucky beat them at home for the first time since 1979.

One Kentucky fan four rows ahead of us kept our section lively all night. He looked like every bouncer at every biker bar in America: an overweight, bald-headed forty-something with a scraggly goatee. But he was decked out in Wildcats gear and spent his evening taunting Florida fans. When Kentucky scored late in regulation, he was heckling loudly enough for us to hear: "Get ready for another 4–8 season, Gators!" When an usher warned him about his behavior and taunts, Grant unleashed a verbal tirade he'd been holding in all night. "First, I've never seen any fan get a warning for anything in the Swamp. They shoulda thrown his ass out. Second, a real fan base wouldn't put up with this shit. At LSU or Bama, this guy woulda been bloody by halftime."

Kentucky scored a touchdown on their first play from scrimmage in overtime. Running back Stanley Williams caught a bubble screen to his right, cut all the way across the left side of the field, broke four or five arm tackles along the way, and dove inside the left pylon just in front of the single section wholly inhabited by Kentucky fans. An audible groan carried through the Swamp. The cue ball man hurled more insults at our section.

Florida's offense sputtered, and they were left with a 4th and goal situation from the 7-yard line. All they could do was hope to score and force a second overtime. They seemed to be in complete disarray; they didn't get the play call in until there were ten seconds on the play clock, and their wide receivers were unsure where to line up. Having used their time-out earlier in the overtime, they couldn't stop to reset the clock, and they didn't want to take a delay of game penalty to force 4th and goal from the 12. Video replay showed that the play clock expired before the ball was snapped. However, the play went off without a flag, and DeMarcus Robinson made a catch in the corner of the end zone, tying the game and forcing a second OT.

During the second overtime, I turned to Grant and said, "I feel bad for Kentucky. They deserve to win this game and they're not gonna." He was engrossed in the game and incapable of talking, but he nodded blankly in agreement. After the teams traded field goals, Florida won the game in the third overtime on a Matt Jones touchdown run. I found a strange albeit familiar type of celebration in my section as Jones crossed the goal line. I've experienced it many times as a Notre Dame fan. It's the kind of celebration that's equal parts relief, excitement, despair, and fear. Relief because your team just escaped a close call, excitement because a nail-biting overtime win is exhilarating no matter what, despair because you know your team had no business being in a game that close, and fear because of what it all portends for the rest of the season.

Leaving the stadium, I couldn't help but think all the fair-weather fans won't have much reason to come back this fall. Florida isn't a good team. They'll win six games this year, maybe seven. When the axe falls on Muschamp in December, the fans will be back on the bandwagon. I've always been conflicted about fair-weather fans. On one hand, I think they're bottom-feeding swine. They're the type that come in and buy up all the good seats when a team's doing well, driving up the price for real fans who have been there all along. On the other hand, I'm reminded of hipsters. They're the people who condescendingly let you know they liked a band before they "made it big and sold out" or hung out in a neighborhood "before it got all yuppie and gentrified." I hate that type of person, and I think that people who judge bandwagon fans are the hipsters of sports. And what self-respecting person wants to be a sports hipster? Point is, a new coach brings the bandwagon fans back and can inject fresh interest in the program. That's one of the great things about being a sports fan: you can always find a reason to believe. Even if you're bottom-feeding swine.

Florida vs. #3 Alabama

September 20, 2014

Tuscaloosa, Alabama

Back in Atlanta Monday morning, I visited the College Football Hall of Fame downtown on Marietta Street. The Hall was established in Kings Mills, Ohio, in 1978. In 1992 it moved to South Bend, where it resided until 2014. Despite whatever practical reasons lay behind the decision to move from South Bend to Atlanta, the move symbolizes the heart of college football's migration South. Through the '60s and '70s and into the '80s, the best of college football could be found in the Midwest,[40] where 3-yard gains under a cloud of dust reigned supreme in places like Columbus, Ann Arbor, Lincoln, State College, Pittsburgh, and South Bend. In the '80s, the success of teams like Miami, Clemson, Georgia, and Auburn signaled the beginning of a Southern-shifting landscape, and in the early '90s, Florida State and Florida piled up wins with their spread attacks and speedy athletes. A new kind of Southern revolution was in full force.

At around this time, the college football player prototype looked increasingly smaller, faster, and more athletic (and black), replacing the stereotype of the stronger, slower, and tougher corn-fed rural white athlete. Granted, these stereotypes don't fully account for a highly nuanced reality, but the point remains that the last decades of the twentieth century brought about major changes in the game. Three-yards-and-a-cloud were traded in for what would become "basketball on grass,"[41] a spread offense, and an up-tempo style that continues to dominate the

---

[40] It should be noted, however, that the '60s and '70s were also marked by a period of unprecedented dominance by Alabama, under Bear Bryant. The Crimson Tide won national championships in 1961, '64, '65, '78, and '79. They also claim a 1973 National Championship because the Coaches Poll declared a champ before bowl games were even played. An undefeated Notre Dame beat Alabama in the Sugar Bowl that year, 24–23. To be clear, Alabama did not win the 1973 National Championship—Notre Dame did.

[41] A cover-all term coined by Purdue's Joe Tiller in the early 2000s, it refers to a variety of spread offensive attacks predicated on forcing defenses to defend the entire 53-yard width of a football field.

game today. To me, the College Football Hall of Fame's move to Atlanta simply finalized the transition and sanctified the South as the epicenter of the college football world.

In the high-ceilinged open foyer at the Hall of Fame, a wall of helmets greets visitors. It stretches forty feet high and includes every current college football team, from Division I down to the NAIA level, 768 helmets in all. By forcing the viewer to tilt their neck back to appreciate the view in its entirety, the exhibit is set up in a way that demands reverence. And rightfully so: the Hall is a treasure trove of college football history, housing artifacts from the game's earliest days and celebrating its greatest players, coaches, teams, and moments. There's a beautiful marriage between the dated with the modern, as black-and-white photographs and placards mesh with computer-generated sights and sounds. In the truest sense, the College Football Hall of Fame is a museum of American history.

The day of the Ole Miss-Vanderbilt game two weeks earlier, I met a social media correspondent working for the website Saturday Down South[42] who was out interviewing fans at different game-day tailgates across the region. Given our overlapping interests (and travels), Ashley and I had kept in touch since our meeting in Nashville. The week before the Florida–Alabama game we met at Nook, a Midtown Atlanta tavern

---

[42] A popular website dedicated to—you guessed it—college football in the South.

across the street from Piedmont Park, so she could interview me for the site and so I could learn from her experience.

Ashley attended Ole Miss but comes from an Alabama family. Her father Tom is an Alabama alum, and his disdain for Auburn and reverence for Alabama came through in Ashley's storytelling in ways that typify a hypercommitted college football fan of the South. Her descriptions and stories cracked me up. Ashley's dad forbade her from attending Auburn for college. She could go anywhere she wanted, he said, except Auburn. As a rebellious teenager in high school, Ashley bought tickets to Rodeo, a massive frat party held every spring at Auburn. Her dad found out and threatened to cut off her credit card. In fact, his wife had to talk him down while he was on the phone with the credit card company. Ashley was eventually allowed to enjoy her weekend in enemy territory.

As is often the case with the die-hard fans, Tom's hatred for his rival is eclipsed only by his love for his own team. While he was a student at Alabama, Tom crossed paths with Bear Bryant once. It was an entirely routine encounter: They passed each other on the steps of the Gorgas Library on Alabama's campus. Tom stopped, shook the coach's hand, and said "Roll Tide." What makes the unremarkable so remarkable is the emotional weight ascribed to the event. For Tom, like so many others who lived through the Bear Bryant era, a chance encounter with the coach was like the heavens parting and God himself reaching his hand down to greet a mere mortal. Having heard the story so many times growing up, Ashley can retell it with crystal clarity. It was and still is one of the proudest moments of her dad's life. That's the power college football wields over so many people in the South.

Fresh out of college, Ashley was living a charmed life by any SEC football fan's standards, and she carries a hodgepodge of SEC loyalties and influences around with her. Even though she's an Ole Miss fan first and foremost, she has more than one SEC team in her life. She covers Ole Miss and Mississippi State for Saturday Down South, attended Ole Miss, was raised in an Alabama house, dates an Auburn grad, and hates LSU and Georgia. Ashley concealed the fact that her boyfriend is an Auburn alum from her dad for months. When I talked to her after the season had ended, Tom had seen the Auburn football mural Ashley made her boyfriend for Christmas. He didn't talk to her for several days thereafter.

⚑

I spent the week in Atlanta back with my buddy Alex. During my trip, these visits with friends were invaluable. They provided a refreshing sense of camaraderie on an otherwise solitary journey. Sitting around watching movies, going out for pizza with Alex's grad school friends and discussing topics had nothing to do with college football, and taking his Jack Russell terrier Carson for long walks at Piedmont Park offered me a bit of distance from this world I'd been immersed in. Still, even in these moments away from college campuses, SEC football found a way of showing up in almost all my interactions.

Alex and his family have their own mixed bag of college football allegiances. Though Alex and I became friends when he lived in Chicago, he and his family hail from Fort Payne, Alabama. Alex is the oldest and attended Auburn. Thus, he's an Auburn fan. His sisters Gina and Carrie both attended Alabama and are Alabama fans. Their younger brother Andrew grew up an Auburn fan, but according to Alex, "He seems to be a Bama fan now for some reason." The most fascinating part of their family fan dynamic comes from Alex's parents. Alex's father is a big Auburn supporter, and his mother was an Auburn fan for years. But when his parents divorced, she remarried an Alabama fan and has since flipped her allegiance. Thanksgiving weekends are always interesting for their family. There have been Iron Bowls in which the kids will watch the first half with one parent and drive over to watch the second half with the other. Nobody in the family is what you'd call a die-hard, so there's no animosity within the clan, but they paint an entirely different picture than any college football families I've seen up north.

⚑

I arrived in Tuscaloosa late Thursday afternoon, parked my Chevy, and strolled around campus as per custom. Simply put: Alabama's campus was gorgeous. In fact, at the end of the season, reflecting on my travels, I would decide that Alabama's was the most beautiful campus I visited. Huge brick buildings featured high-vaulted porches, some columned, and all in pristine condition. There was an endless supply of fraternity houses, each row more impressive than the last, starting down Jefferson Avenue and Fraternity Lane before spilling out onto University Boulevard. Common sense told me that the final houses I passed on University Avenue, the ones directly across the street from Bryant-Denny Stadium, were the top-tier fraternities. Farther on, sorority houses surrounded the east side of the stadium along Magnolia Drive. All the houses are clustered inside a box bounded by Bryant Drive, 6th Avenue, University Avenue, and the Stadium. After my cursory glance at the university, I drove thirty miles to my new guest lodgings in McCalla, where Alex's sister Gina and her boyfriend James were taking me in for the weekend.

I'd never met either of them, so I dropped my things off at their house, played with their dogs Rocky Balboa and Jack, and then got down to talking at El Comal Mexican restaurant a mile down the road. James took a roundabout path to becoming a houndstooth lover, which he charted out over burritos and margaritas. Both his parents grew up in Long Island and attended Auburn, his father on a track scholarship. His parents met at school, married, and had James and his brother. Later on, his parents divorced. James grew up in New York with his father, but his mother stayed in Alabama and eventually accepted a position at the University of Alabama. When James came to Tuscaloosa to finish his undergrad degree at UA, it was love at first sight. Somehow a pair of Auburn alums from New York produced an Alabama fan. You can't make this stuff up.

James and Gina were another great example of the Southern hospitality I received time and again throughout the season. Sight unseen, they took me into their home for three nights and invited me to join them at their tailgate on Saturday.

The first thing I did Friday morning was visit the Bryant Museum, which was right on campus. As I walked in, I reminded myself to start talking to people right away. It seemed the longer in the day I waited to start chatting with the locals, the harder it became. At this point in my trip, there was a momentum and a rhythm to making conversation with strangers. One of the women who worked at the museum was standing out front waiting for something or someone, and I asked her what was special about Alabama to her. "You're not a news reporter, are ya?" she joked. As we laughed, I made a mental note to be more subtle with my questions. But Susie—an Alabama grad, current grad school student, and Bryant museum employee—shared an answer to my question that had nothing to do with football. Instead, she talked about the tornado that hit the area a couple years back. What made the school special, in her view, was that the idea of being Greek or non-Greek—one of the most divisive elements in the Alabama family—faded away during the effort to help rebuild the community after the disaster. Affiliation didn't matter, she told me; it was all hands on deck.

This was one of the two times in our conversation where we talked about Alabama as separate parts of a single family or community. The other was in reference to crazy fans. She asked me not to judge the university based on the few fans who seem to be "off their rocker." She elaborated: "Most of 'em never even attended Alabama, but they show up on game day and do their best to sully the good name of our school." Though I'd been aware of a division between alumni and non-alumni within some fan bases, and I was curious to see where it presented itself, this was the first time the issue came up in conversation.

One of the great things about interacting with strangers is that if the ball starts rolling, the revelations unfold in surprising ways. Somehow, we ended up talking about why the SEC is so dominant, and Susie provided examples from her own life and community to illustrate her thoughts. She made two main points on this topic. The first I was familiar with; the second I had never thought about. First off, Susie declared matter-of-factly, people care so much about college football in the South because there's nothing else to cheer for. In Alabama, there are no professional sports teams. This means there are no other events sucking up people's attention during the off-season. "Y'all have basketball and hockey, the Bulls and the Blackhawks, right? We sort of have the Falcons, Saints, or Titans to pick from, but not really." Professional sports teams reside in the three major Southern cities: Atlanta, New Orleans, and Nashville.[43]

Understandably, it can be hard to get behind a pro team whose home base is so far away. The team doesn't really feel like your own if you don't live or weren't raised in the team's city, let alone its state. Small college towns lend themselves to the sustained fervor of a community that directs all its energy toward one particular outlet. Humans fundamentally crave a sense of pride in their community, and what other opportunities are there in a Tuscaloosa? I don't mean this in a slanderous way, but what outlets for culture really exist in a small Southern town? Scarcely any passion for the arts seemed to exist, and without a professional-level sports team, Alabama appeared to me as a place of bars, churches, and Bryant-Denny or Jordan-Hare Stadium. These are the institutions most people schedule their lives around.

Okay, so that partially explains the passion, but it doesn't explain the SEC's football dominance. Here's where Susie's insights really hit home for me. Because sports are such an integral part of the Southern identity, the passion (and pressure) takes hold early. She told me about her nine-year-old nephew who has to memorize his football playbook, her five-year-old daughter who gets yelled at in softball when she drops a ground ball, and even her three-year-old son who played on a pee-wee football

---

[43] While I never received a fully satisfactory explanation, I learned that many Southerners don't consider Florida a true part of the south. This would omit Miami, Tampa and Jacksonville from a list of major Southern cities. I suppose over the past twenty-five years, Charlotte has established itself as a 4th Southern sports metropolis. However, it wasn't a city I heard many Southerners claim as one of their own.

team. There's a hypercompetitiveness that results from this drive for on-field accomplishment in the South. Granted, this isn't unique to the region, but maybe the emphasis is taken to another level there.

One of the drawbacks of such a focus on sports, and especially football, is that the forced perfectionism stops kids from enjoying their childhood. Hearing about kids who are barely potty-trained already playing football makes me wonder about the downside of parents projecting their unrealized dreams onto their kids. It makes me wonder how many kids grow up dreaming of playing in front of 100,000 people on Saturday afternoons because that's what their parents told them to dream about. Most kids grow up wanting to be superheroes; how many of them picture "superheroes" as star quarterbacks or middle linebackers? All of this raises the question of whether the ends justify the means. I can't help but feel that, as a football-centric society, we're sacrificing the purity and beauty of actually *playing* the sport all for the glory of winning.

After saying goodbye to Susie, I made my way inside the Bryant Museum and swelled up with the same sense of reverence and awe I'd felt earlier in the week at the College Football Hall of Fame in Atlanta. It occurred to me that the Bryant Museum is every bit as important to Alabama as the Hall is to the wider country. A full uniform worn by an Alabama player in 1905 was the first artifact to grab my attention. So much college football history was packed into the building; something caught my eye every two feet. Maybe the most impressive trophy I saw was the 1935 Rose Bowl trophy. I suppose there's something to be said here about the reverence for Alabama football, because the trophy wasn't even encased. The idea of someone stealing or damaging it was inconceivable. Without much effort, you could quite literally reach up and touch numerous bowl game trophies from yesteryear.

Another exhibit that makes this museum unique is Bear Bryant's office, which is preserved nearly in its original state and roped off in one corner of the room. While taking note of the details—Bryant's desk and high-backed leather chair, a Green Bay Packers mug (which I didn't understand or care for), the houndstooth hat and sport coat on a coat hanger—I overheard a man to my left talking with his friends about the display. "Well, the couch wasn't there," he informed his audience. "It was facing the desk and it was sunk beneath the desk, which made looking up at him so much more intimidating. I'm sure that was intentional."

This must have been a person with firsthand knowledge of Bryant. A light went off in my head. A personal account is far more interesting to me than any artifact, so I fixed my attention on their conversation and gradually joined in. The gentleman's name was Dewey Mitchell, and he played linebacker and defensive end for the Tide between 1974 and 1977. A quick Internet search after our meeting revealed that he was also a member of the 1984 U.S. Olympic judo team and had earned the nickname "the Red Fireball" around campus. I got a vicarious high from being included in Mitchell's insider accounts of even the trivial, mundane stories from back in his playing days. It's the same feeling I experienced at the Florida tailgate when Fred Taylor made an appearance. After all, feeling special by proxy is still feeling special. Accordingly, talking with Mitchell and his friends was one of the highlights of my weekend in Tuscaloosa, whereas for him it was probably a forgettable fifteen-minute blip.

Mitchell told a few tales as he went though the museum. I tuned in and out, veering off to look at various pieces of memorabilia, not wanting to be a bother. My favorite story was about spring practice. He said there used to be a chalkboard that would list the next day's practice schedule. Spring practice would often get strung out over the course of two months, so there could've been practice on Monday and Tuesday and then not until the following week. But the players never knew for certain what the dates were, so they had to check the chalkboard each day. "That was so we stayed on campus and out of trouble," Mitchell recalled. One day, Mitchell saw his name on the chalkboard along with about ten other guys on the team. That meant they had to go to Coach's office. You only got called to Bear Bryant's office if you were in trouble, and he couldn't figure out what he'd done wrong. Worried, he walked into the meeting with the rest of the guys. Slowly it dawned on Mitchell that he was sitting in an office full of the "fat guys" on the team. "It was me and the fat guys, I couldn't understand it. I wasn't fat. Maybe five pounds overweight, but I was solid." Once everyone had assembled, Coach Bryant started in on the group. "We can't win championships with turds," he declared. The meeting was about getting in shape and how those assembled would have to go on a diet. When the talk was over, Coach Bryant looked at the physically fit Mitchell standing beside his desk and demanded to know: "What the hell are you doing here?"

On University Avenue, the SEC Network was taping a show. The setup was across the street from Denny Chimes, the landmark bell tower that looms over the Quad, the aptly named public green space in the center of campus. While surveying the scene, I met a ruddy, dough-faced thirty-something Bama fan named Mike. He and his two friends—both Florida fans—flagged me down and had to ask about the Notre Dame shirt I was wearing—and how in the hell I made it to Tuscaloosa. They were jovial and easygoing. Quickly, we jumped on the national college football headline for the week: Jameis Winston. He'd been suspended for the first half of the Florida State–Clemson game for jumping on a table in the middle of campus and shouting obscenities. Winston's display was a nod to a recent viral trend whereby people sneak up on live news reports and blurt out profanity before the camera can cut away. By my non-politically correct standards, the video clips are amusing, if childish. However, by the standards set for a public figure—like, say, a Heisman Trophy winner—and someone who has already been accused of sexual assault and arrested for stealing crab legs, the performance seemed exceptionally self-serving and stupid.

The conversation took an interesting turn when I asked Mike how in the hell Winston, a guy from Hueytown High School, forty minutes from Tuscaloosa, managed to escape the SEC. He explained that Alabama coach Nick Saban only recruits high-character kids, and that probably explains why the school didn't go hard after Winston. I don't know the ins and outs of Alabama football recruiting. I do know that Alabama was among the reported finalists for Winston coming out of high school, but I have no clue how hard they pursued him. Alabama would've had to find some major character concerns to not pursue a bona fide blue-chip quarterback who happened to live right in their own backyard.

Mike's take was interesting for another reason. Most Alabama fans truly believe their school only goes after high-class kids who do things the right way, but the common perception outside the South is that the Crimson Tide are professional cheaters whose primary concern is keeping athletes eligible to play on Saturdays, regardless of any academic, legal, or moral obstacles. Is there a blindness within fans like Mike, or does the rest of the country need to make up some petty justification for why Alabama has been so much better than everyone else over the course of the Saban dynasty?

In the same vein, we discussed Florida State fans' reactions to the Winston suspension. Florida State fans blamed the students who tweeted about what Winston did for getting him in trouble. Rather than holding the culprit responsible for his (dumb) actions, the fans labeled the university students "rats." Mike thought that was ludicrous. "How about [FSU fans] look at what a dumbass their star quarterback is and not blame the kids who tweeted it out?" Well said, Mike. Denial is a sure sign of being out of touch with reality, and there are few clearer indicators of denial than refusing to accept responsibility and blaming others instead. When our loyalties go unchecked, we sometimes end up defending the indefensible.

⚑

Around noontime Saturday, I passed by the impressive-looking frat houses again, the ones across from Bryant-Denny: Sigma Nu, Beta, and Dke. There was something notably smug and condescending about the guys I encountered around the frats. As I passed Sigma Nu, a couple of "brothers" were smoking cigarettes near the fence enclosing the expansive lawn where their pregame festivities were in full effect. They started talking to me in what I guess you'd call caricatured, but clearly fake New York-Italian accents. Most of what they said was unintelligible as they amused themselves finding ways to squeeze two or three "heyyyyyy, ohhhhhhhhs" and "fuhgettaboutits" into every sentence. In under a minute, I felt my internal temperature rising to unsafe levels. I walked away trying to figure out what it was that irritated me so much about some obnoxious frat bros; under most conditions, something like that wouldn't bother me.

As I passed the next couple houses along University Avenue, I saw all the stereotypical bros you'd see in the student section on TV during Alabama games. They looked eerily similar in their getups: black or navy sport coats with white shirts and crimson ties. And as I looked closer, it was clear that a second, older generation of fathers and uncles milled about dressed in the same way. It was as if these fathers didn't only pass on their genes to their sons, but also their fashion sense and demeanor. My temperature began to climb again merely at their sight. I continued on toward Denny Chimes and the Quad. And I started to get a sense of who these Greeks were apart from the wardrobe.

Normally, when you meet someone, you make eye contact or at least look at some part of the person's face. What bothered me most about this fratty type at Alabama was how none of them ever looked at my face. When they were taller than me, they looked down on me, almost past my face to my collarbone. And when they were my height or shorter than me, they looked over my shoulder, like they were waiting for someone to rescue them from an unbearable conversation. I could never put my finger on why, but I left certain that they were fully aware of what they were doing, that looking past people was a conscious choice and a declarative but unspoken statement on their part rather than some benign aloofness.

Crossing the angled sidewalks in the Quad, I noticed two men in their late thirties or early forties. I recognized the symptoms of delusional self-importance from their side profiles. It was dripping from their slicked-back, jet-black hair, radiating out from their puffed chests, and sliding down the exaggerated posture of their spines. As they stood apart from their tailgate sipping Michelob Ultras, first one, then the other, noticed my shirt. "Notre Dame?" one of the men asked. "Yeah, I'm down here from Chicago. Always wanted to see an Alabama game." He looked down at me: "Oh...cool, bro."

In that brief moment of interaction, these two clowns, much like the bros with the fake New York accents, somehow made me feel like they thought I was less than them. They searched past me, looking over my shoulder even as we spoke face-to-face. Right after the "Oh...cool, bro" line, the man locked eyes with his buddy and carried on his conversation, dismissing me entirely. And in that moment I realized the Greek vibe on Alabama's campus is obnoxious and elitist. I still don't know why the exchange rattled me so completely, but it did. Somehow a handful of these brief interactions made me feel completely alone and isolated, apart from everyone around me despite the fact that there were probably at least 150,000 people on campus that afternoon.

⚑

At the back end of the Quad is the Gorgas Library, where I arrived minutes before the Elephant Stomp started. The Elephant Stomp is one of Alabama's game-day traditions during which the band starts off in "Yea Alabama," the school's fight song. Without a doubt, it is the second-catchiest fight song in all of college football—behind the Notre Dame fight song, of course. Thirty seconds into the Stomp the entire crowd was at a fever pitch, pom-poms waving and people cheering and shouting. The Million Dollar Band, as Alabama's marching band is called, was lined up on the stairs of the library with the brass section configured along the back line. The cheerleaders danced on the sidewalk in front of the library, and the dance team, dressed in gleaming crimson tops, shimmied on the side of the stairs on a raised concrete platform.

Big Al, the Alabama mascot, flailed about in front of the cheerleaders. They continued trucking through a series of chants and songs before closing again with "Yea, Alabama."

When they finished, I sauntered back to the stadium to scalp a face-value ticket. Near my section, I met two men in their late forties who both work at the university. Both relocated to Alabama from out of state. One was from Pennsylvania originally, and when he saw my Notre Dame shirt, told me about growing up with Ned Bolcar, a captain on Notre Dame's '88 National Championship team. He also knew the Ismail brothers.[44] After Alabama, he said, he still roots for the Irish, so we got along pretty well. The other fellow, Bill, came from Portland, Oregon, and both said they fell in love with Alabama football almost instantly after they arrived.

As the Million Dollar Band took the field, the men both smiled down on the green field below and explained that their new obsession was unavoidable. They both attended all the home games their first year in Tuscaloosa, and that was all it took to get hooked. "I don't even know how to explain it to you. It just happened. There's something about the spirit of this place. You get swept up in it," Bill offered. We carried on throughout the band's pregame performance until the Crimson Tide took the field, and then discussion switched to Nick Saban. There's an absolute love affair with Saban in Tuscaloosa, and why not? Entering

---

[44] Raghib "Rocket" Ismail played for Notre Dame from 1988–90. He finished second in the 1990 Heisman Trophy voting, despite scoring only six touchdowns during the season. His brother Qadry played football at Syracuse and went on to a successful NFL career, and their brother Suleiman was a walk-on at University of Texas-El Paso.

the 2014 season, he had led Alabama to three national championships in six years. Out flowed an abundance of over-the-top, flattering comments about Saban and how much he means to Alabama: "If he ran for Governor of Alabama, he'd win in a landslide," and "I swear, he'd have to kill somebody to get fired." They really poured it on. "Saban's the best thing to happen to Alabama since Bear Bryant and everybody knows it," I was informed. And then there was this: "Hell, if it came down to it, I'd blow him to keep him from taking another job." Something about the spirit of the place, eh?

⚑

Florida went three-and-out on their opening possession, and Alabama hit an 87-yard touchdown pass on their first play. Florida's next possession lasted only five plays before they were forced to punt again. But on Alabama's first play from scrimmage on their second drive, running back Kenyan Drake fumbled. Florida recovered, and thanks in large part to a short field, the Gators scored three plays later. Receiver DeAndrew White fumbled the next time Alabama had the ball; Florida defensive back Keanu Neal recovered the fumble and scored from 50 yards out. Even after Alabama missed a field goal on their next drive and Florida took over, up a touchdown with decent field position, it never felt like Florida was or should be in this game. After the Gators were forced into another three-and-out, Blake Sims hit Amari Cooper for a 79-yard touchdown on Bama's first play. Alabama scored again on a 2-yard pass halfway through the second quarter, and the game went to halftime with the Crimson Tide leading 21–14. I mentioned to the older man next to me that the score should be closer to 31–7; he grumbled something about how Florida shouldn't even have 7 points. I agreed and strolled to the concourse for a Coke and some shade. After the break, the Tide picked up right where they left off, shooting rounds into their feet. Blake

Sims threw an interception on the first drive of the second half, and Florida scored two plays later to tie the score at 21. From that point forward though, it was all Alabama. The Crimson Tide scored on their next three possessions, smothered Florida's offense, and won 42–21. Cooper, the star receiver, finished the day with over 200 yards and 3 touchdowns, while Blake Sims threw for 445 yards and 4 touchdowns. At the end of the game, I talked with the people around me about how a three-touchdown differential didn't even do justice to how lopsided the game was. Despite all of Alabama's sloppiness, the outcome was never in doubt.

After the game, I found James and Gina with The Dew Crew, their weekly tailgate. Like many fans, they post up in the same spot with the same group every home game. Back behind the Old Row frats on University Avenue, their spread included plenty of food and drinks. I was impressed by their setup. Two connected crimson-and-white tents housed at least a dozen lawn chairs, a 60" flat-screen TV, and stereo system. When I arrived, still an hour before the sun went down on a dry-hot Tuscaloosa afternoon, Gina introduced me to a bunch of the regulars—men and women anywhere from their twenties to their sixties—and everyone shook my hand and said hello. Then a strange thing happened. Everyone I talked to would walk away almost immediatcly after they introduced themselves. They were polite, but uninterested in the stranger in the green shirt.

Most of the people at this tailgate, I gathered, called Tuscaloosa home. And many of them fell into the category of non-alumni fans. As I mentioned earlier, there's a divide in some fan bases between the alumni and the so-called "T-shirt fans." I thought back to Susie imploring me not to judge the Alabama crowd based on this type of fan. A "T-shirt fan" is a slanderous term used by college football fans to indicate an uneducated, oftentimes ignorant type of fan who gives the school's "real" supporters a bad name. I didn't find these people to be that, exactly. I found them leery of a stranger in Notre Dame gear. However, there's a major distinction between the aloofness this group of strangers displayed and the nose-perked Greeks I crossed paths with numerous times before the game. It was plain that the people at this tailgate had no intention of making me feel unwelcome. Rather, they appeared to be the type who were ill at ease with strangers and comfortable only in their own clique. During the couple hours I struggled to kick up small talk, I never took it personally. The reluctance to be any friendlier than curt and cordial was benign. On the other hand, the uppity fellows I encountered earlier in the day, to a man (if you can call them that), seemed programmed to condescend and alienate. Theirs was a malignant sort of unfriendliness.

Late afternoon drifted into night, and as the partiers' daytime buzz gave way to evening drunkenness a funny thing happened: the regulars warmed up to me. It started with a couple of the guys inviting me to throw a game of bags with them. And as one game led to two, they started joking with me a little bit and asking questions about where I was from, and what I thought of Alabama. When the crescent moon overhead and the tiki torches couldn't dispense enough light for us to continue tossing bags, we found seats back inside the tent and watched the ABC featured night game.

A handful of guys called me over to take a pull on the bottle of Fireball they were passing around. They started to regale me with stories of growing up together in Tuscaloosa, causing trouble as teenagers, and then partying on campus in their twenties. The drunker they became, the more likable I was. Glenn, one of the regulars at the tailgate, came up to me when it was his turn to take a swig of the Fireball bottle. He leaned in and whispered: "Tell ya what, Jim. I think I'm too drunk to take any more of this. So I'll show you what I'm gonna do." He stuck his tongue inside the bottle, tilted it back, and pulled the bottle back down without actually taking a swig. Then he patted me on the back and laughed in a high-pitched whinny. "Can't tell nobody, now."

When it was time to leave, I helped pack the tents into the hitched trailer. One of the men offered to drive any stragglers back to our cars. And so my night ended in the only way it could have: sitting in the back of a pickup truck, my forearm resting on a cooler full of beer, driving through downtown Tuscaloosa. I spent my day butting up against cold shoulders from the University of Alabama elite and my night warming up to a group of good ol' boys who grew up in town. As we crossed campus on the way back to James's car, I laughed to myself thinking that in a lot of ways the members of The Dew Crew were like caricature versions of redneck stereotypes I grew up hearing about: a few sat around spitting dip into empty Coke and Budweiser cans, some talked with a thick country drawl, and a couple fellas even stood with their thumbs through their belt loops. I also found myself thinking there's nothing disagreeable or bad about any of that. They might have even been a bit racist in their jokes, but that's everywhere. And then the really puzzling thought occurred to me: how are *these* the people alumni and students worry about giving the fan base a bad name?

⚑

As days passed, thoughts of the overwhelmingly negative interactions I had with the Greek elite lingered in my mind. So I reached out through some connections and eventually made contact with a recent member of one of the more prestigious New Row fraternities on campus. Tom—not his real name—laughed as I told him about my interactions with the fratty elite of Alabama and said that it wasn't surprising at all. He agreed to talk with me about the fraternity culture that runs the University of Alabama and explained why my experience on campus shouldn't be considered an anomaly. He asked me not to use his name because "even though I'm not telling you any secrets or anything that hasn't been talked or written about, I'd still get angry phone calls about it if anyone I know read your book."

Roughly thirty percent of Alabama's undergraduate population is Greek. By percentage, it's easily one of the most Greek-affiliated campuses anywhere in America. The system itself is highly organized and wields tremendous power. "The Machine" is the name that's been given to the power structure within the Greek system, even though its very existence is vehemently denied (at least, publicly). Tom assured me that it certainly does exist. The only thing that's debatable, he insisted, is just how much power it really holds. To be sure, the on-campus power is undeniable. The Machine decides the Homecoming Queen and who's elected to the Student Government Association (SGA) every year. The way they retain that power is every bit as impressive in its organizational prowess as the Democratic machine that controlled Chicago politics and city life throughout the twentieth century. The people who run the Machine are, in effect, the kingmakers on campus. All Old Row fraternities and some New Row fraternities have a Machine representative. When the Machine meets and decides on their slate of candidates to back, they send the representatives back to their frats where the information is relayed. Then, because voting is conducted online, every member of the frat must show the house representative that he voted for the decided-upon candidates. The real question is how far their reach extends. Many speculate that it extends far beyond campus and is responsible for most, if not all, major political decisions in the state of Alabama, including the election of the state's governor.

As Tom tells it, the fraternity system at Alabama propagates an entire culture based on this extended form of nepotism and classism. And racism: Old Row frats and most of the top-tier New Row frats hardly ever allow black people to pledge. The system serves as its own enforcer of social segregation, effectively circumventing the integration forced upon the school and enacted across the country almost sixty years ago. In fact, Tom explained, one New Row frat, Delta Chi, recently admitted a black student. For their trailblazing efforts, they're now known as the frat with a black guy—a stigmatizing distinction within their Greek community.

Of course, the majority of Alabama's student body is non-Greek, and plenty of anti-Greek sentiment exists within that majority. Of those vocally opposed to the Greek culture that dictates so much of life on campus in Tuscaloosa, the loudest voices can often be heard coming from Mallett Hall. Mallett Hall is a dormitory, but also an organization of sorts where people who take issue with the Greeks congregate. They are the students who stage protests and write editorial pieces for the *Crimson White*, the Alabama student newspaper. If anyone stands in the way of Greek life running roughshod over the university, it's those inside Mallett Hall. To the Greeks, they're simply known as GDIs, or God Damn Independents.

But other than the occasional hiccup, there isn't much interference with the Greek system and its heartbeat, the Machine, as it calls the shots in Tuscaloosa. It's clannish in the most extreme sense. Outsiders are made to feel unwelcome, and it's extremely difficult to find yourself on the inside. If you do find yourself behind the curtain and follow the extensive rules of social control meant to dictate every aspect of your behavior, I'm told the payoff is incredible. With membership comes access to sororities with the best-looking women on campus and the best parties (fraternity entertainment budgets are regularly in the mid-six-figures per semester), and graduates get access to a social network made up of the who's who of the Southern aristocracy. Unsurprisingly, this makes finding a choice job after graduation quite a bit easier. Like so many other families, the Machine takes care of its own.

Beyond directly making decisions on campus by controlling student government, there are other ways the Greek system maintains its influence. When you walk around campus, all you'll see are guys in Vineyard Vines shirts and boat shoes. During the day, girls are in oversized T-shirts and Nike shorts. At night, the same girls are in dresses and heels with their hair and makeup done up like it's prom night. There's a huge amount of social pressure to wear what the rest of the Greeks are wearing. It's like a uniform that lets you know at a glance whether someone is a part of the society or not. Tom said that he had to buy a whole new wardrobe when he was inducted into his frat. He didn't wear button-down shirts and boat shoes in high school, but if you're going to fit in, you have to look the part.

The conformity extends beyond the dress code. Tom explained that there are message boards within the Greek community that let everyone know who's sleeping with whom and who has said or done anything that doesn't fall in line with the social norms. They also keep a register of which Greek members have been seen socializing with black students on campus. Not only does the Greek system not want black students in their closed community, they don't even want the members of their community associating with black students at all. With few exceptions, the only black people on guest lists at frat parties at Alabama are their drug dealers and football players.

And when it comes to recruiting, the Greek system pursues its own blue-chip prospects and tunnels pipelines into talent-rich high schools with almost as much enthusiasm as college coaching staffs do in assembling championship-caliber teams. Pledges from north of the Mason–Dixon Line are almost never accepted into any decent fraternity at Alabama. At first glance, this reads like lingering anti-Yankee sentiment. While that surely still exists, Tom offered a more practical explanation for why this happens. The majority of Alabama students come from Alabama, Mississippi, Tennessee, Georgia, and Florida. When pledges are inducted into the frat, it's expected that they will bring high schoolers from their school or town down to visit. When that happens, they're looking for "cool" kids of course, but much more importantly, they're looking for kids whose parents have money or political connections. And when such a valuable prospect is visiting campus for a weekend, every member of the frat knows about it. The rule is for everyone to make sure the prospect has a good time, gets drunk, and is surrounded by girls who will (hopefully) get him laid. The motivation behind this is clear: the more kids in the frat whose parents are extremely wealthy or have political clout, by proxy, the further the fraternity's reach will be.

What's the point of all this? I made a phone call and found out some background information that explains why I was made to feel unwelcome on campus on one Saturday in September. So what?

Well, I'll tell you what. Clearly, the Greek system procures the best sections and seats in the student section of Bryant-Denny Stadium. So, when I (and the rest of America) turn on ESPN or CBS on a Saturday afternoon, I see what appears to be the face of Alabama football as the camera pans the crowd. That face is well-dressed, attractive, and almost exclusively white: guys in sport coats and ties, their mop of hair combed over, and girls in black or crimson or white sundresses and cowgirl boots with their hair and makeup done, all of them with their perfect white smiles beaming. At the beginning of my stay in Tuscaloosa, I heard about the white trash and poor black Alabama fans, and how they sully the good name of Alabama football by allowing people all over the country to think that there's nothing but backwards-assed hillbillies in Alabama. After a weekend on campus, I think Susie and others like her have it all wrong. Her conclusion about which kinds of fans give Alabama a bad name is the only thing backwards-assed about it.

Missouri vs. #13 South Carolina

September 27, 2014

Columbia, South Carolina

I knew that, if possible, I wanted to visit a number of Southern cities away from the college towns. The number one city on that list was Charleston, South Carolina. Though I couldn't pinpoint where I got the impression, I'd always envisioned Charleston as a Southern paradise. So I made plans to stop through for a day or two before riding into Columbia again. I'd kept in touch with Jenny, the girl I met at Starbucks the morning of the A&M–Carolina game, and invited her to meet me in Charleston—or Chuck-town, as she called it.

Stormy weather kept Jenny and me largely confined to our hotel after dinner Tuesday night, but first thing Wednesday morning we found coffee and began touristing around downtown Charleston. We had four or five hours until our afternoon boat tour to Fort Sumter, and I wanted to breathe in as much of the city as possible. Palmetto trees lined walkways as we passed opulent centuries-old mansions along the waterfront. Pearly-white outdoor patios ran the length of almost every property, in many cases on both the second and third floors as well. And it was almost impossible to walk two blocks without spotting a cathedral, some of which had cemeteries in their backyard. Some cemeteries had headstones from as far back as the late 1600s. All the history would have made me feel like I was in a time warp if not for the brightly painted houses in yellow and pink and baby blue and lilac intermingled with the traditional brick and whitewashed homes down on Rainbow Row.

Before we boarded the boat tour to Sumter, we stopped at the City Market, where I bought my sister, Ryanne, coasters for her apartment. Jenny explained that the marketplace used to be an auction site where slaves were bought and sold upon arriving in America. It's always been easy to not fully grapple with the reality of slavery, easy to see it as some abhorrent abstraction I only read about in history classes, easy to keep it on the far fringes of my consciousness. Out of sight, out of mind. Stepping through places where slavery thrived struck a sadness into me that no textbook, no college lecture, and no History Channel documentary ever could force upon my psyche. Slavery became real to me that morning, and that afternoon at Fort Sumter, the Civil War did, too.

On the boat trip to Sumter, a prerecorded narrator provided the background, explaining how Union Major Robert Anderson brought his men from nearby Fort Moultrie to Fort Sumter, a man-made island fortress. Anderson found Moultrie indefensible and believed Sumter a better place to station his troops. After South Carolina seceded from the Union—the first state to do so—it demanded Anderson and his men leave Sumter. Following orders from President Lincoln, Anderson refused. Lincoln sent supplies to Anderson and his men so they wouldn't starve. On April 11, 1861, a Union ship approached Sumter to deliver goods. General Pierre Beauregard, commander of the Confederate troops at Charleston, blocked the ship's passage and demanded Anderson surrender Fort Sumter. When Anderson refused, Beauregard gave orders to his men, and at 4:30 am they fired the first shots of the Civil War. After thirty-four hours, Anderson and his troops surrendered the fort. Over the next four years, the Union, having realized the strategic significance of Fort Sumter, made numerous unsuccessful attempts to retake the island stronghold. It wasn't until February 17, 1865—when General Sherman's infamous march from Savannah arrived to Charleston—that Confederate troops finally abandoned Fort Sumter. Walking around the island, I couldn't help but feel the full weight of the fortress. The events on this tiny, man-made speck of land charted the course of our nation's history. Peering out a hole in the brick exterior through which cannons fired once upon a time, I let the waves roll over in my mind. As each wave crested and broke, I felt a little smaller, a little more insignificant. That William Blake line about "a grain of sand" kept running through my mind.[45]

⚑

Back in Columbia, I said goodbye to Jenny and made my way to my Airbnb lodging for the week. I was staying with a Columbia native in his sixties who spoke with a thick country twang. Larry told me stories

---

[45] "To see the world in a grain of sand, / And heaven in a wild flower, / Hold infinity in the palm of your hand, / And eternity in an hour…." –William Blake, "Auguries of Innocence"

about his sons—whose framed pictures lined the walls—while he gave me the house tour. He called me buddy in nearly every sentence, and the only Gamecock memorabilia in his house was a lamp made out of an old South Carolina helmet in his living room. Larry wanted me to feel at home and when his friends came to visit throughout the week, he'd always introduce me the same way: "This here's my buddy, Tim." He was so earnest and hell-bent on making me feel welcome, I never had the heart to correct him.

On Thursday night, I met Missy, my former Airbnb host in Columbia, for dinner at Hunter-Gatherer in Vista. We had a great time catching up; she told me about the play she was opening the next night, and I told her all about getting robbed in Atlanta and the interesting people I'd met over the past month. After dinner, we went to a bar called Jillian's to dance. The Carolina Shag is the official state dance of South Carolina and is almost exclusively limited to the Carolinas. Shagging is another one of those regional traditions I wouldn't know about if I hadn't seen or experienced it firsthand. Watching couples glide across the floor to beach music brought me back to iconic images of a bygone America: cheerleaders wearing their boyfriends' lettermen jackets, poodle skirts, and carhops serving milkshakes at the drive-in. What kept producing this effect? What was it about my surroundings in so many different locations in the South that made me feel like I'd tapped into the halcyon days of 1950s teenage Americana? I couldn't understand. On a regular basis during my trip through the South, I was reminded of, and sometimes even transported to, a state of nostalgic innocence. It wasn't my nostalgic innocence, but even still I couldn't keep from being swept up into it.

The dance itself has a one-and-two, three-and-four, five, six cadence, with a simple pattern of shuffle steps and single steps. But from this simple outline, I looked out on the dance floor and saw incredibly smooth and rhythmic dancers making the pattern their own in every way imaginable. They had, in effect, learned the rules so that they could break them, and the people transformed this basic formula into a silky glide that line dancing or a two-step would never allow. I, on the other hand, was terrible at shagging. When I focused on the steps, I was stiff and robotic, and when I was loose and having fun dancing, I'm sure I wasn't keeping rhythm with the pattern at all. I found I couldn't have both the first time learning shag, so I rolled with the latter, deciding it was much better to enjoy what I was doing than to do it the "right" way. Missy didn't seem to mind, and we had a good time. She introduced me to one of her professors who teaches most of the dance classes available at USC, and he offered to give us a free lesson if I'm ever back in town. So I've got that going for me…which is nice.

After catching the opening of Missy's play on Friday night, I had a late dinner with her and her stepbrother. Knowing that *College GameDay* would be airing on Saturday morning from the Horseshoe (the historic and imposing quad), I dragged Missy along to view the late night setup. We found a veritable alien invasion as we drew near at midnight: tents arranged all through the quad emitting the strange, almost primitive cacophony of eighteen- to twenty-one-year-olds camping on campus; glow-in-the-dark footballs and Frisbees flung and zipped in every direction simultaneously; and a pair of belligerent undergrads being dragged out in handcuffs.

Once we adjusted to the lights and sounds, our attention naturally fell on the signs scattered throughout the quad and leaned against tents. Missy had a lot of questions. The first was about a real attention-grabber: a ten-foot-tall goalpost with a football on the left upright and a poster below that said, "Remember this, Mizzou?" I explained that the sign was a reference to Missouri's missed overtime field goal in the 2013 Mizzou–USC game, which sealed a South Carolina victory. Missy nodded. The multiple "Hoosier Daddy, Mizzou?" signs caught her attention as well. Those were a nod to both Indiana's upset win over Missouri the week before and the lack of originality in so many college kids. Missy rolled her eyes. Then she spotted one that read "Tigers Love Cocks," which had a picture of former Missouri defensive end Michael Sam, and asked: "Do I even want to know?" I told her that Sam was the first openly gay player drafted into the NFL. Missy sighed and said, "Oh, brother!"

On Saturday morning I got over to the Horseshoe in time to catch the second half of the *College GameDay* broadcast. A Mizzou flag waved high above the crowd along with the infamous Washington State flag that flies at every *College GameDay* stop.[46] My top priority was to meet

---

[46] Initially, the Wazzu flags were flown as part of a push to bring *College GameDay* to Pullman, Washington, in 2003, when Washington State was ranked as high as No. 3 in the nation. It quickly became a tradition adopted by Cougar alums around the country, who volunteer to handle flag duties if *College GameDay* is broadcasting near them on a weekend. The WSU flags have been raised high on over a hundred consecutive *College GameDay* broadcasts. Despite this, the program still hasn't broadcast from Pullman.

some Mizzou fans, so I made my way to the pocket of golden-yellow T-shirts. Missouri and Kentucky were the two SEC schools I wouldn't be visiting, and with all due respect to UK football, they're a basketball school. Mizzou was the school I felt bad about not checking out.

Like most of my Saturday chats, my first conversation of the day started when someone took notice of my Fighting Irish shirt. Meg and Phil were a couple from northern South Carolina who were back on USC's campus for the first time in over a decade. Though both attended Furman, a private school in Greenville, South Carolina, they grew up big Gamecock fans. Then their son went to Mizzou because the family all liked its broadcast journalism program. Maybe it's because their money goes to the University of Missouri, or maybe it's an expression of love and support for their son. Who knows? But Mom and Dad are Missouri Tiger fans now. Sometimes when a family member goes to another SEC school, the other members transfer their allegiance and become fans of that school. Some people can change their allegiances like changing pants. Consequently, their story raised a very serious question: can people who switch sides so easily even be considered fans?

On the opposite side of the spectrum, I've met people whose parents refused to sign the tuition check when the child attended a rival school, parents who wouldn't talk to their kid for two or three weeks after finding out where they decided to go to college, and siblings who didn't communicate at all during football season because their colleges hated each other. I wasn't expecting a stock answer to how fans handled these situations, and where college football fit in the pecking order of the important things in life. After all, what's the criteria for being a "fan"? Is a lifetime commitment to one team a prerequisite for calling yourself one? Are casual supporters considered second-class fans because they don't put their sports teams on a pedestal, like others do? The couple I met who switched their allegiance didn't see anything wrong with changing who they rooted for. And I'm not sure I do, either. Still, something about rooting for a new team against your old team—and in the place where you grew up, no less—felt sacrilegious.

As our conversation wound down, I began to notice a Mizzou student news reporter interviewing a spunky middle-aged lady. I overheard bits and pieces of the interview. They were fairly routine questions, like: "How long did the drive down take?" and "Who do you think's gonna win tonight?" From what I heard of the responses, the lady put dramatic flourishes on even the most basic questions, and I loved that. At the end, the interviewer asked the woman if she had anything else to add: *"M-I-Z!"* the woman screamed at the top of her lungs. *"Z-O-U!"* the densely packed gold-and-black pocket of fans shouted back.

I sought out the interviewee after the student reporter left. Her name was Darlene, and she was the type of person who feels like an old family friend two minutes into a conversation. We talked about life in Columbia, Missouri, and life in Chicago. When I pressed her about Mizzou, she explained how Mizzou's been consistently good for a decade, but they only started to get respect once they joined the SEC. This sounded like another one of her dramatic flourishes. When I raised an eyebrow, she got specific. "We were #1 in the BCS in 2006 headed into conference championship week. If we won that game, we would've played Ohio State for the national championship. But we lost and that 2-loss LSU team snuck in and won it all. Nobody even knows about that." It's true: I had no idea what she was talking about. When I Googled it, I found she was right about almost everything. Mizzou did come *that close* to a national championship berth, and they had three 10-win seasons over the previous decade. The only part she got wrong was overstating the impact of Mizzou's move to the SEC. Doesn't matter what conference they're in—the Missouri Tigers are still an afterthought.

Something else stuck out to me about Darlene, or maybe it's that she was the access point to something I'd been noticing in general. When you're on the road by yourself, the strangers you meet have way more power to affect the quality of your experience than they do if you were to meet them in your own community. I suppose the contrast between Alabama and South Carolina illustrated this for me. I did meet some friendly folks at Alabama. For the majority of the day, though, I was eyed suspiciously and made to feel like an outsider. I think everybody knows what it is to be an outsider; it's another thing altogether to be made to *feel* like one. I was an outsider everywhere I went on this trip. I hardly knew anyone at any of these schools, but the great thing is that people with open and engaging dispositions, people like Darlene, made me forget my circumstances. Still, it's hard to accept the reality that the quality of my experience was dictated simply by my interactions with the strangers around me.

⛳

After *College GameDay* ended I walked over to the Five Points area and eventually found myself sitting at the bar at the Village Idiot pub, yukking it up with a middle-aged man on his third scotch and soda. I wondered why I ended up talking to middle-aged people so often. They were old enough to have interesting stories of yesteryear, and young enough to not repeat themselves every five minutes, I suppose. Carter and I were discussing all things Carolina football while we watched the Georgia–Tennessee game on TV. At one point he mentioned how it'd be so much easier to root for a tradition-rich school like Tennessee or Georgia. To make his point, Carter asked me if I knew the first time Carolina ever won a bowl game. It was 1994.[47] I knew the Gamecocks had a history of mediocrity and the current "era" represents the peak of their football history, but I had no idea things were that bad back in the day.

As we talked, the bar owner, Brian, jumped in and out of conversation while he served drinks and took food orders. At one point, we all marveled as Todd Gurley II, Georgia's all-everything running back, hurdled a defender in the open field. Brian started in on how Gurley likes coming to the Village Idiot, and that he's been seen hanging out with South Carolina players Mike Davis, Shaq Roland, and others a handful of times at the bar. Carter and I were speculating on why a Georgia player would come up to South Carolina to hang out when Brian said something that made perfect sense: "People still know who he is here, but there's not that hero worship that he gets everywhere at Georgia. Ya know, these are twenty-year-old kids trying to figure all this stuff out."

I'd never given much thought to how difficult it is to be a star athlete at any college, especially at an SEC school, where the spotlight burns so much brighter. It's easy to buy into everyone around you telling you you're the greatest. How do you keep your ego in check when people fawn over you everywhere you go? And how do you get away if you just want to be a normal college kid for a weekend or even a day?

---

[47] Coincidentally, South Carolina honored the 1994 team at halftime during the game Saturday night.

Brian shared a story about the last time Gurley and his Georgia buddies visited the Village Idiot, the previous spring. While Brian recounted which players were in attendance that night, he peppered in little details about some of the players. Specifically, he informed me and Carter—who by this point seemed more interested in his fifth scotch and soda than anything being discussed—that Mike Davis never drinks when he goes out. He always eats sausage pizza and drinks sugar-free Red Bull when he's at the bar. Brian was proud of being in the position to share this detail with us. And in that moment it occurred to me that when we're dealing with star athletes, the focal point of our fan's gaze, even the most mundane factoids about them become worthy of retelling. If he wasn't a star athlete, would anyone care at all what some guy named Mike Davis ate or drank at the bar? Absolutely not.

Anyway, the story goes that while the crew hung out at the bar, Gurley requested a red Village Idiot T-shirt. When Brian returned with the shirt, Gurley asked how much, and Brian replied: "Tell you what, go out and light up Clemson in the opener and we'll call it even." In the season opener, Gurley racked up 293 all-purpose yards and 4 touchdowns in a 45–21 drubbing of the Clemson Tigers. Later, Brian received a text message from Gurley: "Good enough?"

Did Todd Gurley II, Heisman Trophy front-runner, really keep a South Carolina bar owner's phone number and remember to text him months later? Who knows. It sounded a bit far-fetched to me, but hey, never let facts get in the way of a good story.

After the Georgia–Tennessee game I headed to the stadium. On the walk I called Jim, the fellow originally from the Chicago suburbs Brandon and I met in August. (He's the one who gave us his parking pass for the A&M game.) I made plans to stop by his tailgate, and when I arrived, Jim was already manning the grill. He introduced me to his wife and pointed out which kids were his within the cluster of seven- to fourteen-year-olds kicking a soccer ball around on the grass nearby.

I introduced myself to some of the other fellows at the tailgate. Turns out most of them, including Jim, played soccer together at USC and get together once or twice a year to catch up on a football weekend. There was a split USC–Mizzou family in the group: the husband and wife both attended Carolina, and their son was a current Missouri student. They'd driven down from St. Louis for the game with the husband sporting a South Carolina shirt, the wife a Missouri shirt, and a caravan full of Mizzou students piled in the back.

It was as though there were two separate tailgates: the South Carolina fans in their mid-forties and the Missouri students. All the Carolina fans were easygoing and relaxed in making conversation while the Missouri fans had a rowdiness about them that was tempered by the exhaustion of their fourteen-hour drive. I'd catch a glimmer of collegiate spirit with a round of shots or Mizzou chant, but in each instance, the flame was short-lived. What energy they had was spent trying to stay awake long enough to make it through the game. Talking to one of the Mizzou girls, I discovered she and her friends were "Golden Girls," members of Missouri's dance team. Since the dance team doesn't travel, they trekked to South Carolina to be normal tailgating college kids for a weekend. When she started pointing out which girls in the group were on the dance team, I stopped her: "All the tan ones, right?" She looked over at her friends and laughed, "Yeah, I guess so."

Three of the Mizzou kids came over to where Jim, the Golden Girl, and I were talking, and then one of them started introductions: "Guys, this is Jim. It's his tailgate. He was in Hootie and the Blowfish." Jim shook their hands, offered them a hot dog or sausage, and completely ignored that last part. Sure enough, my new buddy Jim was Jim Sonefeld, the drummer from Hootie and the Blowfish.

For some reason—maybe I felt a connection because he was originally from Chicagoland, or maybe I liked how he was so nonchalant about his celebrity—I told Jim about my book. He proved to be an insightful sounding board about Northern and Southern living, and shared his thoughts on what it means to be a fan. Later, over e-mail, Jim was kind enough to elaborate on some things we'd discussed at the tailgate.

I told him how I'd been passing through these Southern college towns and cities and sizing them all up, wondering whether I could set down roots in them. I left Chicago knowing that I don't feel particularly tied to the city I was born and raised in anymore. He told me how it worked in his family, how one person moving away opened a channel for others to move. It all started when his brother came down to live with an aunt in Columbia. This helped Jim feel comfortable enough to attend South Carolina and then walk on to the soccer team, which in turn led to his younger sister attending South Carolina a couple years later.

I decided after college that I couldn't and wouldn't get stuck in the neighborhood I grew up in. I had no interest in doing the same things, hanging with the same people, at the same neighborhood bars, for the next forty years. I'm sure a ton of people would disagree, but I feel there's something inherently sad about a person who never experiences life outside the community they were raised in. Besides, I can always go back and connect with the people I want to see.

There's a lot of staying put in the South. People are born and raised in a small town and never leave. I suppose the illusion of security afforded by routine and familiarity make the outside world an undesirable, even scary, place for many people. The comfort in having a clear identity within the community you grew up in makes it hard for many people to strike out and forge a new one in a different place. But so many people who have done exactly that, people like Jim, swear they're better for it.

Jim described his experiences with whatever "good ol' boy" network exists in the South. His description made it sound a lot like the neighborhood communities I've always known in Chicago. "It's not too different than any other regional group of cronies who like to hang out with people who are just like themselves. It's comfortable to be around people who think and act and sound like you. You get to agree wholeheartedly with each other on most subjects and point the finger at everyone outside of your group when there is someone to blame. I was an outsider when I came to South Carolina in 1983, and to some degree I always will be. You can only be from one place, and if it ain't here then you'll always be an outsider."

Once Jim made the decision to move to Columbia, he became a Gamecocks fan almost instantly. This is another common story I've encountered among transplants. When you move to one of these SEC college towns and the football culture permeates everything you do and see, it just happens—you almost can't help becoming a fan. He made the point that the Southern football schools are similar in other ways, too: "I think all the fans of big Southern schools are actually more similar than we'd like to believe. We have insane fan support, lots of partying around the game, Southern traditions, trash talking, hope, expectations…"

Given our shared regional past, and the fact that we both grew up Chicago Cubs fans,[48] Jim likened rooting for South Carolina to rooting for the Cubs (until the Spurrier era, that is). But in sharing how tough it's been stomaching disappointment and heartache year after year as a Gamecock, Jim stumbled on one of the mystifying aspects of fandom. "There is ALWAYS hope and expectations, no matter how bad we were the previous season," he said. "Crazy how quickly we're willing to forget our recent failures and replace them with dreamy hope."

It's easy to have a rabid fan base when you've experienced 10-win seasons or contended for a championship in recent years. But until three years ago, South Carolina fans couldn't say that. Jim struck a familiar chord, one that Susan and Holly touched on back in August, when he said that the expectations and excitement never diminished all through the decades of forgettable Gamecock football.

⚑

I had broken my code for the Missouri game by pre-purchasing tickets. I found face-value seats online and made a regrettable impulse decision. My seats were in the nosebleed section, which offered me quite a different perspective of the stadium than my first time, when I was on the 40-yard line five rows up from the field. I sat two rows from the top on the 30-yard line of the South Carolina sideline. My sight line was partially

---

[48] November 2, 2016: the Chicago Cubs win their first World Series since 1908.

blocked by the aluminum awning overhang, so I had to squat down to see replays on the jumbotron.

I found myself chatting up a woman next to me throughout the game. She wore pearls and a patterned dress and sat with her husband and daughter. But as she talked, I could clearly see her as a frog-gigging,[49] baseball-playing tomboy in her adolescence. I don't remember what we started out talking about or when, but during time-outs and at halftime, we ran the gamut. She introduced herself at halftime: "My name's Kevin, like a boy." Of course it was.

Kevin introduced me to the verb form of Clempson. *Clempsoning* means to screw something up that you'd have to be a complete idiot to screw up. To cross sports streams for an apt analogy, it's missing a wide-open layup. I'm not sure this is a universal term, but rather one South Carolina fans coined in their distaste for their intrastate rival. Kevin and most other South Carolina fans also think Clemson Head Coach Dabo Swinney is a moron. I wondered aloud if that's because Swinney actually says and does idiotic things, or whether the description is simply given to anyone with his job title.[50] Our conversation continued to revolve around Clempson, and after a bit Kevin began to reexamine how she felt watching Clempson play for the national championship in 1981.

---

[49] Gigging is hunting small game, often frogs, with a spear. Apparently, this is a popular pastime in parts of the South.

[50] January 11, 2016: Alabama defeated Clemson 45–40 for the national championship. January 9, 2017: Clemson defeated Alabama 35–31 for the national championship. I'm not sure a moron could make it to back-to-back national championship games.

Like a repressed memory bursting forth in a therapist's office, Kevin's face turned to a grimace and her body shuddered when she was transported back to the day she watched Clemson win the big one. She couldn't recall who the Tigers played that day (Nebraska), but she remembered her feelings and passionately rooting for Clemson's opponent—whoever it was—with crystal clarity. Kevin relived Clemson's Orange Bowl victory the exact same way.

Her reaction was completely relatable to me, and probably most serious sports fans. The particulars may be different, but the feelings come from the same place and often manifest themselves in the same way. I remember watching the 2006 National Championship game between Southern Cal and Texas and wanting Southern Cal to lose almost as badly as I would've wanted Notre Dame to win. That was the year of the classic "Bush Push" game between No. 1-ranked Southern Cal and No. 9-ranked Notre Dame, during which Southern Cal running back Reggie Bush helped shove his quarterback, Matt Leinart, into the end zone for the game-winning touchdown with less than ten seconds to play at Notre Dame Stadium. I remember being positively giddy when Texas quarterback Vince Young broke contain and ran for the right pylon to beat the Trojans in the final minute but having to contain myself because I was in a room full of die-hard Southern Cal fans. I didn't like seeing my friends dejected, but because it was the Trojans, I was almost as happy that their team lost as I would have been if the Irish had won.

Sometime into the second half, Kevin and I canvassed South Carolina history. She explained the destitution of the South Carolina economy after the Civil War and said the South only truly recovered in the 1970s. We talked for a bit about the importance of high school football in South Carolina. National high school powerhouse Byrnes came up, which is the school that produced Gamecock legend Marcus Lattimore. I asked if it was named after South Carolina Senator James Byrnes, and Kevin nodded yes. I said I had heard that Byrnes was almost the de facto president for a while during the Truman Presidency, and that he had a huge influence on Truman's decision-making. Was that true? She turned to me all alight with gratification and replied, "Oh yes, that's all true."

Then Kevin told me she was a direct descendent—the great-great-great-great-granddaughter, to be exact—of former South Carolina Governor John Drayton, the man who founded South Carolina in 1801. I asked her whether a direct line to the founder shouldn't get better seats at football games, and she threw a playful "oh, hush" glance in my direction as we both squatted down to catch a replay on the jumbotron.

South Carolina looked in command of the field most of the night. Missouri's offense couldn't move the ball after scoring a touchdown on a short field their first possession of the game. With a little more than seven minutes left South Carolina scored, taking a 20–7 lead. Because of how inept Mizzou looked on offense all night, the touchdown seemed to seal a Gamecock victory. I remember thinking to myself that Mizzou would open the playbook up now—they had no choice—and they would either rip off a big chunk play or turn the ball over within two downs. There's no margin for error when you're down two scores with seven minutes left, especially when your offense has been trash all night. It was quick strike or bust for the Tigers. 68 yards and thirty-eight seconds later, Missouri answered with a touchdown of their own, closing the gap to 20–14. When South Carolina took the ball and went three-and-out, it let all the air out of the stadium. 80,000-plus decked out in garnet, black, and white tried to breathe life back into Williams-Brice for the defense, but the shouts were choked with worry and doubt. Everyone knew what was coming next. Missouri running back Russell Hansbrough plunged into the end zone on 4th and goal from the 1-yard line with just over a minute remaining. An extra point made the score 21–20 Missouri. South Carolina turned the ball over on downs and the Missouri Tigers took two knees in the victory formation to seal their comeback win.

The anguish hung heavy at Williams-Brice Stadium and crept out into the Columbia night. It was a different sort of despair than I'd seen when Texas A&M beat the brakes off the Gamecocks on opening night. I surmised two reasons behind the change: One, a blowout hits people in a different way than a last-second heartbreaker. It's often much easier to accept and deal with the blowouts. Two, a second conference loss before October effectively ended South Carolina's season. Any hope of participating in the inaugural College Football Playoff vanished with the loss. The bigger they are, the harder they fall, and South Carolina's preseason expectations had never been higher than they were in 2014.

When you consider where South Carolina was in 2014 and where they'd been previously, it makes for an interesting meditation on perspective. Had this been five years ago, a 2-loss Gamecock team with a realistic shot at an SEC East title would have brought a great deal of hope and excitement heading into October. This year, however, a second loss before October stings—a lot. Three seasons of fielding 11-win teams will spoil you, I suppose. The hard truth is that this season will be considered a letdown, because losing hurts that much more when you've grown accustomed to winning.

#15 LSU vs. #5 Auburn

October 4, 2014

Auburn, Alabama

Before I left Chicago, one of the people I befriended through the college football websites I frequented was a Texas A&M die-hard named David. David's brother Charlie attended Auburn, and before I arrived on campus Charlie was gracious enough to let me pick his brain about Auburn football. Predictably, he emphasized the rivalry with Alabama as the most important facet of AU fandom. After forty years of immersion in the rivalry, however, Charlie had some nuanced justifications for why Tigers feel such contempt for the Crimson Tide. His take provided a valuable insight into the mind of an Auburn fan. It will also surely fire up anyone reading this from the Crimson side of the fence.

"First, the vast majority of Auburn fans are graduates or are connected to the university through family. At Alabama, the vast majority are sidewalk fans and have no connection to the school other than the football team. I think this is because during the Bryant years they had great success and the locals adopted Bama as their rooting interest. The breakdown of the fan base in the state is probably something like 75–25 Bama. It tends to give Auburn folks a siege mentality. The second factor is an overwhelming bias toward Alabama in the state press because covering Bama brings viewers and readers. This tends to give Auburn folks a chip on their shoulder. Auburn leads the series since Bryant's death 17–14, but I don't think that is the general perception."[51]

A prevalent dynamic in sports rivalries is a "big brother–little brother" relationship between teams. No better example exists in college football than the Alabama–Auburn rivalry. The "chip on the shoulder" Charlie described is a hallmark of every team that feels disrespected or looked down upon by one of their rivals. South Carolina feels it with Clemson, which is strange because USC is the state school and was founded before Clemson (but that's another matter altogether). Texas A&M feels it with Texas (again, TAMU opened its doors before UT), and Mississippi State with Ole Miss. The best way to reinforce a pack mentality with fans is to marginalize them and paint them as the red-headed stepchild of the rivalry, state, region, or conference.

Even sports fans in the North have heard about the absurd levels to which the rivalry between Auburn and Alabama can reach. So, while I understood that the antipathy towards Bama was a huge piece of the

---

[51] "The media's ALWAYS out to get us." —Every sports fan, ever.

puzzle in what makes an Auburn fan tick, I wanted to see what else I could uncover while I was in Tiger country.

⚑

Auburn opens Jordan-Hare Stadium for locker room tours on Fridays before home games. A few steps outside the entrance, I stopped to photograph Auburn's tiger statue. It's an impressive beast, made in faded black with its teeth gnashing and front right paw batting the air. I finished taking my picture before a group of middle-aged LSU fans swarmed the tiger, climbing on it in their loud LSU visors (the ones with fake Guy Fieri-style blond hair[52] sticking out on top), gold shirts, and purple pants. Watching the LSU fans' mockery toward one of Auburn's sacred symbols irritated me, but my anger wasn't about LSU and Auburn fans. I'd started to grasp why certain aspects of a team's history and various traditions are so esteemed. Traditions and symbols are meant to endow college football with meaning; this, in turn, gives fans (especially throughout the South) a reason to attach such deep significance to them. This reverence—and in some extreme cases, worship—for said traditions and symbols transforms a seemingly innocuous, if annoying, act like climbing on the tiger statue leading into the Auburn locker room into a highly disrespectful one. If you understand how much a campus symbol can mean—and being a fan of another SEC team means that you absolutely do—then there's no excuse for such behavior. But if you're the type of individual who wears Guy Fieri-style

---

[52] Despite being a world-class chef who owns multiple restaurants, has hosted numerous food-related TV shows, and penned two *New York Times* bestsellers, Fieri is best known for his trademark late-90s-skater-punk bleached-blond spiked hair.

visors in public in your mid-forties, I guess this type of common sense might escape you, too.

When I first walked in to the lobby through the Mike and Jane McCartney Plaza entrance, I noticed a massive TV with ESPN playing and about twenty high-top tables and chairs straight ahead. Scanning the lobby, I found a display of All-Americans running the length of one of the walls, with pictures of Heisman Trophy winners Bo Jackson and Pat Sullivan displayed prominently in the top right and bottom left corners.

A pair of tour guides escorted roughly thirty of us to the field. We all took pictures, and I'm fairly certain one man, who, I gathered, had never seen Jordan-Hare in person, had a spiritual experience. His statuesque pose of stunned silence was only occasionally interrupted by the low sounds of hyperventilation and incoherent mumbling to his wife. After some small talk, the guides herded us into the locker room. Oversized painted murals occupied the space on either side of the doors. One showed Bo Jackson leaping over Alabama linebacker Robbie Jones for the game-winning touchdown in the infamous and aptly named "Bo Over the Top" 1982 Iron Bowl. The other was of Chris Davis running with the ball in his right arm during his 109-yard game-winning touchdown with 00:00 remaining on the clock in the 2013 Iron Bowl. No game means more to Auburn than the Iron Bowl, so it only makes sense for two of the greatest moments in the history of the rivalry to serve as a visual reminder for every Auburn football player who steps into their locker room.

Inside, the encased Bo Jackson and Cam Newton Heisman Trophies caught my eye. I couldn't imagine the thrill of suiting up every week with testimonials to your school's legacy of excellence ten feet away. Nearly everyone stopped to take pictures with both the trophies, along with various pictures of star players' lockers. This year's picture-worthy lockers belonged to Nick Marshall and Sammie Coates. Next year, who knows? It doesn't matter. Fans will make these same stops in the same locker room year after year. The true believers keep coming back to pay homage every fall.

Most players had their own locker with a nameplate as identification. Lockers appeared to be sectioned off by position group. In the center of the immaculate room, a circle of roughly twenty chairs faced outward, with a helmet and shoulder pads on the floor in front of each. These were, I assumed, for the non-scholarship players who dress for home games. A couple around my age, P. J. and Brandy, came in from Mobile for the game. As we realized why these players didn't have their own lockers, P. J. looked at me and said, "Man, can you imagine walking on and then seeing your name on the back of the jersey?" A long silence ensued, and I think we were both content to let it linger. There's something romantic about the story of the underdog who works hard, pays his dues, and gets his name stitched onto the back of that Auburn jersey (or really any school's jersey). I have to believe dressing for a game means just a little more to those twenty guys in the circle than it does to the four- or five-star recruit who had his pick of schools.

Outside the football complex a couple blocks down Donahue Drive, the Reverse Walk was kicking off. It's a tradition unique to Auburn so far as I've seen. During the event, people line the sides of the walkway leading out of the football complex and toward the buses waiting to take the football team away for the night. The team spends each night before a game in a hotel outside of town, a common practice because it takes players away from any potential distractions they might find Friday night on campus. Pretty girls in burnt orange and navy with Auburn logo stickers on their cheeks waved pom-poms and cheered as the players emerged from the building in a slow trickle: one and two at a time over the course of a half hour. These young women are called Tigerettes, and they function as hostesses for recruits on visits, tour guides for families around campus, and a general spirit squad for the football team. As the team departed, the Tigerettes took their families inside to tour the complex. Not wanting to miss out, I tagged along.

When security announced that only guests of the Tigerettes were allowed in the building, I stood next to a Tigerette and her family to blend in. The trophy room we started out in housed a large portion of Auburn's physical football history. I was awestruck by Pat Sullivan's Heisman Trophy, the 1957 National Championship trophy,[53] and the faded Associated Press teletype from the infamous "Punt Bama Punt" Iron Bowl in 1972. Auburn won the game 17–16 on the heels of two blocked punts returned for touchdowns. Alabama was undefeated and ranked No. 2 in the country entering that game, and a 14-point favorite over the No. 9-ranked, 1-loss Auburn squad. Alabama dominated the game for three quarters, leading 16–0. After an Auburn field goal early in the fourth quarter, Alabama was forced to punt on their next two possessions. Both punts were blocked by Bill Newton—and returned for touchdowns by David Langner. As a result, the game remains one of

---

[53] Auburn was the AP National Champion that year, while Ohio State was named national champ by the Coaches Poll. The Tigers were ineligible for a bowl game during the 1957 season because of recruiting violations.

the all-time classics in Auburn history. There's even a bar on campus called "1716," a nod to one of Auburn's most sacred football memories.

In one of the film and meeting rooms, big charts hung on either side of the wall near the doors. One was a percentage chart showing how often the Tigers can expect to score points and touchdowns based on where they take over possession on the field, and the other was a list of explosive special teams plays and where they took place on the field. Each big kicking game play was marked by the opponents' decal. Sure, I could have read the placards and gleaned all the fascinating play information, but I chose to listen to the Tigerettes educate their families about the trophies and charts. Everything sounds better in a sweet Southern drawl...

After spending a minute at the indoor practice field, I left the Tigerette groups I'd been glomming onto and headed back into the main building. I noticed an upstairs area in the complex with various offices and headed in that direction. Being alone and only seeing one tour group on the floor, I walked briskly past a security guard and someone who seemed to be an actual police officer as if I were catching up with my group. The tour group walked into a set of offices in the back right corner. I opened the door and passed Auburn Head Coach Gus Malzahn in the entryway. At least, I was pretty sure that was him. When I glanced up and saw the Tigerette's family standing next to the secretary's desk with their jaws agape, I took that as confirmation. I turned and followed him back out before asking if I could take a picture with him. He glared at my ND T-shirt for a few seconds, peeked over to the officer—presumably his police escort—and said, "Somebody's gotta get this boy a new shirt." He was gracious, though, and took a picture with me in spite of my offending attire.

Southbound Traveler

I cut through Auburn's campus at dusk, craning my neck like a pelican scanning the water for its next meal as I examined the burnt-brick classroom buildings and read commemorative plaques alongside various statues. While wandering about in full tourist mode, I met a group of students dressed in tuxedos and fancy evening gowns taking pictures and milling about before a sorority formal. Apparently I was doing everything short of carrying a camera around my neck and squinting at an oversized paper map, because the undergrads knew it was my first time on campus. They offered suggestions on places to eat—like Momma Goldberg's Deli—and sights to see over the weekend, and as we parted ways, they sent me off in the direction of Toomer's Corner, the iconic drugstore and restaurant founded in the 1890s.

While the drugstore is rightly famous for its history, it had long been known for the beautiful oak trees that sat caddy corner. Over the years, the Auburn Oaks had become a cherished symbol of the school. After the 2010 Iron Bowl, however, a middle-aged Alabama fan named Harvey Updyke poisoned the trees. I knew all that, but I didn't know the trees had been removed, so I wasn't sure I was in the right place when I arrived. I stopped in front of a barbershop that had posted the final scores of all Auburn's Iron Bowl wins on its door and took a picture. A man around my age in a cut-off T-shirt and an Auburn hat sat on a bench alongside the storefront. I asked him if this was, in fact, Toomer's Corner and if so, where the Oaks were.

The man, Travis, was born and raised in Auburn, and he attended the university for a couple years before dropping out to take care of his mother when she fell ill. He painted houses for a living and had no particular place to go as he waited for his wife to finish work at the nail salon a couple doors down. It's safe to say I liked Travis instantly. Some people are open to making conversation with strangers, and Travis was one of them. He had an air about him where he seemed present in the moment and simply responded to what the world placed in front of him. He had no agenda, and no pretense, and since the universe presented a stranger to talk with, he engaged the conversation.

We spent the better part of an hour shooting the breeze. I could tell Travis was a born raconteur by the way his mannerisms sharpened throughout the course of a story to underscore key moments and by the way his voice rose and fell at the appropriate beats. He painted a vivid picture of the rowdiness at the intersection of Magnolia Avenue and College Street after an Auburn win: how there might be 87,000 people in the stadium and then nearly double that rolling (that is, toilet papering) the trees down on College Street after the game. Despite the Oaks being poisoned and subsequently removed, Tigers still roll every other tree nearby. They also roll street signs, lampposts, and anything else within throwing distance that will hold toilet paper after a victory. The bigger the game, the bigger the crowd, the bigger the roll.

During the 2010 National Championship Game between Auburn and Oregon, Travis decided to joyride on one of the Auburn Police Department's Segways. He showed me a picture of himself standing in front of the two-wheeler moments before he took it for a spin around the block. He was arrested of course, but the funny part to both of us was the judge's final reaction. The judge was initially matter-of-fact, telling Travis, "You can't go around taking police vehicles, son." Given the circumstances, however, the judge showed leniency and levied only a $500 fine with no charge. Basically, the justice of the court did everything but yell "War Eagle" (the Auburn fan cry)[54] at the hearing, according to Travis. By his estimation, there must have been over 200,000 people lining College Street on that January night when Auburn hoisted their first national championship trophy in over fifty years.

While we were on the subject of the 2010 National Championship, I felt compelled to ask him about Cam Newton and the pay-for-play scandal. Travis was candid: "Oh yeah, we did that shit. We paid for him and I'm good with it. No way we woulda won it all without him." According to Travis, Cam Newton arrived on Auburn's campus riding a moped. He wrecked the scooter—and then began driving a brand new Corvette around shortly thereafter. Many college football fans belligerently deny any illegal activity takes place when it comes to courting top recruits. There's nothing you can do to convince or reason with these people. And even if you somehow manage to persuade such a naive individual that paying players is a real thing, that boosters dole out cash to help their university sign top recruits, you won't be able to convince them it's *their* kids who are accepting favors. "We don't do that here. We do things the 'right' way," is a refrain I heard over and over. For a

---

[54] According to Auburn's website, the chant originated in 1892 when a Civil War veteran attended an Auburn–Georgia game with his pet eagle, which he'd kept as a pet since the war. Late in the game, the eagle broke free and began flying around the stadium. As the eagle flew, Auburn drove for the game-winning score. Fans cried "War Eagle!" and the legend was born. Oddly, the upshot to the story is that the eagle crashed into the field after the game ended and died. Still, "War Eagle" lived on.

die-hard, there's often more at stake than meets the eye in such an admission. If you're forced to acknowledge that your team pays players, then you might have to conclude that *your* team is the "bad guy."

It's rare to find somebody who wants to root for the bad guy, but not impossible. We've seen teams and programs embrace the bad-guy persona: the Oakland Raiders, the Detroit Pistons, and the Miami Hurricanes have all fed off the negative energy of being cast as the "dirty" team that opposing fans boo a little louder than everyone else. By and large, their backers have followed suit and embraced the image. Hell, some sports fans switched over and became Raiders, Pistons, and Hurricanes fans purely for the bad-boy image. Still, such examples are exceptions to the rule. If you envision yourself as a good and decent person, and you're forced to confront the fact that the team you've spent years rooting for, whose games you've attended, whose gear you've worn with pride, cheats, the knowledge creates a disconnect.[55] The more invested the fan, the more steadfast their denials, and the more obstinate they become in rooting themselves in the narrative of "I pull for the good guys." People spin the facts, no matter how concrete, to fit their preexisting assumptions and beliefs. It's that simple.[56] Sports fans make for great case studies in human behavior and, I'm sure, clients for therapists.

Since our conversation had legs and neither of us was in a rush to be anywhere else, Travis and I walked down the street to a bar where he bought two beers. He casually brought them back outside so he could chain-smoke Marlboro Reds as we carried on. "You can't do this at a lot

---

[55] The psychological term for this is cognitive dissonance.

[56] The psychological term for this is confirmation bias.

of schools, ya know," he said, gesturing to the beer in his right hand with an air of impunity. "At Georgia, cops'll pull you over, write you a ticket. They're kind of hard-asses down in Athens." I told him I remembered students telling me I'd get pulled over for jaywalking in downtown Athens. "Yeah, damn right they will," Travis agreed. "I love that school though. My daddy went to school there so I love Georgia, too." And again, like so many SEC fans, Travis's personal experiences charted out his personal road map of college football loyalties. For him, Auburn comes first, Georgia second, whoever's playing Alabama third, and whatever SEC team is playing fourth. Discovering people's layers of fandom and how they arrived at their allegiances had become one of most enjoyable aspects of meeting fans down South.

One of the last things Travis and I chatted about before I wandered on down Magnolia Avenue was Alabama and the Iron Bowl. He dated Bama girls in the past, but said he's happy he settled down with an Auburn gal. One of his buddies, another Auburn fan, married an Alabama alum. Travis watched last year's Iron Bowl with the two of them and a few other friends. When the game ended, his friend's celebration escalated to taunting his wife. The teasing between husband and wife turned ugly and personal in a hurry, to the point where Travis said he became so uncomfortable he left. Travis found out later that it got even more venomous after he left the scene, with both parties spewing hateful words they couldn't take back. The couple divorced this past winter. If I didn't know what I know about what this game does to emotions, and how much it means to people down here, I would've called B.S. on Travis's story. But after six weeks on the road in the SEC, if you're gonna tell me that an Iron Bowl broke up a marriage, I'll buy it.

Right before we parted ways, Travis left me with a prophecy: "Oh and you watch—Ole Miss is gonna beat Bama tomorrow." I disagreed. "They can't run the ball between the tackles, no way they win that game." Travis shook his head and chuckled: "I fuckin' guarantee it. You'll see."

🏴

My hotel was forty miles away in Columbus, Georgia. I suppose I wasn't surprised that this was the nearest cheap hotel room for the biggest home game of the year. Before I hopped on I-280 and took the hilly, picturesque drive from Opelika east to the Alabama–Georgia border, I drove through the Chick-fil-A on campus. I couldn't help but think of Cassanova McKinzy, the Tigers' starting middle linebacker who signed with Auburn over Clemson in 2012 because Auburn had a Chick-fil-A on campus and Clemson didn't.[57] Don't get me wrong: I've been driving through and ordering one Chicken Sandwich and one Spicy Chicken Sandwich with extra pickles about three times a week since I've been down South, and I'm hooked. I just don't think I could ever be *that* infatuated with a chicken sandwich to base a major life decision around it.

Later Friday night, as I sat in my hotel room in Columbus, my buddy Alex called me with some bad news. He was driving down to meet me for the game Saturday, but he'd gotten pulled over and had his car towed on account of some nonsense not worth retelling. A little after midnight,

---

[57] Best part of this story: Clemson actually does have a Chick-fil-A on campus.

Southbound Traveler

I drove forty-five minutes to pick him up at a Waffle House in Hogansville, Georgia. As we sat there, I scanned the room. I noticed an engaged or newly married couple engrossed in each other on the stools next to us. They couldn't have been older than twenty two, and appeared to be settling into their comfort, relaxed in their basketball shorts and hoodies, hair down, flip-flops over mid-calf socks. I could see how they were both probably a few pounds heavier than they were in high school, and I could also see them in the future: fat and happy or fat and miserable, depending. They looked happy, for now. I saw a group of high school kids in the far corner joking around with a waitress they knew. I saw a two guys in their late twenties in the booth next to them, their eyes a fiery red, devouring over-syruped waffles. Alex turned to me: "Yeah buddy, this is a redneck town in the South. I would know—I grew up in one." I remember thinking to myself that this was small-town America, and that there was really no regional distinction. I asked Alex, "How's this any different than sitting in a Denny's once you get to the small towns past the suburbs outside Chicago?" He pondered a minute before answering: "Huh. I'm not sure."

As Alex and I passed through the basketball arena parking lot across from the baseball and softball stadium, a tricked out[58] car in Auburn styling caught my attention. The blue paint job glinted and the orange trim reflected sunbeams. Small Auburn logos brought the color scheme together, and the hood was popped so everyone could see it was there for show. I don't know enough about cars to remember the make and

---

[58] Accessorized to a gaudy, extravagant degree.

model, but it reminded me of the General Lee, the late-'60s Charger from *The Dukes of Hazzard*. The owners, Paul and Brenda, a couple in their late forties or early fifties, were only too happy to show and tell all about the car. The interior featured leather seats that had the cowhide texture of a football with the AU logo on the headrest. An Auburn helmet signed by the school's Holy Trinity of Heisman winners (Sullivan, Jackson, and Newton) sat in between the seats. Brenda joked that Paul loves that car more than her, and that he'd sleep in the garage with it every night if he could. As with most jokes, I felt a hint of truth contained within this one. Paul's eyes lit up as he told me the story of how he restored the car over a year and a half, then won Best Interior at the first car show he took it to. He touted the machine like he was bragging on his first-born child.

As Paul and his buddies told me about their tailgate's history, a small group of LSU fans passed within earshot of their spread. "Hey LSU fans, thanks for coming today. Hope y'all enjoy yourselves," Paul half yelled, without a hint of sarcasm in his voice. The Bayou Bengals stopped to look at Paul and each other before walking away confused. Everyone laughed. "Happens all the time. They think we're messin' with 'em or something. I do hope they have a good time." This brief interaction set the table for what I was to experience the rest of that day and evening at Auburn.

Alex and I split up for a while: he went to visit a relatives' tailgate and I set off to explore. Campus lawns on the south side of Jordan-Hare Stadium were packed with premade tailgates, each set up complete with standard-issue white tents, chairs, tables, and big-screen TV. I noticed these prefab deals at Alabama, too. Clearly, providing tailgating packages is a growing business. I'm sure it's far more convenient to not deal with transport, setup and break-down, but there's something impersonal and generic about these tailgates that makes me sad about the trend.

One of the white tents had a sign that read "Sweet Home Chicago Auburn Tailgate." There couldn't have been a clearer indicator of where I needed to be. The first lady I met was an attractive middle-aged woman named Marilyn. She was from Libertyville, Illinois, an affluent suburb, but was born in the Beverly neighborhood on the South Side of Chicago. Her daughter attends Auburn, so the family are all converted Tigers fans. I walked around and met people from various Chicago suburbs. As we chatted about Sweet Home Chicago, I felt a sense of community I'd been lacking since I hit the road. Even though I'd never met them, it felt like I had stumbled upon my people. Our overlapping experiences gave me a sense of connection I didn't know I'd miss when I left the Windy City. To a lesser degree, I experienced a sense of fraternity when, at every single school I visited, an SEC fan wearing colors different than the home team's would see me and shout or whisper, "Go Irish!" The shared connection between fans of the same team is a critical part of fandom's allure. It generates an instant brotherhood that you can take with you wherever you go.

Alex and I had decided on the drive to campus that we were both perfectly okay sitting separately, since individual tickets tend to be cheaper than pairs or group seats when you're scalping. It took no more than five minutes to find Alex an end zone seat for $80, and a front row upper deck seat at the 20-yard line on the Auburn side for $95 (face value) for me. I wound up buying my ticket from Marilyn's husband Steve, who had an extra, which meant I would be watching the game with people from the tailgate. Sitting with the Chicago-based crew occupying the seven or eight seats to my left made me feel like a regular, as did all of my interactions inside Jordan-Hare Stadium.

During the first couple drives of the game, the woman sitting to my right kept refreshing her phone every minute or so in order to follow the end of the Alabama–Ole Miss game. As Auburn moved the ball down the field for their first score, Alabama was minutes away from being upset by Ole Miss in Oxford. When the Rebels intercepted Alabama quarterback Blake Sims in the end zone with a minute left in regulation, the play was broadcast over the jumbotron in the south end zone, setting off a powder keg of cheers and applause. Somewhere in the stadium, I thought, Travis was both overjoyed and self-satisfied, reminding his wife: "I told you. I fuckin' told you that was gonna happen."

As the crowd died down and Auburn's defense took the field, I began chatting with my neighbor, the avid score-checker, about the day's college football games. Her name was Aimee. She saw my yellow-gold Notre Dame sweatshirt, which she originally mistook for an LSU shirt, and checked the Irish score for me. Apparently Notre Dame put together one of their better game-winning drives in recent memory against Stanford. When the final registered, I let out a Nature Boy-style "Wooooo,"[59] which drew awkward looks from the people sitting around me who knew nothing about the ND game but heard a loud, giddy yawp

---

[59] Ric Flair's trademark shout. A "rolex-wearin', diamond-ring wearin', kiss-stealin' (woooo), wheelin-dealin', limousine-ridin', jet-flyin', son of a gun…havin' a hard time holdin' these alligators down," Flair (not his real name) is a former professional wrestler whose shtick has become a pop-culture staple in recent years.

after an uneventful second down. Sensing my need to celebrate with somebody, anybody, Aimee reached back and high-fived me.

Halfway through the first quarter, the game was clearly a blowout in the making. Auburn moved the ball at will through the air. LSU committed to stopping the run, and their talented albeit young defensive backfield had no chance of containing both Sammie Coates and Duke Williams downfield. Both receivers are definite mismatches against single coverage and because of sheer numbers, LSU couldn't simultaneously bracket or shade zone coverage toward both receivers and defend against the run. As a result, one of the two Auburn playmakers was continually open, ready to rip off another big chunk of yardage downfield. On the other side of the ball, LSU connected on one explosive pass play but neither half of their young and ineffectual quarterback tandem of Anthony Jennings and Brandon Harris was able to throw the ball consistently. Even with budding superstar Leonard Fournette toting the rock, LSU couldn't get a run game together. LSU never had a chance.

With five minutes to play in the first half, Auburn safety Nick Ruffin dislodged the ball from an LSU receiver over the middle of the field with a jarring hit. Flags flew and Ruffin was called for targeting. Subsequent review both confirmed the call and resulted in Ruffin's ejection from the game. The replay was shown on the jumbotron a few times and what I and every other paying customer in the stands saw was a thing of beauty: Ruffin's shoulder driving squarely into the shoulder pads of the LSU receiver, the force slamming the receiver into the ground. It was devastating—and legal. So it was understandable that Auburn fans were upset when the call on the field not only stood, but was confirmed. When a play stands, it means the officials don't have sufficient evidence to overturn the call. Confirmation is confirmation.

Fans all around me spent the rest of the evening stewing in a nasty a persecution complex. From that point forward, every call against Auburn was a bad call, and every call against LSU was a "make-up call."[60] The fans were justifiably angry, but their fury grew to cartoonish, comical proportions. The rest of the evening, a man two rows behind me called for Auburn players to hit the ref after every penalty against Auburn. An eye for an eye, I suppose.

The concession stand lines were obscenely long with a couple minutes left in the first half. I was cold and hungry but I felt no particular urge to deal with the twenty-minute wait, so I found the smoking area and bummed a cigarette from one of the guys there. The cast of characters in the smoking section of almost any entertainment venue could star in their own production, and I found myself in a veritable rogues' gallery. For this reason alone it's unfortunate that smoking is gradually being banned from all public venues.

When I arrived, the topic of conversation was lucky bounces. An Alabama fan had told one of these fellows that Auburn's run to the title game in 2013 should have never happened. They all conceded the Georgia game was a lucky bounce. Late in the fourth quarter of that game, a Georgia defender tipped a Nick Marshall pass up over his head and directly into the hands of receiver Ricardo Louis, who took the ball in stride into the end zone for the game-winner. Losing to Georgia would almost certainly have dashed Auburn's championship aspirations. One of the men insisted, "Every team that's ever won anything caught a few

---

[60] The term for when a referee tries to compensate (make up) for previous bad calls by penalizing the other team.

breaks along the way, but we were better than Alabama that night anyways. No doubt about it, we were the better team."

Auburn was quickly growing on me. Everyone I met radiated a warmth that made me feel right at home, and they had no problem including me in their conversations and tailgates. When I returned to Tuscaloosa in late November, I already knew I'd be rooting for Auburn. However, I can't agree that Auburn was better than Alabama in the 2013 Iron Bowl. I remember watching the game at home thinking it was only a matter of time until Alabama pulled away. Expecting a commercial break before overtime, I flipped the channel and missed the final play when Chris Davis returned the missed Alabama field goal 109 yards and became an instant legend. I wasn't going to argue the point with my newfound friends, though.

We stood around talking about our seats and how great or lousy they were. A man named Jay—he could've passed for forty but was probably fifty-five—took the lead, explaining how he's had the same seats nine rows up on the 50-yard line of the upper deck since the '80s. "Yeah, I pay $3,600 a year for the opportunity to pay $3,600 a year for season tickets.[61] Turns out to be a pretty big investment. But it's all worth it, ya know?" Not a word of dissent. At a glance, Jay had all the characteristics of the smarmy aging frat "brothers" at Alabama: slicked, jet-black hair, a sleek slim-fit polo, and immaculate posture. The similarities ended there, however, as Jay was as chummy as the Bama brothers were cold.

---

[61] Season tickets typically require a sizable donation to the university in addition to the cost of the tickets themselves.

Before we all headed back to our seats, dispersing at once like we were breaking a huddle, Jay asked me if everyone was treating me well. "If you don't feel like going to the bars after the game, we're over at tent 33—that's Bo minus one.[62] Come on by, we'll be there after. We've got beer, liquor, probably still some food. Whatever you need, man. We want you to have a good time while you're here." How could I not be drawn in when Auburn fans had treated me this way all day long?

The second half was much like the first: fans screaming at the refs like a drunk parent embarrassing his son at a Little League game; Auburn's offense marching down the field and scoring almost at will; and LSU's offense sputtering, unable to sustain a drive. I picked up my conversation with Aimee and her husband Rob, who drove in from suburban Birmingham for the game. Both Auburn alums in their thirties, the couple didn't meet until after college despite having mutual close friends at school. As we talked, I realized we each had something the other wanted. They'd love to be able to take a year off work and go to college football games (who wouldn't?), and I'd love to settle down and raise a family with a woman whose idea of a fun night out is hiring a babysitter so we can go to a college football game. They only bring their kids, ages seven and nine, to cupcake games, because at big-time games the kids would "see and hear things children shouldn't see and hear." Just then, the man two rows behind us who'd been calling for Auburn players to spear a referee ever since Ruffin's ejection in the second quarter let out

---

[62] A reference to Bo Jackson's college jersey number, 34.

a profanity-laced tirade about the ref's most recent call, completely underscoring their point.

As we joined the masses hurrying for the exit after Auburn finished their 41–7 beatdown of LSU, Rob took down my number. Later he texted me: "Rob and Aimee in Auburn, live in Birmingham. Call us if u need a place to stay." Again, the people I met at Auburn University epitomized Southern hospitality.

In the chaos outside Jordan-Hare after the game, I found Alex and we hurried to Toomer's Corner. After all, a trip to Auburn isn't complete without seeing Toomer's Corner rolled. It happened quickly. I remember arriving and the trees down College Street were already rolled. I saw a roll on the ground and tossed it back into the nearest tree, contributing my own part to the cause. We walked down a ways and I saw this striking white-trimmed red brick building with two spires, one of which had a giant clock and a weathervane at the peak. It was Samford Hall, and I stood and stared up at it for a good two minutes, admiring how the silhouette cast the building in a burnt-orange light. For a building to have that kind of effect over me at all, let alone in the middle of something as silly as rolling Toomer's Corner, it had to be special. And as I stood there marveling at the scene, a thought occurred to me for the first time on my trip: I've got to come back here for another game weekend when this trip is over. I have to get back to this town *someday*.

#2 Auburn vs. #3 Mississippi State

October 11, 2014

Starkville, Mississippi

I spent the week leading up to game day in Starkville visiting my grandma in Long Beach, Mississippi. A small coastal community with a slow-moving pace and rhythm of its own, Long Beach was hosting Cruisin' the Coast, their annual classic car showcase and parade, the same week I was visiting. On Monday evening, I drove downtown to the four-block-long strip that leads directly to the white sands and Gulf Coast waters. Families lined the streets on either side with small children and grown-ups alike waving their arms and calling for beads and stuffed animals from people in the cars crawling down the strip, showing off their old muscle cars. There was something decidedly small-towny about the spectacle that made the big city in me roll my eyes. The whole thing was a little silly. At the same time, there was a wholesome and pure quality to this type of community gathering, something innocent and joyous in seeing middle-aged men and women as engaged and excited as small children. Such events don't happen in big cities these days (if they ever did). Walking up and down both sides of the strip, searching the faces that were searching the cars, I found what I'd only seen in movies or read about in books. There's a steeled cynicism in a city like Chicago that doesn't allow for this kind of simple, earnest fun. In that moment, I glimpsed the appeal of small-town living.

In the same four-day stay, I also understood why so many people prefer the hustle and bustle of sprawling metropolises over the quaint and understated charms of small-town life. Apart from the job opportunities that keep people in and around big cities, I found it boring as hell being stuck in a small town. After four days in Long Beach, I felt like I'd lose my mind within the week. I was so bored I started eating as a way to pass the time, and I found myself craving some sort of entertainment or diversion beyond what a parade of classic cars had to offer. Comedy, sports, culture, something—*anything*—would've sufficed. This boredom, however, helped me wheel back around to why college football fanaticism is so intense in the South. Granted, small towns exist everywhere in America, and a general list of pros and cons that weighs big-city living against small-town living would probably be wash. (For many people, at least. Just not me.) But in a small town, you almost have to actively seek out pastimes to be super-passionate about. And in the South, unlike other sections of America, there aren't many professional sports teams to get behind. So if sports is your thing, you're probably going to be a college football fan. A big one.

⚑

Living in a small town, there's a degree of isolation from the outside world that can be liberating or suffocating, depending on how a person relates to it. My grandma Maggie left Chicago for the Mississippi Gulf Coast a decade ago, just before Hurricane Katrina hit. Good timing, Mags. Our relationship, though always warm, had been distant since she relocated. As we moved past catching up, trading memories and opinions on people and events within the family, I started to observe my grandma's natural rhythms and routines. During the day, she watched FOX News and the Home Shopping Network, and at dinner one night I noticed how she parroted what I'd overheard on FOX News earlier that afternoon. She was stating opinions from a cable news program as fact. I knew instantly it was relevant to my project, but I couldn't figure out why right away.

A couple days later, I flipped to the Paul Finebaum Show on the SEC Network. As I listened in to the topics of the day, which included the Auburn–Mississippi State game I'd be attending on Saturday, I made the connection between cable news and what it has to do with college football fans. Cable television channels dedicated to a particular collegiate conference, or team—looking at you, Longhorn Network—serve the same function as a cable news channel: both are designed to tell the viewer exactly what they want to hear. And increasingly as a society, our demand for instant gratification—in this case, information spun to fit our preconceived biases—is being catered to by media outlets only too happy to tell us what we want to hear, all of which is (conveniently) dressed up as irrefutable fact.

A key characteristic of true believers (which most die-hards represent) is that there's little to no room for doubt in their world. Things must be black and white, good and evil, 'Murica[63] and the terrorists, us and them. If you want to believe that liberals or conservatives are trying to drag this country to hell, we've got a station for that. If you want to believe that the SEC or the Big Ten or the Pac-12 is the premier power conference in the collegiate landscape, we've got a station for that, too. And if you want to believe that Mississippi State or Auburn or Missouri or South Carolina is the premier school within that premier power conference, well we don't have a cable channel for that yet, but we've got two or three websites just for you. As fanatics, we're really only interested in seeing the news privately viewed from our own lens.

Driving under the cover of darkness on two-lane highways with minimal lighting, my sense of isolation was almost complete. I called friends back home to check in and feel connected to somebody. I was so bored I listened to the Colts–Texans *Thursday Night Football* game on the radio on the four-hour trip up to my hotel in Columbus, Mississippi, twenty miles outside Starkville. During the drive, I made the decision to stay up all night Friday night and camp out with the Mississippi State fans for yet another *College GameDay* experience. In order to do that, I'd have to stay up all night Thursday and sleep all day Friday. So as I approached my hotel, I stopped for gas and coffee just before midnight.

Staying up all night, writing the last of my initial thoughts on my Auburn weekend, I felt twenty again, like I was pulling another all-nighter

---

[63] A caricature of the United States of America; a place where we're incapable of wrongdoing and all our actions and policies are good and just. A living, breathing modern-day utopia.

in Raynor Library at Marquette University to finish all the work I'd put off all semester. In the morning, after writing for a couple hours and reading most of *Mississippi Mud*, a true-crime thriller set on the coast in Biloxi, I decided to go for a drive through downtown Columbus.

The town had the look and feel of a different era. An old football field grabbed my attention so completely that I pulled over and hopped out of the car to investigate. The abandoned stadium had chipped concrete-slab seating and a six-foot-high, weather-worn concrete wall surrounding the field, which was complete with outdated goal posts and patches of crabgrass growing high in between dead spots. I stopped because I was all but entranced when I caught sight of the old field. Maybe it was the antiquated feel of the town and the dilapidated field before me, or maybe it was my diminished state after an all-nighter; I don't know. But I slipped into a reverie.

I never figured out exactly how to describe the feeling. I'm not a science-fiction writer and I don't know much about time travel, but there were moments traveling through the South when I felt transported to another time and place. And whenever that happened, I was always taken to the '50s.

Picture small-town America before the Civil Rights Era, Vietnam, and the various cultural revolutions of the 1960s teased, poked, prodded, and shook change out of it. In this vision of rustic American life, there's clear-cut right and wrong. You can tell good from bad just by looking at a person; the divide isn't only between black and white, but between flattop and collared shirt and greasy, slicked hair and wife-beater. It's understood that white folks born and raised in town are to be trusted and welcomed, while all others aren't. This simplicity provides immense comfort. It's no wonder that in a world of increasing ambiguity and complexity, simple folks clamor for simpler times.

Friday nights are eagerly anticipated, even more than Saturday afternoons down the road in Starkville, and local boys are the heroes of the community. The starting quarterback might as well be John Wayne. Hero worship in football may have started nationally with the Red Granges,[64] but it was soon replicated in small towns all over. Here in the South, residents had finally established a literal and figurative proving ground upon which they might assert their physical dominance. This was a battlefield on which they could determine their own fate, before the John F. Kennedys and Lyndon Johnsons forced the George Wallaces and Ross Barnetts to allow black kids into their Wonder Bread world.

I was so immersed in this dream state that I failed to notice the old lady dragging a pull-cart behind herself until she was three feet from me and commented on the weather. I mumbled, "Nice day," and walked back to the car feeling like I'd just seen a ghost.

⚑

I woke up a little after 8 pm Friday, thoroughly rested but disoriented. After watching the first half of the Stanford–Washington State game in my hotel room, I showered and headed over to Mississippi State's cam-

---

[64] The Galloping Ghost. Grange was a University of Illinois halfback in the early '20s before playing for the Chicago Bears and arguably the first American football player to cast a larger-than-life shadow.

pus. When I arrived, Bulldog fans were departing Cowbell Ring Practice at Davis-Wade Stadium. I was aware of the event, but felt no particular urge to attend because it's exactly what it sounds like: fans all congregate in the stadium the night before home games and practice ringing their cowbells.

The student dorms weren't being monitored for parking yet, so I posted up around 11 pm and stumbled into a group of freshmen headed to the Junction, the tailgating hub that leads directly to the stadium. They had set up shop next to the *College GameDay* countdown timer, which read eight hours when we arrived. James, Jesús, Zach, Hernandez, and the rest of their crew were discussing pacing themselves to be able to keep drinking straight through the game, set to kickoff in fourteen-and-a-half hours. After finding out I'd never been to Starkville, they quickly informed me they start drinking at eight or nine years old in Mississippi and they can drink all night and day and of course, Hail State. "There's really only two things to do in a town like this: drink and smash," James declared. Everyone else nodded their heads in agreement.

That's the thing about Mississippi State: they have no real football history to speak of. They're conditioned to expect losing and keep a "win or lose, we still booze" mentality about it. So a day like this was nearly unfathomable to many of the people I met in Starkville. They simply couldn't comprehend being one convincing win away from becoming the No. 1-ranked team in America.

The 2014 season started in typical-enough fashion for Mississippi State football. They beat up on in-state little brother Southern Miss 49–0 before inexplicably finding themselves in a tight game against Alabama-Birmingham. State won 47–34 but was out-gained by UAB 548–516 in the game and surrendered 435 passing yards. In that moment, fans and pundits alike began to write Mississippi State off the same way they do most seasons. But something unexpected happened next. Instead of fading away to the depths of the SEC West, the Mississippi State Bulldogs traveled to Death Valley on September 20th and beat No. 8-ranked LSU at night. LSU had never lost a home night game to an unranked team under Les Miles. What was most promising (and perplexing) to all those who expected the same ol' Mississippi State was the way the Bulldogs won. The 34–29 final belies the fact of the matter, which is that State whipped LSU in all phases of the game. Mississippi State pounced on the Tigers early and never let up. Two last-minute touchdowns let those who didn't watch the game believe it was close. It never really was.

After a bye week, Mississippi State was now ranked twelfth in the country. Let the record show that this is the exact type of situation fans outside the SEC who allege that media bias and an ESPN hype machine surround the conference cite when lodging their complaints: unranked to No. 12 with one convincing top-10 win and 3 wins over patsies. I understand their frustration here. I don't believe a perennial cellar-dweller in the Pac-12 or Big Ten would've had the same meteoric rise if they'd knocked off an Oregon or Ohio State. All the same, when Mississippi State took the field again, they commanded the nation's attention as they demolished No. 6-ranked Texas A&M. The game was over with ten minutes left in the fourth quarter as quarterback Dak Prescott crossed the goal line for his third rushing touchdown of the day in addition to the two he threw. A&M trailed 48–17, and their two late scores didn't fool anyone. On the same day that in-state rival Ole Miss beat the No. 3-ranked Crimson Tide, Mississippi State annihilated Texas A&M. Mississippi football was back on the map.

Mississippi State tied for third in the AP poll with the Ole Miss Rebels, a coincidence befitting the tumultuous relationship between the Rebs and the Bulldogs. Even in their brightest moment, State's highest ranking in the seventy-eight-year history of the Associated Press poll, they still had to be tied to their antagonistic, uppity big brother. The hatred between Mississippi State and Ole Miss is real. Maybe the only thing that could have put a damper on this unprecedented high was being grouped with "that other Mississippi school" up the road in Oxford all week. *Sports Illustrated*'s "Mississippi Mayhem" cover highlighted both Mississippi schools' signature wins from the previous Saturday and sold out in bookstores all over the state in record time. If ever there was a time to be a Mississippi State football fan, this was it.

You'd think that this level of attention surrounding a program not used to the spotlight would be unbearably bright. If it wasn't true for head coach Dan Mullen and his Bulldog team, it was certainly true for the fans camping out all night for *College GameDay*. There's an old football adage attributed to legendary Green Bay Packers coach Vince Lombardi: "When you get into the end zone, act like you've been there before." Still, as a fan, how do you act if your team has never actually been there before?

Most people I met—the dreamers, the level-headed folk, and the naysayers alike—were all overjoyed at how high they'd already climbed and were content to hedge their bets. "If we lose to No. 2 Auburn this week, so be it. We're already way ahead of where we thought we'd be" was the general sentiment. And while some people genuinely believed that State would win the following afternoon, everyone made it clear that a loss wouldn't dampen the spirit and excitement running through Starkville. "But if we win tomorrow," one of the half-cocked freshmen bellowed at 3:30 in the morning, "we're gonna burn this city to the ground." On this point, as well, all the overnighters agreed.

As entertaining as the blustering drunken freshmen were, their talking points had started to repeat themselves and our interactions had hit a point of diminishing returns. I noticed a group across the lawn tossing a football, and like an overeager puppy, I scurried across the field to play catch. The guy next to me, Daniel, was an MSU senior. As we chatted and tossed the pigskin, I noticed his cooler, which was sitting next to me, was locked. "Hey man, what's up with the lock on the cooler?" I inquired. He looked confused by the question, as if I'd asked him why he's wearing shoes. "Oh, everybody does that here. People will jack your stuff if you don't keep it locked. Some guys don't go to the games so they can go around and take people's booze from unlocked coolers and tailgates." I let the idea sink in before responding: "That's kinda messed up." Daniel shrugged, "Yeah, but that's why you get a lock."

He asked me to keep watch on the cooler while he went back to his truck for his cowbell. Ringing the cowbell is the foremost football tradition in Starkville. It traces its roots back to the pre-World War II era of Bulldog football—specifically, to the time when a cow supposedly made its way onto the field as the Bulldogs whipped the Rebels. The "apocryphal event that happened during a meaningful victory a long time ago" seemed to provide the template for so many college football superstitions, including Auburn's War Eagle. At any rate, the cowbell has become one of the hallmarks of attending a game in Starkville. It also serves as a symbol for passing fandom from one generation to the next. It's bad luck to buy your first cowbell; it has to be a gift. Most of the guys I talked to received their first cowbell from a parent or grand-parent. Bequeathed like a family heirloom, it cemented in place the allegiance of another in a long line of proud, if browbeaten, Mississippi State Bulldog fans.

When Daniel returned from his truck, he handed me a cowbell that was maroon with a long handle. It was also bare. Most of the cowbells I'd seen were decorated with stickers from various games or painted with the signs of their frat or sorority. This was another facet of the cowbell tradition, one that I was rather fond of. Each person decorates their cowbell with memories of the games they've attended. This way no two cowbells, much like no two fans' game experiences, are exactly the same.

With my new cowbell in tow, I felt like a part of the Mississippi State family. I never would have asked to be initiated into the fan base that makes the most annoying sound in all of sports, but since it happened, I figured I might as well roll with it. I hunkered down with the guys who had been tossing the ball around earlier. It was 4:30 in the morning, and everybody kept themselves warm with shots of Fireball and a steady stream of cigarettes. By 5:30 a couple guys had fallen asleep in their chairs, grinding our conversations to a halt. Everyone was sick of talking, sick of being awake, sick of waiting. It was around this time that I began questioning my decision-making: *Who cares about being on TV for* College GameDay? *Is there even anything worthwhile in this experience? Who cares about Lee Corso's picks, and how did he get so popular anyway? If I'm tired now, how am I going to be able to stay up through the game and into Saturday night?*

The gates finally opened and security vetted us two at a time as we passed toward the barricade separating fans from the stage. The two hours leading up to the show dragged on interminably despite all the diversions. The speakers pumped in pop music that was much more enjoyable than at any other time in its existence. When you've been up all night and you're dragging ass as the sun's rising, Iggy Azalea suddenly isn't so bad. The Mississippi State cheerleaders and dance team made their way into the space between the barricade and stage, and, more than anything, they provided much-needed relief for weary eyes, especially after being around dudes talking football all night. Something they don't tell you about these overnighters for *College GameDay* is that they're sausage fests. I saw all of ten girls the entire night. As the sun drew near, all those plus-fours[65] arrived, many of them girls appearing well-rested with a fresh coat of makeup on and Mississippi State stickers on their cheeks. They served as a sharp contrast to me and all the other guys who'd stayed up all night, as haggard, beat-up, and in desperate need of a shower and nap as we were.

The crowd went through the whole routine. Mississippi State people handed out Stark Vegas[66] shirts to the first couple rows and then ESPN people handed out the orange Home Depot hard hats. I grabbed the shirt but not a hard hat. David Pollack stepped on stage first and filmed a segment for the SEC Network around 7:30 am and everybody rang the cowbells like their lives depended on it. My ears were humming, and if I were the claustrophobic type I would've bugged out. Everyone pushed toward the front, screaming and ringing, swinging their signs around wildly, hoping theirs would appear on TV. And when the crew

---

[65] Four people whose spot in line was saved by one person who stayed up all night.

[66] Not to be confused with Nashvegas.

came out, it was more of the same. Chris Fowler walked along the barricade, shook hands with the first two rows, took a selfie with one fan's phone, and headed up to the podium. The others, Corso, Herbstreit, and Howard, all walked up the back stairs away from the cowbell-clanging masses. Lee Corso started his shtick early, taking a cowbell and ringing it, then picking up a Mississippi State helmet and kissing it. It's amazing how easy it is for this man to provoke a reaction. Fans all across the country eat it up season after season, and for the life of me, I still can't understand it.

(My favorite Lee Corso story is from when he was coaching Indiana University in the 1970s. Corso's Hoosiers were playing the No. 1-ranked Ohio State Buckeyes, who were led by legendary coach Woody Hayes. Indiana wasn't very good and was a big underdog in the game. The story goes that Ohio State scored first on a pick-six but missed the extra point; 6–0 Ohio State. Indiana then drove the ball down the field and scored, making it 7–6 Indiana. Corso called time-out, and then took his entire team down underneath the scoreboard to take a picture of Indiana beating the number one team in the country. As you might imagine, the Hayes-run Buckeyes didn't find the antic amusing, and proceeded to throttle Indiana 47–7. But the story captures the essence of Lee Corso's TV persona as I see it: a showman who does stupid things for attention, but is ultimately harmless and annoyingly lovable.)

As *College GameDay* kicked off, the whole event felt anticlimactic. Sure, the cowbells rang louder and the signs waved in a frenzy. I was a full-fledged member of the State crowd sporting my new Stark Vegas shirt and flicking my wrist to join the cowbell chorus. My spot in the sardine can was third row center in between Chris Fowler and either Lee Corso or David Pollack as the main camera panned in on the four men at their desk. And a couple buddies back in Chicago texted to let me know they saw me waving my green ND shirt overhead on ESPN. Still, after an hour, I'd had my fill of *GameDay*. I headed back to my car and fell asleep for an hour in the driver's seat with my feet on the dash, waking up in a cold sweat confused as to where I was. Such is life on the road.

Heading back to the Junction, I was still disoriented. The grill belonging to the freshmen guys I'd spent the first part of the overnighter with was still where they'd left it, but they were nowhere to be found. Other tents cropped up around their abandoned tailgate. It's like they were never there.

⚑

The Auburn-Mississippi State game was the first of the trip where tickets were genuinely hard to come by. It was no surprise in a game matching the No. 2 and No. 3 teams in the country. On top of being a top-3 matchup, it was arguably the biggest contest in the history of Mississippi State football, and in a stadium that seats only 62,000. I had to lap the stadium numerous times as the countdown to kickoff approached. With thirty minutes until kick, usually prime buying time, scalper tickets were still between $175 and $250 and nobody on their way in had any extras to get rid of. It wasn't until fifteen minutes before kickoff that I found an Auburn fan who approached me and sold me his extra for $100. Davis-Wade Stadium was confusing, as the upper deck doesn't wrap around, and by the time I found my seat on the ten-yard line on the Mississippi State sideline, there was 12:30 left in the first quarter and State had already raced out to a 14–0 lead.

FOX Sports columnist Stewart Mandel tweeted after the game, "Loudest game I've ever attended, start to finish, even postgame." His assessment was spot-on. Even from the upper deck in a mostly Auburn section, it was incredibly noisy. When the rain poured down late in the second quarter with Mississippi State leading 21–13, the fans never wavered in their intensity, ringing with all their might between plays and as the Auburn center lined up over the ball. Then the jumbotron read, "No Bell, Just Yell," so the cowbells stopped instantly and a deafening roar took their place, barely missing a beat. Mississippi State quarterback Dak Prescott broke loose for a 15-yard touchdown run into the north end zone, where the student section is located. With 3:58 remaining in the first half, State led 28–13. Pandemonium ensued in the middle of a downpour on Davis-Wade Stadium. The Auburn fans around me fell silent again.

The stadium grew tense as Auburn marched the ball 99 yards on their first drive after halftime. Monsoon-like conditions had driven many of us to the concourse, where we watched the third quarter on the jumbotron under concrete cover. With 6:09 remaining in the third quarter, Auburn's Duke Williams capped a drive with a physics-defying 15-yard touchdown catch to make the score 28–20, a one-possession difference. At that moment, Bulldog anxiety reached its peak inside the concourse.

The Tigers would come no closer, however. Mississippi State's defense stiffened, and the Bulldogs followed up an early fourth-quarter field goal with a fumble recovery and subsequent score to make the game 38–20 with 11:00 to play. Unlike the previous two games, where Mississippi State surrendered multiple late fourth-quarter scores, the Bulldogs finished off the No. 2 team in America decisively, 38–23.

I still get chills writing about what I witnessed next. With the stadium lights on and the rain stopped at last, Mississippi State fans sang and danced and rang their cowbells with the type of jubilation that can't be replicated. This type of unbridled glee only happens once in a generation. It was a coming-of-age moment; I might never bear witness to something like it again, and Mississippi State fans probably won't either. The day your team reaches the mountaintop for the first time in its history produces sheer ecstasy. Singing along to Journey's "Don't Stop Believin'" after the alma mater[67] and watching Coach Dan Mullen carry his young daughter in one arm while lapping the stadium shaking fans' hands, I felt like I was witnessing a moment of total synchronization between fans and team. Everyone rode the same wavelength, fully present, absorbing a surreal moment.

I wandered around the Junction for a while after the game despite being beyond exhausted. I'd now been awake for over twenty-four hours save a power nap in my car. The atmosphere outside the stadium gave me a third wind and I stopped at various tailgates, checking in on the closer-than-expected Arkansas–Alabama game and congratulating fans, feeling genuinely happy for the moment they were experiencing. The last man I talked to on the way back to my car seemed a little guarded when I told him I was happy for them becoming the No. 1 team in the country, happy I could be in Starkville to share in the experience. He stammered a bit, looking down at the sidewalk, kicking one of his feet ever

---

[67] The school's official anthem. This is different from—and nowhere near as catchy as—a fight song.

so slightly. "Yeah, we're gonna be No. 1 tomorrow but you know there's only one place to go from there…down."

Decades of being conditioned to lose will do that to you. I hope he found a way to enjoy the moment. But I left with the distinct impression that he'd wake up the next morning convinced that it was only a dream, that it had never really happened.

Tennessee vs. #3 Ole Miss

October 18, 2014

Oxford, Mississippi

You only have to spend five minutes in Starkville and Oxford to begin to understand the differences that make the two schools such bitter sports rivals. Most obviously, there are the clear social and cultural lines: blue collar and white collar, mudflap country hillbilly and refined posh socialite. Mississippi State is the countrified, cowbell-ringing college that reflects its rural surroundings. Ole Miss is the cultured, fashionable seat of refinement that presents itself as a wealthy suburban oasis surrounded by country roads and two-lane highways expanding in all directions back into the void of simpler country living. If you choose to focus on the differences, they're everywhere. If you choose to focus on the similarities though, you could find those everywhere, too. But as sports fans, and especially when we're talking about rivalries, we magnify the differences and trivialize the similarities. It's easier to deal in absolutes.

When I pulled into the Square, the historic center of downtown Oxford, I was immediately struck by the beauty of the elegant whitewashed courthouse that serves as the Square's centerpiece and focal point. It took nearly half an hour to find parking on Friday morning, which speaks both to what happens to Oxford on a game weekend and what happens when a team is ranked in the top-5 for just the second time since 1970.

Ajax Diner, a country and soul food restaurant in the Square, had a line out the door within twenty minutes of opening at 11 am Friday. But Ashley, the reporter from Saturday Down South I had met in Nashville and Atlanta, had a two-seater table for us in the back. She was the only person I could compare notes with. Her tailgate piece for SDS this week was on a topic we'd discussed back in Atlanta: multiple generations at one tailgate. As I devoured my Big Easy, a country-fried steak burger with mashed potatoes, gravy, coleslaw, and lima beans, Ashley dropped assorted Ole Miss knowledge on me, including the fact that Ajax was Eli Manning's favorite restaurant when he was on campus.

Somehow we wound up on the topic of mascots, which at Ole Miss meant we were talking about Colonel Reb. Without question, Reb serves as one of the more literal and complicated symbols of Ole Miss history, offering a telling glimpse into the ever-present elephant in the room: racial tension. Ashley brought me up to speed on the history of the mascot. Created in the 1930s, Colonel Reb was used in a popular but unofficial capacity for decades before being adopted as the official Ole Miss mascot in 1979. In 2003, however, the mascot was abandoned by Athletic Director Pete Boone and Chancellor Robert Khayat because, Boone explained, "it didn't fit anything we do." To move past niceties and political phraseology, the mascot—with his crisp suit, string tie, country hat, and cane—smacked of plantation-era slavery.

Removing Colonel Reb was one of the least popular decisions in school history, and it spawned grassroots campaigns to restore the mascot. These took the form of pushing for state legislation, harnessing pressure from the student body and alumni associations, and withdrawing booster donations to the tune of $50 million. Websites like saveolemiss.com sprung up to garner support for the cause while preexisting sites like confederatewave.org subsumed the cause as part of a larger agenda.

I won't pretend to fully understand the intricacies of the topic after spending a weekend on campus and reading some articles and trading a few e-mails with people online. But as far as I've been able to wrap my head around the strongly held beliefs on all sides of the issue, I do think I've grasped one of the fundamental misunderstandings, a piece of what's lost in translation and has opposite sides talking past each other.

Those opposed to Colonel Reb, especially outsiders, have the following point of view: It's emblematic of the nasty, deep-seated racism that ran to the core of the South in another era. If we truly want to move past that time and place, isn't it better to cut ties with such a clear and visible reminder of such an ugly chapter in history, one we aim to transcend? To go no further leaves a person with the impression that everyone who helped get Colonel Reb removed is on the side of good and everyone against his removal is on the side of evil. Such a snap judgment would suggest that anyone still shouting for Colonel Reb is masquerading the racist values they still hold at their core but can't flaunt as openly because of the slowly shifting social climate over the past half century. Certainly, plenty of people fall into this category, but it doesn't account for the more innocent perspective on why Ole Miss fans still clamor for Colonel Reb.

Some of the main characteristics I noticed about people in the South—again, not across the board but generally speaking—are that they're slow to change, they hang on to tradition and history, and they're defiant toward authority figures telling them what to do. In fact, so many of the charming aspects of the Southern demeanor stem from this resistance to change. Southern gentility—chivalry and manners—is a living, breathing part of the culture, and it comes from a bygone era in our society. These admirable traits have been lost in so many other places across the country. In many ways, the desire to cling to something that holds historical weight and significance, like a school mascot, comes from the same instinct that preserves other traditions, ones that are desirable and even admirable. The racist undertones or overtones are secondary to most when considering the issue.

Despite doing my best to understand both sides of the argument, I still can't force myself to side with the Colonel Reb crusaders. To me, it's the same as the "heritage, not hate" argument defending those who choose to fly the Southern Cross. I can see why hanging onto your traditions and the past is important, and maybe even more so for Southerners than many others across the country. But when the way in which you cling to your heritage serves as a terrorizing reminder to an entire race of people of a time when they were enslaved, it seems the harm done by these emblems, no matter how well intentioned, far exceeds any perceived benefit.

If Colonel Reb's removal represents the divisiveness coursing through Rebel Nation, then his replacement, the Black Bear, offers a common ground where all Ole Miss fans can come together. Nobody supports or even accepts the Black Bear as their mascot. "What does that even have to do with Mississippi?" Ashley wondered aloud in between bites of her biscuit. "There aren't even black bears in Mississippi. Why not Kodiak bear or polar bear for Christ's sake?"

Though the final poll somehow brought the Black Bear[68] to the Ole Miss sidelines, one of the runners-up, the Landshark, is a recent and enormously popular piece of the Ole Miss football culture. "Fins Up" is a persistent reminder on the jumbotron in Vaught-Hemingway Stadium, a command to the crowd to put an open hand perpendicular to their forehead akin to a shark fin. The term and tradition originated in Ole Miss lore with linebacker Tony Fein in 2008. An Iraq War veteran, Fein came to Oxford after transferring from a community college in Arizona. He coined the term "Landshark" for the Rebel defense during the resurgent 2008 season, where Ole Miss finished 9–4 after four consecutive losing seasons. Fein died of an accidental overdose days after being cut by the Baltimore Ravens in 2009, bringing a disheartening end to a feel-good story. The Landshark took on greater significance to the Ole Miss community after Fein's death, serving as both a rallying cry and celebratory gesture by the defense and fans alike, as well as a way of

---

[68] The Black Bear's connection to Mississippi has two supposed points of origin. One is a William Faulkner short story, "The Bear," from the larger work, *Go Down, Moses*. The other is a 1902 hunting trip to Mississippi during which President Theodore Roosevelt refused to shoot a bear. I don't get it, either.

honoring the memory of one of their own. If finding something meaningful to the Ole Miss community to replace Colonel Reb is the goal, a Landshark would certainly fit the bill.

⚑

After lunch I made my way to Vaught-Hemingway for a tour. A friend of a friend named Angela was waiting for me; though we had never met before, she had very generously welcomed me to stay with her for the weekend. She worked at the stadium and was finishing her undergrad degree that fall and somehow had downtime to show me around. We started on the field, and I headed straight for the 50-yard line in the middle of the Ole Miss logo. I kicked up pieces of the chewed-up rubber in the field turf and took a couple pictures before heading upstairs with Angela through the tunnel where the Rebels take the field. On our way, we stopped at the "NEVER QUIT" Chucky Mullins statue where the team gathers before rushing out. The bronze bust is removed during the week and placed back atop the brick monument on game day. Angela told me about Mullins's story and the legacy of No. 38 in Ole Miss football. In October 1989, Mullins, a defensive back for the Rebels, was paralyzed while making a tackle on a Vanderbilt player. He was airlifted to a hospital and had surgery to repair the four shattered vertebrae in his spine but never regained sensation or movement below the neck. He returned to school in June 1990, but died on May 6, 1991, after suffering a pulmonary embolism. In tribute, the Chucky Mullins Courage Award is presented to one player every spring, and that player has the honor of wearing No. 38 in the fall.

We made our way up the ramps to the private suites and press boxes and coaches' booths. I stood over the 50-yard line in front of the green screen where ESPN announcers would call the game the following evening. I parked myself in the coaches' booth where coordinators survey the game below as they call plays and relay information to coaches and players on the field. In Ole Miss's coaches' booth, I even found a laminated special teams depth chart and play call sheet left behind from the Alabama game. Souvenir.

The privately owned suites had varying degrees of decor, ranging from simple couches and a TV to elaborate, interior designed touches with Ole Miss football artifacts and team color-coordinated couches and area rugs. We walked into the Tuohy family's booth, which identified itself with oversized photos of Michael Oher and his adoptive family. The book *The Blindside* (and later, the movie version) chronicled the true story of how the well-to-do family took in the homeless Oher during his high school years. Oher was a unanimous All-American at Ole Miss before the Baltimore Ravens drafted him as their 2009 first-round pick. In another suite, I noticed a framed photo of a young Elvis Presley playing backyard football with friends while wearing an Ole Miss sweatshirt. In *these* halls of power and influence, it didn't matter so much how many number one hits you had or whose number one pick you were in the NFL draft; what counted was your ties to the Ole Miss Rebels.

After the tour, I ventured back to the Square. When I got there, the radio host Paul Finebaum was signing copies of his new book, *My Conference Can Beat Your Conference*. A chatty mother and daughter behind me in line made the time spent waiting to meet "The Mouth of the South" fly by. As has been par for the course on my travels, I found in Caroline and Marie people exemplifying every positive stereotype about Southerners: they were sweet and charming, warm and hospitable. And as mothers will do, Caroline spent a good deal of our time bragging on her three children, all of whom attended or currently attend

Ole Miss. Caroline bragged on her daughter Marie so much you'd think she was a homely child in need of validation and self-esteem. To the contrary, Marie was an impressive, accomplished, and attractive young lady. I thought I'd misheard when Caroline told me Marie was Miss Mississippi. Nope; I'd heard right. I was standing in line with a former Miss Mississippi, though you'd never know it by her aw-shucks humility.

When I finally stepped up to Finebaum's table, I told him what I was doing and asked him what he'd key in on, what he'd look for if he were an outsider trying to grasp Southern football culture. He affirmed something for me that had been driving me nuts. According to Finebaum, Notre Dame fans can, and in many cases do, *get it*. "Notre Dame's it's own thing, it has that cult following. That's pretty much the exception up north, [except for] maybe Ohio State or a Penn State." He went on to explain the contrast between the North and the South to me in terms of Big Ten and SEC: "Up there, you have your Iowa fans, your Wisconsin fans and they care about their team. They care if their team wins or loses, but they have plenty of things going on in their lives outside football. Down here…"

As he trailed off, he made eye contact to ensure his point was received. He sounded like a man slandering his own target audience, saying they had no lives. But was he? Many of the die-hard fans take such words as a high compliment. They'd see it as saying that they have correctly prioritized college football in their lives. And therein lies a big piece of what's lost in translation as you cross the Mason-Dixon line.

We chatted for another minute or two before Square Books owner and Oxford Mayor Richard Howorth shooed me along. There were others in line, after all. I moved on, grateful for Finebaum's ear. I will say that he seemed fully engaged in our conversation. If he had no interest, he was a convincing actor.[69]

℞

I tried to walk around most of the college campuses I visited in Notre Dame shirts, but there are exceptions to every rule, and Ole Miss was one such exception. When people talk about Ole Miss, they talk about the Grove. In fact, it's arguably the single most hyped college tailgate in America. Despite having heard the hoopla, I only knew a few particulars about the Grove in advance: One, men wear collared shirts or sport coats and bow ties and women wear sundresses. It is clearly a classy affair. Two, the pop-up tents are more ornate than at other schools. I'd heard rumblings of chandeliers inside the tents, but that was only speculation. Three, there are more attractive women per square foot in the Grove on a fall Saturday than anywhere else in America. With that in mind, I packed a sport coat when I left Chicago, bought a blue-and-gold bow tie upon arriving in Oxford, and used an iron for the first time in months. I'd never worn a bow tie, so I had to Google how to tie one on Saturday morning. And despite the fact that I looked good dressed up for the first time in a while, I felt like an idiot knowing that I was headed to a tailgate looking the way I did. But dressing for a cocktail party was far from the silliest tradition I'd encountered over the course of my travels.

---

[69] In our picture Finebaum looks like he'd rather be in the middle of a double root canal than standing next to me. But then again, he isn't exactly known for his cheery disposition.

Red brick buildings with impressive white Greek-style columns appeared everywhere on my stroll around campus Saturday morning. It's not just the Square; there's an elegance about the entire campus. While giving myself the tour, I found the James Meredith statue. Meredith was the first black student enrolled at Ole Miss, an event that caused a riot on campus when he enrolled in 1962 and required the National Guard's presence to restore peace and ensure Meredith's safety. Over fifty years later, Meredith is still a fixture on campus, attending various events and even Ole Miss football games.

In February 2014, three Ole Miss students, all freshmen from Georgia, were expelled from the university for hanging a noose around the Meredith statue. Depending on whom you ask, this act and its aftermath is either a symbol of the school's racial progress or its lack thereof. Angela, the girl I was staying with, hails from the Upper Peninsula in northern Michigan but has lived in the South for a number of years now, in Memphis, Southaven, and now in Oxford. To her, the fact that a noose was hung shows just how backwards some people in the South still are. "I mean, it's the twenty-first century. How is this still happening? How is this not a bigger deal to people?" she fumed. When I asked Ashley about the incident, her point of view was the polar opposite of Angela's. The noose hanging, though disgusting, was a case where the university showed itself to be proactive and socially just in its response. The school promptly expelled all three students, she noted, and they weren't even Mississippi kids. "They were three morons from Georgia," Ashley said, "and it's like a couple bad apples are giving a bad name to the whole bunch. Their entire frat was disbanded, too."

I was completely overwhelmed by my first sight of the Grove. There's something about how compactly the tents folded, almost on top of each other, that's truly stifling. And looking inside, what I'd heard about the chandeliers was true. Practically every other tent had a chandelier hanging from the ceiling. Two of the major differences between the Grove and everywhere else I'd been were that everyone drank their alcohol out of red Solo cups and there were no grills to be found anywhere. It was explained to me that both open alcohol containers and open-flame grills were banned because of some antiquated Oxford laws.

Marie and Caroline had invited me to join them at the Delta Gamma sorority house where Marie's younger sister Lizzy was a member. Like anywhere else I went in Oxford, I felt awestruck walking through their extravagant home, like I was walking around a country club or a museum. It was foreign in the sense that their college living situation was 180-degrees from the way my friends and I lived back then, with dirty dishes always in the sink and empty pizza boxes stacked high in a corner of the kitchen.

When I met Lizzy, she told me about the sorority and how theirs was the first national Delta Gamma chapter. Then I met Nana, the girls' grandma, who complimented my "gorgeous blue eyes." What can I say? Grandmas like me. We spent the next few hours together, first at the sorority house and later at various tailgates around the Grove. As socialites do, the gals made the rounds, chatting with old friends and dragging me along for the ride. I didn't mind being led around, as I often felt overwhelmed trying to process all the stimuli, starting conversations with groups of strangers by myself all day while never telling anyone why I was really there.

I met a couple interesting people along the way. At one of the tailgates, a lady in her sixties named Barb told me about coming to the Grove with her parents as a little girl. "Back then, you could drive right up on the lawn and unload your tailgate. We used to come to almost every home game." Barb recalled how Archie Manning was a celebrity in Oxford when he played for Ole Miss, and confided that Archie was her first crush. "When I was 12 years old, I told my mother I was going to marry him someday," she said, giggling and blushing at the memory. But as she carried on, I could feel her spirit being transported back to childhood, reliving her first Ole Miss football moments. She got that faraway look, like she'd gone a million miles away. Barb had the rare quality of being able to transmit her emotions in her storytelling, and with each passing anecdote I caught myself growing more wistful, almost as if I'd grown up watching ol' No. 18 electrify Oxford myself.

At another tailgate, where my hosts talked with two men involved in the Miss Mississippi pageant in some form or another—you gotta politick, right?—I met a fellow named Chad. He was around my age and wore standard Oxford Saturday attire: a striped button-down with the Ole Miss logo on the breast pocket and tan slacks. Between sips of bourbon on the rocks out of his red solo cup, he reminisced about how he sat through the Ed Orgeron[70] era as a student, which included a 2-win season. "We may not win the game, but we ain't never lost a party. You

---

[70] Bruce Feldman's book *Meat Market* explores Orgeron's time as head man at Ole Miss, and portrays Orgeron as one of the most fascinating characters in all of college football. The story that always sticks out in my mind was when the coach reportedly ripped off his shirt and offered to fight any his Rebel players in the locker room. On November 26, 2016, Orgeron was named head coach at LSU.

ever heard that? It meant a lot more back then, when we were terrible." He touched on the solace fans take in little victories when their team doesn't produce all the time. You can take comfort knowing the party's always there.

Besides, when a team wins all the time, the law of diminishing returns and increased expectations can make the high life of a fan virtually unsustainable. Finebaum's book explored this phenomenon through the Alabama fan base, and he argues that fans' demand for perfection will eventually get the best of Nick Saban. There's no threat of that happening anytime soon in Oxford, however. The Ole Miss Rebels haven't had a 10-win season since Eli Manning donned the Yale blue and crimson. I'm sure a 10-win season would be met with greater appreciation and enjoyment in Oxford or Starkville than Tuscaloosa any day. Win the party, and anything else is just a bonus.

As it became clear Chad knew plenty about recruiting, I brought up the 2013 Ole Miss recruiting class. I asked if he thought boosters had paid to bring in top recruits that year, and Chad waved me off. "C'mon man, why you gotta bring that shit up? I remember Quon's stack of cash[71] on

---

[71] One of the more questionable recruiting moments came when Laquon Treadwell, a highly touted prospect from Illinois, posted a picture of a stack of hundred-dollar bills while on his recruiting visit to Ole Miss. He deleted the photo almost immediately, but not before some sports fans (and the media) got wind of it.

Instagram or whatever. What's that prove?" I shrugged: "Nothing, I guess. Just curious."

I'm fascinated by college football recruiting. I hound Notre Dame football message boards in the days leading up to National Signing Day, worried about other schools poaching our commits, excited about the prospect of us poaching others. I'm also fascinated by the idea of boosters working under the table to illegally entice recruits. I'm of the opinion that the NCAA's recent treatment of schools like North Carolina and Miami,[72] as well as its lack of sanctions for other offending schools, demonstrates that it's an ineffectual governing body and that there's no teeth in its bite. University of Southern California is the last school to really feel its wrath[73]—and said wrath was only felt after hard evidence of illegal activities tied to the recruitments of Reggie Bush (in football) and O. J. Mayo (in basketball) was supposedly dropped right in reporters' laps at Yahoo.com. If the NCAA doesn't have the punitive authority it once did, then it serves to reason that there is no motivation for boosters to stop cutting corners to snare top athletes.

As well, the current college football landscape has become a facilities arms race where big-time schools compete with each other to gain a competitive advantage. New facilities and athlete dorms and stadium upgrades are being built all over the country at an incredible rate, and

---

[72] Both schools effectively received "slap on the wrist" punishments for major violations in recent years. No-show classes and booster-supplied benefits were among the violations.

[73] Penn State's recent sanctions had nothing to do with recruiting violations.

they tend to be a little pricey. Let's be clear: college football is a multi-billion-dollar industry. As a result, there's never been more monetary incentive to cheat. Winning brings money to the program, from bowl appearance payouts and (aboveboard) booster contributions to merchandise and TV contracts. The best way to win is to have the best athletes and coaches. The process cycles through, and the ends justify the means. Or so the thinking goes.

In April 2014, Steven Godfrey wrote an article for SBNation.com titled "Meet the Bag Man." It chronicled a series of off-the-record interviews Godfrey had with football boosters from various unnamed SEC schools. The article goes into detail about how the process of paying players has evolved to where it is in today's game. According to the story, the boosters involved in these schemes operate with the clandestine precision of a crime syndicate: payoffs are delivered in ways that allow for suspicion but never proof of illegality. These payments are made by upstanding citizens with discretionary income who care more about the condition of their alma mater's football program than adherence to NCAA rules, which they consider outdated and optional, anyway.

I'm shocked when fans claim to honestly believe that everything is aboveboard. Has history taught them no lessons? A look back at bygone eras shows players and boosters owning up when the statute of limitations can no longer penalize them. But players aren't paid today because why? Because programs know what can happen to them? Okay.

I have no issue with the illegal paying of players. Above all, I believe that student-athletes are underpaid and undervalued. I personally understand the importance of a college degree and that, depending on what school they attend, these young men are receiving the equivalent of a living wage for what they do. Sure, they're being compensated for their time—at least, in a way. But when you consider the amount of time they spend on football-related activities in a given week, a number of hours certainly similar in commitment to a full-time job, it's not hard to see how education could take a back seat. Many big-time college football players never end up receiving college degrees. And many more who do earn degrees earn them in general studies-type disciplines that have little real-world applicability. What these athletes have is a highly coveted commodity unique to an exceptionally small percentage of the population. If they're able to exploit their unique ability to better their lives and the lives of their families while they're being exploited for their talents, good for them, I say. It's unfortunate that only a select few programs have the means, the willingness, and the passionate fan base to make such payments happen. This creates an oligarchy in the college football world. But in an imperfect system, I'm all for the have-nots squeezing all they can from the willing haves.

Still, ask almost any school about their team and whether they pay players and you'll encounter steadfast denials. Like many others around the country, I have questions about that 2013 Ole Miss recruiting class. It included the number one player in the country, Robert Nkemdiche, the country's top receiver Laquon Treadwell, two of the top three offensive tackles in Laremy Tunsil and Austin Golson, and the number two safety in Tony Conner. Coming off a 7–6 record and with a new coach in Hugh Freeze, how does a team that hadn't had a 10-win season in a decade land a consensus top-10 recruiting class? Nkemdiche makes sense when you consider that his older brother was already on the Ole Miss squad. But the others?

Asking about this in casual conversation around Oxford, people like Chad had ready explanations. The ones I heard most were that Hugh

Freeze is a spectacular recruiter and that good players want to follow the number one recruit wherever he's going. I suppose these answers possess a certain plausibility, but I'm skeptical. I'm skeptical because we're talking about a landscape where the underhanded practice of paying players is simply the way of the world and a standard practice of business. This rationalizing isn't unique to Oxford, however. I had no intention to attack the Rebels' class, season, or current success. They simply represented a readily available case in point. I wasn't looking for people to hand me documentation proving that their school does, in fact, pay their players. I just wanted to have this conversation without people looking at me like I'm some cockeyed, possibly unhinged conspiracy theorist. Bless my heart, right?[74]

⚑

Ten minutes before kickoff, the Ramblin' Rebel, a 1930 Ford Model A car inspired by Georgia Tech's famous Ramblin' Wreck, crept out from the visitors' entrance into the south end zone. It had a Yale blue and Harvard crimson paint job, white wall tires and a No. 18 Archie Manning decal on the hood, and came fully equipped with a cheerleader riding on the steps of either side. Around the same time, the Pride of the South, the Ole Miss band, lined up diagonally, making a path for the team when it ran out of the entrance. The Ole Miss Rebels huddled in the southwest corner of the stadium at the Chucky Mullins "Never Quit" bust while the stadium proceeded to Lock the Vaught. The football team linked arms and began swaying side to side as Puff Daddy and

---

[74] February 22, 2017: The NCAA cites Ole Miss with violating thirteen of the twenty-eight rules governing universities. Nine of the thirteen violations occurred during Coach Hugh Freeze's tenure.

Jimmy Page's "Come With Me" blared through the sound system with a bass I could feel emanating up through my feet. When I looked over toward the student section, I saw one of the most memorable sights in SEC football: an entire quarter of the lower bowl with locked arms swaying in near-perfect harmony, the rows of fans moving in alternating directions.

Ten minutes after kickoff, however, the pregame excitement and energy gave way to the monotony of a boring football game. Ole Miss couldn't move the ball early and Tennessee triggerman Justin Worley would follow up his big-chunk plays with turnovers. Tennessee scored the game's first points on a field goal early in the second quarter. But these would be the only 3 points of the game for the Volunteers, as Ole Miss started moving offensively, and would eventually tally the next 34. Down 3–0, Bo Wallace connected with receiver Vince Sanders on back-to-back vertical routes; the second went 39 yards for a touchdown to make it 7–3. After Ole Miss scored again before half to make it a 14–3 game, I nearly left. There were three reasons why: One, the game was boring. Specifically, the Ole Miss offense couldn't run the ball between the tackles. This made the team entirely dependent on quarterback Bo Wallace's ability to exploit man coverages, find soft spots in zones, or take the top of the defense with deep vertical throws. And on this night, Bo Wallace didn't bring his "A" game. He missed open receivers, made dumb decisions, and finished the evening completing less than 50 percent of his passes. Two, the game was over at 14–3. Despite all of Tennessee's offensive weapons and their solid defensive play, Justin Worley made too many careless throws (read: interception-prone ones), and the young offensive line wasn't experienced enough to give Worley the time he needed to get the ball into his playmakers' hands. Against a top-notch speedy defense like Ole Miss, there was no chance of overcoming these hurdles. Three, Notre Dame and Florida State were playing in Tallahassee, and for the first time all season I felt physical discomfort—tightness in my chest and a pit in my stomach—not watching an Irish game. FSU was ranked No. 2 coming in and the Irish No. 5.

For the second half, I found myself standing atop the section at the 45-yard line on the Tennessee sideline along with a few Ole Miss fans. This had a much better view than the corner of the end zone. By the time the third quarter kicked off, my attention was split almost evenly between the game on the field and the scoreboard scrolling across the bottom of the jumbotron.

Notre Dame–7, Florida State–0.

Notre Dame–7, Florida State–7.

Notre Dame–14, Florida State–7.

Notre Dame–14, Florida State–10.

Somewhere in there, Ole Miss kicked a field goal and then scored a touchdown to go up 24–3 late in the third quarter. I couldn't stand it any longer; I had to catch the rest of the Notre Dame game. Ole Miss would tack on another ten points in the fourth quarter, making the final 34–3.

I walked back into the Grove in time to see the last couple plays of the first half of the Notre Dame game. The Irish were leading Florida State 17–10 going into the break. I had to see the second half, but to be perfectly honest I didn't want to be in the middle of some bar in the Square with my emotional well-being on the line, so I power-walked to my car and drove back to Angela's house. Watching Notre Dame's final drive, I paced back and forth across Angela's living room like I was waiting for the doctor to tell me a family member was out of surgery. When Irish quarterback Everett Golson converted to Corey Robinson on 4th and 18, I was frozen, believing Notre Dame was actually on the verge of punching it in to knock off the defending champs.

Golson hit Robinson on 4th and goal inside of fifteen seconds left for the game-winning touchdown, Robinson's 3rd touchdown catch of the game. However, an offensive pass interference call took the score off the board and forced a 4th and goal from the 18 that Notre Dame couldn't convert. I don't have Notre Dame blinders on to the point where I'm going to deny that C. J. Prosise interfered by running into his defender, making no effort to run a route. What I will say is that the call is sad for two reasons: One, you hate to see the officials determine the outcome of the game; and two, Robinson would have scored even without the interference. Florida State corner Ronald Darby, the outside defender, stepped inside to defend Will Fuller's slant route and nobody could have reached Robinson before he crossed the pylon regardless of the pick. Florida State won the game 31–27, extending the Seminoles' unbeaten streak to 23 games. I spent the rest of my Saturday night moping.

⚑

On Sunday, I explored the rest of Oxford and the surrounding areas. A few miles from campus there's a little town called Taylor that emits an old-timey, rustic feel. The main square extends maybe a block long, and the buildings stood faded white and red bricked and in need of tuck-pointing. Aluminum siding crept up the two steps leading to the Taylor Grocery and Restaurant. An old stand-alone gas station pump rusted in front of the diner, whose specialty is fried catfish; the view belonged on a postcard. After my meal, I headed a few miles farther down the road and found the Casey Jones Railroad Museum in Water Valley. I climbed aboard the train car, and read about the night Jones died after his train collided with another one. He's regarded as something of a folk hero because he was able to slow his train down enough so that all the passengers aboard survived; Jones, the conductor, was the only casualty. There was a peacefulness in driving through small towns across the South. Each location had its own particular way of washing over me with the same calming feeling.

Later, back in Oxford, Angela and I visited William Faulkner's home at Rowan Oak. The cedar tree-lined walkway to the home put blinders on me. It offered a tunnel vision to the front door of the white house, while the Greek Revival-style columns framed the front porch. As I approached the front door and peered inside the green-shuttered windows, my mind reeled back to that ever-famous Faulkner line from *Requiem for a Nun*, "*The past is never dead. It's not even past,*" and I explored his estate wondering what he'd think about his hometown these days.

When we'd finished strolling the grounds, we sat down at Gus's Fried Chicken for dinner. While there, we ran into one of Angela's friends. After she explained why I was in town, he commented on the various wood-carved Colonel Reb statuettes he'd seen all weekend. "You see it everywhere with the mascots, but when I saw them carved out of tree stumps, it made me realize how much all this sports stuff is really tribal. Seeing it in wood made me see that these are just like the icons primitive cultures would carve out." We talked a while longer about how fans magnify the 0.1 percent difference between themselves and fans of different sports teams. Fans are alike in so many ways that in order to fuel rivalries and give us a reason to want to beat the other guy, we have to focus on the differences, no matter how insignificant they are. It all made sense to me, but try explaining to an Ole Miss fan that they're 99.9 percent similar to a Mississippi State fan. The meaning we take out of that fraction of a percent of difference carries a great deal of weight.

George Rogers: 1980 Heisman Trophy winner,
1981 No. 1 NFL draft pick, and 1987 Super Bowl champion.

August 30, 2014: Sanford Stadium. Georgia outscored Clemson
21–0 in the fourth quarter to win 45–21.

The Holy Trinity of Florida Gator quarterbacks: Tim Tebow, Steve Spurrier, and Danny Wuerffel.

Bo Jackson: arguably the greatest college football player of all time.

"Somebody's gotta get this boy a new shirt." —Gus Malzahn, Auburn Head Coach.

Fans roll Toomer's Corner in Auburn after a Tigers win—a must-see SEC football tradition.

A night game at LSU's Tiger Stadium has
the best stadium atmosphere in American sports.

The Million Dollar Band pregame show at the Iron Bowl.
Auburn–Alabama is the marquee rivalry in the SEC.

The Helmet Wall at the College Football Hall of Fame in Atlanta, Georgia. 768 helmets in all.

Postgame celebration at the 2014 SEC Championship game. Alabama defeated Missouri 42–13 to punch their ticket to the inaugural College Football Playoff.

Florida football legend Fred Taylor amassed 3,792 total yards and 31 touchdowns between 1994 and 1997.

Former Notre Dame coach and ESPN commentator Lou Holtz has a pronounced lisp. This sign, found at the Junction in Starkville, Mississippi, was the funniest I saw all season.

Paul Finebaum, host of The Paul Finebaum Show,
is one of ESPN's best-known radio personalities,
and clearly excited to be taking a picture with me.

Tennessee's Pride of the Southland Band puts on the most
entertaining halftime show anywhere in the SEC.

Though not university-sanctioned, the Texas A&M bonfire before their Thanksgiving weekend game remains a sacred tradition in Aggieland.

Mike "Big Dawg" Woods was a permanent fixture on Georgia game days for twenty-five years before he passed in January 2017.

#4 Alabama vs. Tennessee

October 25, 2014

Knoxville, Tennessee

I arrived back in Memphis in time to catch some blues on Beale Street with my friend Anne. Full of bars and blues venues, Beale Street is kind of like a smaller, less debauched version of Bourbon Street and is the city's main tourist drag. We saw Dr. Herman Green, who plays with a group every Sunday night. He's played with all the legends: Thelonious Monk, John Coltrane, Miles Davis, B. B. King. One of the things I liked best about my trip were the adventures that came during the week, between the games. While I was in the South to witness the best of college football and take in each school's traditions, I was seeing more of the American landscape and the people who fill it on my supposed "off" days.

Memphis combined that sense of exploring new places with the comfort and familiarity of a grooved routine. During the day, I explored the sights—Sun Records, the Stax Records Museum, the Lorraine Motel (the place where MLK was assassinated)—and at night I'd go out to dinner or join in board game night with my friend Anne and her crew. Strange as it may sound, a sense of community, of having a group of friends, is what I missed most about my prior life. I made fast friends on the road, sure, and met plenty of interesting people, but I took comfort in knowing that the following night we'd be going out to Central BBQ or down to Beale Street, or maybe just bumming around playing Balderdash.

⚑

The drive from Memphis to Knoxville—clear across Tennessee—took six hours on Thursday. The only remotely interesting thing I saw on the trip was a sign for Nathan Bedford Forrest State Park. Of course, he's best known in pop culture as Forrest Gump's namesake. After reading up on him, I learned that Forrest was a Lieutenant General for the Confederacy in the Civil War and an innovative and resilient battlefield presence. He was also the first Grand Wizard of the Ku Klux Klan. In the twenty-first century, how does the state of Tennessee reconcile this fact with their public tribute to him? Is it rationalized because he later distanced himself from the Klan? I drove along for miles thinking about that park, wondering how and why a figure so closely linked to what is arguably the most hateful, bigoted organization in our nation's history has a state park named after him. The rest of the United States tends to dump on the South at times, painting it in a certain unflattering light: slow-moving, poorly educated, stuck in its good ol' boy racist past. In my travels I met a handful of characters who fit the stereotype, but they were the exception to the rule. I hadn't seen anything institutional that felt like a nod to segregation or slavery until I passed Forrest State Park. Some things are beyond my comprehension.

⚑

Part of surveying the landscape outside college towns in the South led me to Civil War forts and battlefields. Ironically, they served as a serene retreat from the perpetual din on SEC campuses. While these markers are reminders of where we were as a country 150 years ago—the bloodshed, atrocities, and heartbreak that occurred at those sites were the manifestations of a nation divided—I found a strange, almost meditative tranquility in retracing the steps through this utterly conflicted land.

The road sign read "Fort Dickerson 1 Mile Ahead" as I cruised through Knoxville on the lookout for a greasy spoon Friday morning. I pulled off, traveling up a steep gravel hill and over a paved asphalt road to a small graveyard-like enclosure. It was reinforced by large flat stones around the perimeter, and showed the markings of where small cannons once laid. Fort Dickerson functioned as a Confederate post until 1863, when Lincoln decided Knoxville was a key strategic location. He was right: it was a linchpin of the Confederacy's communication, transport, and food distribution systems. With Knoxville in Union hands, a crucial link in the Confederacy's supply chain had been severed.

The placard at the fort referred to it as the "Back Door to Knoxville." Back door, perhaps, but the fort itself was the size of a backyard, wider than long. There was a trail for visitors to follow in order to preserve the grounds in a semi-natural state. I stood overlooking the valley below and thought—about the strategic use of high ground in this fortification, about what I might find compelling this weekend at UT, and about how a true rivalry is only one in which records and rankings don't matter; one where no matter how lopsided the game is on paper, anything can happen because it's such an emotionally charged atmosphere. Would that be the case here in Knoxville this weekend?

About a hundred yards from the fort, there was an infographic about the Civil War. It had pictures of what Knoxville looked like in the 1860s from where I stood: what occupied the space where Neyland Stadium, the home of the Volunteers, stands now; where the original courthouse stood; and so forth. I stared out over the valley for a while contemplating how completely different Knoxville, or any city, now looks compared to 150 years ago. It's a couple lifetimes, sure, but it's also the blink of an eye in our collective history. Perspective is a funny thing, I guess. Maybe it was these shifts in consciousness, more than anything else, that quieted me at the Civil War sites.

⚑

Besides the university and its football team, the main appeal of Knoxville lies in its Old City with it's loft-style buildings, kitschy one-story facades housing upscale clothing stores and restaurants and, of course, cobblestone streets. Well-dressed Tennessee and Alabama fans lined the streets and occupied the patio chairs at every upscale restaurant. Making my way through Market Square, I explored Old Knoxville. Bama fans were out in almost equal number to Tennessee fans early Friday afternoon. That's one of the things I liked about SEC football: the visiting team's fans travel as well, which makes for a livelier atmosphere on Thursdays and Fridays before games. I made small talk with some Alabama fans about the rest of their conference schedule, looking past the 3–4 Tennessee team to bigger obstacles ahead. Then I made small talk with some Tennessee fans about whether they should pull the redshirt off quarterback Josh Dobbs and whether they'd make a bowl game this year. I made a lot of small talk.

Casual conversation revealed that the current status of the schools represents a reversal of fortunes from a decade earlier. In 2004, Tennessee beat Alabama 17–13 in Knoxville, their 9th win in the previous ten games in the series. Before that, between 1986 and 1994, Alabama had their own streak of 8 wins, 0 losses, and 1 tie. The rivalry, known as "The Third Saturday in October," has run in streaks throughout its history. In the current era, from 2007 to the present, the Crimson Tide have been ranked in the top-10 when the schools have met every year but '07, and the Vols have always been unranked.

A look back at the history between the schools shows it to be one of the more heated and anticipated rivalry games in the SEC, but the atmosphere around Knoxville this weekend betrayed no real hint of antipathy. I didn't meet a single Tennessee fan who claimed to hate Alabama, nor a single Bama fan who claimed to hate the Vols. The word "hate" *was* thrown around quite a bit throughout the weekend, it just had a different target: Alabama Offensive Coordinator Lane Kiffin. On Saturday Kiffin would be making his first appearance in Knoxville since leaving Vol Nation high and dry in 2010, when he departed his head coaching job after one season under the cover of darkness, shuttling recruits with him across the country to his new job as head coach at the University of Southern California.

Some UT students I met that afternoon told me that Chancellor Jimmy Cheek had sent a school-wide e-mail earlier in the week imploring the fan base to refrain from foul language. Head Coach Butch Jones also called on the Volunteer faithful to not make the game about Kiffin, asking fans to leave Kiffin out of their chants and cheers. Three weeks earlier, Tennessee lost a 10–9 game to another rival, the Florida Gators. Not only did they lose to one of their most hated rivals, but the loss made it more difficult to reach the six wins necessary to be bowl eligible. Bowl berths not only bring money to the school, but also provide extra practice time that's critical for a coach trying desperately to rebuild a program. Losing to a lower-tier SEC squad after they pulled their embattled quarterback for a true freshman who had never played a college down only poured more salt in the wound. As the game's final seconds ticked away, the Tennessee student section began chanting "Fuck You Florida" loudly enough that it could be heard on TV. It's no wonder the e-mail went out. I have to say, given the fairly weak matchup (compared to the previous games I had attended on my trip), what I was most interested in was seeing how this subplot played out on Saturday night.

Neyland Stadium is one of the older structures in the SEC, and a walk around the outside easily confirmed its age. From the time-worn chain-link fences around the back to the support beams overhead and the chipped concrete on the stairwells, I gathered as much a sense of history from the building itself as I did from talking to longtime fans. Multiple school buildings are built into the backside of the stadium as well. I walked through what I surmised were professors' offices and down hallways that haven't been renovated since, I'd guess, the '60s. It's wild to consider that this stadium has held over 100,000 people for each game since the mid-'90s. Only in the past few years have other traditional powers caught up to this trend toward gigantism, with Alabama, LSU, and Texas A&M all making renovations to put themselves in the same 100,000-plus club that Tennessee's been occupying.[75]

The Vols are a once-proud national power in the midst of a period of dormancy and a struggle to rebuild. With the exception of Peyton Manning-worship, these fans don't seem lost in the past, however. There is a reverence for the heroes and the great moments like anywhere else with a rich football tradition, but I never got the sense that UT fans are living in the past to comfort the pain of their current mediocrity. Rather, nearly everyone I met was sifting through the present moment for glimmers of hope that bode well for the future of the program.

At the front of the stadium there is a statue of the building's namesake, Robert Neyland. The bronze sculpture portrays Neyland on a knee with his arms crossed, wrists resting on his knee, a hat in his left hand, and a whistle around his neck. The concrete base of the statue holds Neyland's Seven Maxims. They served as Neyland's guiding principles for playing the game of football and are as follows: "1. The team that makes the fewest mistakes will win. 2. Play for and make the breaks, and when one comes your way—SCORE! 3. If at first the game—or the breaks—go against you, don't let up...put on more steam. 4. Protect our kickers, our QB, our lead and our ball game. 5. Ball, oskie, cover, block, cut and slice, pursue and gang tackle...for this is the WINNING EDGE. 6.

---

[75] Michigan has been housing over 100,000 fans per game since 1956. Tennessee became the second member of the 100,000 Club in 1996. Penn State and Ohio State were next in 2001 and 2005, respectively. Between 2010–2014, Alabama, Texas, Texas A&M, and LSU all completed renovations that pushed their seating capacities past 100,000.

Press the kicking game. Here is where the breaks are made. 7. Carry the fight to our opponent and keep it there for 60 minutes."

In the same way that Peyton Manning is the gold standard for on-field performance at Tennessee, Robert Neyland is the gold standard for coaching excellence in Knoxville. Through his stints as head coach between 1926 and 1952, Neyland amassed an incredible 173–31–12 record. Some coaches cast larger-than-life shadows and others recede into the annals of history as the forgotten greats. It's not to say that Neyland's legacy has been forgotten in Knoxville—the stadium is named after him and there's a massive bronze statue of the man outside the front entrance, after all. But people don't talk about Neyland like they do Bear Bryant. In that sense, Neyland is like longtime Georgia Head Coach Vince Dooley. People worship Bryant and Steve Spurrier—and yes, they're Nos. one and two in all-time SEC victories, respectively—but somehow Robert Neyland and Vince Dooley fall by the wayside in the broader conversation. Part of the amnesia could be explained by the fact that Neyland coached so much earlier than all the others. But to be honest, I'm not sure how to account for the gulf in perception between legendary coaches.

Later on Friday night, I drove over to the airport Hilton, where Alabama's football team was staying. One of the people I had chatted with over message boards and social media during the spring and summer was a man named Matthew who operates the headsets for Alabama. Obviously I asked for details, but he's contractually obligated to stay hushed about what he hears during games, at least until he leaves the job and, presumably, Nick Saban leaves Alabama. Matthew and his friend Jackie were sitting at a table next to the bar watching the Oregon–

Cal game when I joined them. Within minutes, one of the guys brought up the Ole Miss–Alabama game from a couple weeks earlier, the one where Ole Miss stormed the field and tore down the goal posts after beating Alabama. Neither had much to say about the Ole Miss—Alabama game itself, other than it was a blip and that Bama would run the table. But Matthew and Jackie both insisted the Rebs' celebration was a sign of respect for the Alabama program, that because they are the gold standard in college football beating them warrants this type of celebration. This is a uniquely Alabamian point of view. I had never heard this perspective in any national or local account of the game; in fact, I had never heard it anywhere but from die-hard Alabama fans. My new acquaintances provided a wonderful illustration of how fans see the college football world around them. In the case of Alabama fans, perspective is filtered through a lens of smug, matter-of-fact superiority, making it all the easier to throw crimson-colored shade on everyone else in the college football world.

As an outsider, I didn't see Ole Miss storming the field after beating Alabama being about Alabama. It was about a team on their way to a top-5 national ranking for only the second time since Archie Manning's playing days. It was about beating a top-5 team at home on the same day that *College GameDay* broadcast from the Grove for the first time in the twenty-one year history of the national pregame show. It was about was the fact that Ole Miss hadn't won ten games in a season since 2002, when Eli Manning was a senior quarterback, and there was finally something worth celebrating in Oxford. But it most certainly was *not* about Alabama. Swap in another top-5 team, say Auburn or Mississippi State that year, Georgia or Florida or LSU some other year, and I'm certain the same celebratory spectacle would've ensued.

It's part of every Alabama fan's mental make-up to firmly believe they'll "win a national championship every year," Matthew declared. Jackie nodded in agreement and reached back into his memory for the last time Alabama fans rushed the field. As best he could recall, Bear Bryant's all-time record-setting 315th win against Auburn in 1981 was the last time it happened. This, they insisted, demonstrates a mentality of expecting to win. "There's no need to storm the field," Jackie insisted, "if you walked into the stadium knowing your team is going to win." Fair point.

Moments later, an absolute hulk of a human being in an Alabama tracksuit came strutting through the lobby into the bar and took the seat on the stool over my left shoulder. Matthew leaned in and told me that it was Chris Samuels, former Alabama offensive tackle, NFL Pro-Bowler, and current Alabama grad assistant of some sort. What happened next helped redeem the reputation of Alabama fans and showcased one of the things about die-hard fans in general I love the most: Matthew turned to Jackie and asked if he remembered a crushing key block Samuels made to spring running back Shaun Alexander for a touchdown sometime in the late '90s. Without missing a beat, Jackie nodded, "Mmmhmm. Oh yeah!"

They both had total recall of a *block* that happened over fifteen years ago—not a game-winning touchdown, not a pick-six, not a record-breaking catch or completion. A block. These two remembered a pancake block over fifteen years after the fact without even having to think about it. When I meet people like these two, I always wonder what their memories are like in regards to getting the transmission fixed on their cars, or how well they can recall arguments they've had with their wives, or memorable frames on league bowling night. Is the memory only laser sharp when it involves something the person feels this passionately about? It has to be. Either that, or I've met dozens of people with photographic memories in the past two months.

One thing all Alabama fans have an absolutely clear vision of is the day they met Paul William Bryant, if in fact they have. If not, they likely have someone else's account of meeting Bryant impressed upon their consciousness as firmly as if it were their own. Jackie was no different in this regard. He met Bear Bryant the morning of the coach's final game, the Liberty Bowl victory over Illinois. As he talked, I could see Jackie retracing his steps from that morning. Slowly, he began to share his story, taking his time as if he was savoring every detail that passed his lips. Jackie was staying with friends in Memphis, and the night before the game he declared that in the morning he'd go to the hotel where Alabama was staying and meet Bryant. Sure enough, like something out of a movie, as Jackie walked into the hotel, the coach was walking down the front stairs by himself. Coach Bryant sat on the couch in the lobby and Jackie sat beside him a minute later. Presumably, Jackie needed that minute to work up the courage to introduce himself to his hero. Bryant leafed through Jackie's program and autographed the page with his picture on it. They made small talk—about the weather and the hotel—for about three minutes before others started arriving, thus ending the special moment only the two of them shared that morning. This is the nature of legends in sports; in the exact same way that Ashley's father's interaction with Bear Bryant will never be forgotten (by him *or* his family), this was one of the proudest moments of Jackie's life. When we build our heroes into godlike figures, it's a life-altering experience—almost by definition—when they step down from their pedestals and interact with us mere mortals.

Jackie told me that he has a picture with Coach Bryant from that morning hanging up in his home. I've never been to his house, but I'm positive I know just how it's framed. It's displayed in some combination of Alabama colors, crimson-matted with a white background and maybe a black or houndstooth frame, and both the photo and the autographed page in the program are encased. I'm equally positive that it's prominently displayed in his home, maybe in the front hallway or the living room adjacent to a family portrait, his wedding picture, or his kids' graduation photos.

When fans down South tell me I can't ever comprehend what it's like to live an existence where your college football team means more than anything else, I get annoyed. What can't I understand? What don't I get? I'm starting to recognize it when I see it, and I understand that even as a die-hard Notre Dame fan who takes Fighting Irish losses hard, takes them personally, there's something that separates the true fanatics from a guy like me. Not every fan has it, not every fan base in the SEC has it, and it doesn't look the same among the ones that do. But it's here. Its essence is fleeting, but I can see it in individual examples even if I can't define it in clear and concise terms.

⚑

Tailgating at Tennessee has two unique features: it takes place in a four-floor parking garage and on the Tennessee River. The majority of the tailgates populate the garage roof. Other than the odd location, however, the tailgate isn't much different than those at other SEC schools. I spent about an hour on the roof, threw a game of bags with a group of UT grads in their late-thirties, and cracked jokes with the guys and their wives. But what I really wanted to see in Knoxville was the Vol Navy. For a half-mile stretch, boats docked along the Tennessee River getting ready for the game. The boats came in various sizes, ranging from twenty-footers to cruise liner-sized ships. Fired-up grills, full bars, live music, bags games, and all the other trappings of a great tailgate marked the decks.

On the dock alongside a massive barge that read "It's All About Me" around a monogrammed Tennessee "T," I met a couple fresh out of college. Garrison and Becca were decked out in Vols gear, like most people. But it turned out Garrison was a big Arkansas fan. He'd made a bet with Becca, his girlfriend: Whoever's team had the worse record in 2013 had to wear the other's team colors every Saturday for the 2014 season. Since the Vols' 5–7 record bested the Razorbacks' 3–9, Garrison had to pay up. I couldn't imagine wearing another team's shirt and hat for a full season.

When I told him I was from Chicago, we started talking about Northern coaches and if being from the North is an obstacle coaches have to overcome when they take over an SEC program. Both his and Becca's schools currently have Northern coaches. Butch Jones ran the Cincinnati and Central Michigan programs before accepting the UT job. Bret Bielema played at Iowa before taking over the reins at Wisconsin, and then at Arkansas. 2014 marked both Jones's and Bielema's second season as head coach of their respective SEC programs. I had wondered about Northern-born coaches and if their origins were an issue for SEC fans, but the topic hadn't come up much on the trip outside of my discussions about Urban Meyer at Florida. Garrison put it succinctly, speaking for his Southern brethren: "Yeah, it's a thing. But it's mostly an ego thing. We get over it pretty quick if the coach is worth a damn." As to whether or not Bielema and Jones are worth a damn, the jury's still out.

Southbound Traveler

An hour and change before kickoff, I retraced my steps along the waterfront, up through the parking garage, all the way back to Neyland Stadium. I arrived in time to see the Pride of the Southland Band step off into the stadium. As the band made its way into the stadium, people lined the streets on either side just like they did at every other school. Some of the traditions are universal across the SEC. There was no reason to think this band would be any different than the Pride of the South at Ole Miss or the Million Dollar Band at Alabama or any other talented but ordinary college band. By the time their halftime show ended, though, I knew I'd been wrong about that assumption. Without question, the Pride of the Southland was the most impressive and talented college band I'd ever seen, forming intricate patterns as they played, shape-shifting with amoeba-like fluidity before re-forming in a new and equally impressive arrangement—and all without missing a beat.

Shortly after the band finished their step-off into the stadium, I found a ticket on the 45-yard line on the Tennessee sideline twenty-three rows from the field. Okay, to be honest, I bought a ticket at the corner of the end zone for face value and walked to an empty seat near midfield that nobody ever moved me from. Sitting next to me was a high school girl who happened to be one of the funniest people I met on the entire trip. I chatted with Kelly and her mother throughout the game. Kelly told me all about Tennessee and shared stories about her go-go dancer sister, and I told the two of them about teaching and coaching football in Chicago. The thing about this girl was that she blurted out *the* question I felt lingering in the air a majority of the time when I met strangers on the road and we were feeling each other out. We were talking about different places to live in Tennessee, what each is like, and then she put the hammer down: "So are you racist, or do you like black people?"

In her mind, the answer to that question was of vital importance for deciding which cities would be good places to live if I ever wanted to move to Tennessee. One of my favorite things about teaching and coaching is that teenagers have a candor about them that's lost as they become adults. They're willing to say what decorum and social norms often stop grown-ups from saying. And it was a fair question, albeit a difficult one to answer. That's one of the functions of polite society: it keeps us from having to directly address difficult questions and engage challenging situations for comfort's sake. I pondered for a minute before answering. "Both, I think."

Sounds awful, right? Let me explain. I was raised in a predominantly white Chicago neighborhood where racist jokes were an accepted norm. When you live in a homogenous culture—all white people in a low-crime, upper-middle class neighborhood—many people assume that the neighborhood stays that way because it's only white people living there. It wasn't until I'd been away from the neighborhood for some time that I began to question and eventually reject the beliefs I held growing up. And even now, despite the fact that my friend group is fairly diverse—not just an "I have a black friend" scenario, which so many white people use to deflect the notion that they might be racist—I still wonder what lingering racist beliefs I haven't yet stamped out. I spent most of the first half thinking about this. There's no way to excuse who I was as an adolescent; no way to excuse my ignorant worldview and all the racist jokes I laughed at and retold. Because I hadn't reflected on it in so long, the waves of embarrassment and guilt hit me hard. Eventually, I took some measure of comfort in the fact that I'm not that man as an adult; that once I knew better, I began to do better. There was no way she could've known, because I never let on, but Kelly's question made me uncomfortable than I'd felt in a really long time. Who knows? Maybe that was a good thing.

༄

Right before kickoff, as Alabama took the field, there was a brief "Fuck You Kiffin" chant from the student section. As far as I could tell, it came from the end zone. I believe that means it was younger students. The student section wraps from the end zone to about the 25- or 30-yard line on the visitors' sideline. From what I know of how student sections work, they're either first come first served, or upperclassmen get priority seating. Either way, it was brief. It happened only once before the TV cameras were rolling, but that was the anticlimactic end of the Kiffin-versus-the-crowd saga. And Lane Kiffin did his talking with his play calling. On Alabama's first offensive snap, he slid All-American receiver Amari Cooper across the formation through the backfield on a fake zone-read rollout. To oversimplify matters, the play used a simple concept that optioned the edge rusher. If the end dropped off to cover the receiver slipping out of the backfield, the quarterback would've either had time to survey the field and allow a deep route to develop, or take off running. Because the end pursued the quarterback, however, it was an easy dump-off pass. Blake Sims flipped the ball out to Cooper in the right flat. Cooper broke one tackle and blew down the sidelines for an 80-yard touchdown.

Meanwhile, the Volunteers were in the middle of an offensive identity crisis. Quarterback Justin Worley, who had started the first seven games, was benched for backup Nathan Peterman. Two drives into the Alabama game, Peterman was benched for Ricky Dobbs. While Tennessee was playing quarterback roulette early, Alabama dominated and led 27–

0 by the start of the second quarter. But the Vols never shut down, and they played hard for the full sixty minutes. Once he settled into his season debut, Ricky Dobbs became the catalyst Tennessee needed, and in the third quarter they closed the gap to 10 points, making it a 27–17 game. They wouldn't get any closer, however, as Alabama converted third down after third down on a backbreaking drive that chewed up nearly six minutes at the end of the third quarter and put Alabama up three scores, 34–17. Over and over during that game-clinching drive, the play clock wound after second down, ticking the seconds before Alabama needed to run their third-down play. Every time this happened Lil' John's "Turn Down for What"—adapted by the Tennessee crowd as "Third Down for What"—blared over the sound system. The crowd whipped itself into a frenzy, providing the deafening wails that signify home-field advantage. With each successive third-down conversion by Alabama, however, the orange-and-white-checkered maniacs' voices died down, their hopes receding deeper into the night. Third down for what, indeed.

⚑

I woke up early Sunday morning, bought a Clif Bar and a Gatorade and set off for a day in the Smoky Mountains. In late October when the leaves are changing, there are few more spectacular sites anywhere on God's green earth. Despite being bored and lonely at times on the road, often I couldn't be any happier seeing what the South had to offer all alone. I drove for a while through the hilly, winding roads, stopped, hiked a couple miles, came back to my car, cruised along, stopped, took pictures, got back in the car, and did it all over again. I needed these moments to balance out the college town game weekends and constant chatter with strangers. Whether it was sitting in Southern churches or walking through Civil War battle sites or hiking in the Smoky Mountains, these retreats allowed me to stop and process everything I was seeing and sensing along the way. Days like these helped all the other days on the road sink in with a little more depth. In the quiet and newness of these jaunts, I was overwhelmed with gratitude for being able to take this trip. By late afternoon, I'd passed through Cades Cove and hiked through a trail in the Cataloochee Valley, seeing the leaves in all their oranges and reds, golden yellows and browns. I returned to the car to begin the four-hour drive to Atlanta at sunset, tired and happy.

#3 Auburn vs. #4 Ole Miss

November 1, 2014

Oxford, Mississippi

I'd always wanted to see Savannah, so I made plans to meet Missy from South Carolina there on the Tuesday before the World's Largest Outdoor Cocktail Party (WLOCP), the nickname for the annual Florida–Georgia matchup held in Jacksonville. We spent the day exploring the Historic District. I craned my neck to soak in the antebellum homes up and down tree-lined streets and gazed at the spacious beauty of various squares—Madison and Chippewa, Columbia and Ogelthorpe, Warren and Reynolds—filled with trees, statues, and park benches. We strolled the perimeter of the Green-Meldrim House, on Macon Street, taking pictures and appreciating the view. The house served as Sherman's Headquarters from late 1864 to early 1865, and the pristine landscaping inside its wrought-iron fences made me appreciate gardening in a way I didn't think possible. Missy and I shared the same sentiment at the Comer House, which is where Jefferson Davis stayed when he visited Savannah in 1886. Crossing the cobblestone streets on our way to the Savannah riverfront at sunset, it hit me: my God, this might be the most beautiful place I've been in America. Everything about downtown Savannah had that same effect. The city's Southern charm and historical weight left me in an awestruck, stunned silence. Late Wednesday morning, Missy and I ate at Mrs. Wilkes Dining Room, the famous brunch spot in the Historic District.

After brunch she drove back to Carolina and I roamed Savannah alone, looking ahead to the weekend I had planned in Jacksonville. The World's Largest Outdoor Cocktail Party is one of the premier events in college football and Florida–Georgia is one of the marquee Southern rivalries. Coming into the season, I was excited to see the 50-50 crowd split, attend the beachfront parties, and hear stories of memorable WLOCP weekends through the years. Beneath the excitement however, I was dying for a great football game.

The past two games on the trip had bored me, as Ole Miss and Alabama handled Tennessee with relative ease in consecutive weeks. I wanted barn-burning, back-and-forth, down-to-the-last-minute SEC football. When you boil it down, without the instant classics the appeal of SEC fanaticism fades and Southern football as a way of life looks pretty ridiculous. It's all about the epic battles, which is what fans down here live for—and relive for years.

It was within this context that I made my next big decision. The Playoff Committee's Tuesday night standings had come out, and they ranked Auburn third and Ole Miss fourth nationally ahead of their prime-time Saturday night matchup. Since both teams had already suffered one loss on the season, somebody's championship dreams would crash and burn in Oxford.

On impulse, I cancelled my Jacksonville hotel room late Wednesday night and called my friend Angela in Oxford to see if I could stay at her place again. On Thursday morning, I hit the road. Sure, it was a nine-hour drive from Savannah to Oxford, but behind the decision to quit my job, drive over 10,000 miles throughout the course of a season, and write a book whose very publication was uncertain—behind all that was a deep and abiding love for college football. I knew that however this trip worked itself out, I'd never have any regrets about any of it because of nights like these.

Once I arrived at the Grove, it only took me two minutes to find a face-value ticket about thirty rows up on the Ole Miss sideline at the 15-yard line. The usher scanned my ticket and bounding past her, I realized I was more excited about this game than I'd been since opening weekend. You know how they talk about energy being infectious? The vibe at Vaught-Hemingway Stadium lifted me up the second I stepped inside, swung me around for three hours, and didn't put me back on the ground until the clock read 00:00. When I found my seat, the older lady sitting next to me looked down at my Notre Dame sweatshirt, cocked her head, and asked, "Now who are you rootin' for, dear?" When I told her I didn't have a dog in the fight, but thought Auburn would win, she looked at me with the disappointment of a parent whose teenager just got brought home by the cops. "Oh, that's the wrong answer. I don't think you should tell people that," she said. When it was time to Lock the Vaught a few minutes later, though, that sweet lady who was so disappointed in my assessment of the game hooked her arm in mine and we swayed to the beat along with most of the 62,000 people in attendance. Vaught-Hemingway bounced. Despite the cold, the collective anticipation was a live wire ignited by bundled-up Rebel supporters rocking back and forth in time with the team, which was standing by the Chucky Mullins statue. At the Tennessee–Ole Miss game a couple weeks back, not many people locked arms outside the student section, and the energy in Vaught-Hemingway Stadium sagged. It was obvious, as I panned the shivering masses beneath the lights before kickoff, that the Auburn game mattered more. Have you ever heard of teams playing down to their competition? There's something to that, being unable to get pumped up for an inferior opponent and not playing your best as a result. Stadium atmosphere is palpable, and when the home team sleepwalks through a game, the thousands inside the stadium feel and reflect that lethargy. At the Tennessee game a couple weeks back, the student section was loud throughout, but the energy was missing. Ole Miss coasted through that game on autopilot, uninspired and unenthused.

The difference a few weeks makes. Even if you knew nothing about college football and found yourself in Vaught-Hemingway Stadium this Saturday night, you'd still know this game mattered. Every moment I spent in that stadium as Auburn battled Ole Miss was a reminder of all the things people love so much about college football.

Once the game started, nobody had time for small talk and trading stories. We were transfixed. The weather hovered around 35 degrees, and we all pulled our hats and hoods tight with each new cross breeze, our eyes glued on the battle unfolding before us. Occasionally, we'd turn to exchange commentary on big plays or confer with the lady who was listening to the radio broadcast on her headphones during on-field reviews. The interplay reflected the synchronization between the fans and the players that's so crucial toward building up the crowd's energy. On the field, the game lived up to its billing as a fifteen-round heavyweight fight with all the high drama of a Hollywood blockbuster.

⚑

Auburn won the coin toss, elected to receive, and marched down the field with surgical precision. Nick Marshall plunged into the end zone on a 2-yard run less than three minutes into the game to cap an 8-play, 73-yard drive. *Auburn 7, Ole Miss 0.*

The teams traded punts on brief two-minute drives, then Ole Miss took over at their own 8-yard line. The Ole Miss offense kicked into gear behind quarterback Bo Wallace and receiver Vince Sanders. Sanders caught four passes on the drive for a total of 66 yards, and on 3rd and goal running back I'Tavius Mathers scored from four yards out. *Auburn 7, Ole Miss 7.*

After the Mathers touchdown, the teams punted back and forth for the next ten minutes before Ole Miss's All-American cornerback Senquez Golson intercepted Nick Marshall as Auburn approached the red zone. Ole Miss took possession with a little over six minutes remaining in the second quarter and after a false-start penalty, Bo Wallace, the lumbering, rifle-armed quarterback, broke contain and ran 59 yards down the left sideline to the surprise of everyone, most of all himself. Some 35 yards into the run, Wallace looked over his shoulder as if to say, "How has nobody caught me yet?" With a late hit out of bounds penalty added on to the end of Wallace's run, the Rebels snapped the ball from the Auburn 10-yard line and Wallace hit Laquon Treadwell on a screen pass for a 10-yard touchdown. Two plays, 74 yards. High-fives and hugs all around. *Auburn 7, Ole Miss 14.*

After trading three-and-outs again, it felt like Ole Miss had figured out the Auburn offense. The Rebels sported the nation's top defense entering the game but many expected the explosive, if inconsistent, Tiger offense put up points regardless. In the matchup of strength on strength, it started to look as though the Rebs held the upper hand. But just like that, Auburn struck. With 1:36 remaining in the first half, Nick Marshall took the first snap of the drive, rolled right, and threw deep to Sammie Coates, who beat Senquez Golson on a deep post. All-American safety Cody Prewitt was late getting over the top and in one play, Auburn beat the two best players in the Ole Miss secondary for a 57-yard touchdown. Fans grumbled about Prewitt not getting back in time. Meanwhile, in the north end zone the Auburn sections celebrated. *Auburn 14, Ole Miss 14.*

Ole Miss drove to the Auburn 30-yard line in their two-minute offense and kicker Gary Wunderlich drilled a 47-yard field goal as time expired in the first half. *Auburn 14, Ole Miss 17.*

The blow-by-blow account of the first half doesn't do the experience justice. What I remember clearly is pulling the hood of my sweatshirt tight to fight off the cold and letting out deep breaths at the end of every scoring drive throughout the game, as if to remind myself to appreciate every second. I knew leaving Savannah Thursday morning, I knew before kickoff, and I knew all throughout the game that it would come down to the final possession. It's an odd feeling knowing you're witnessing a classic as it happens. I remember wanting to turn to someone around me and mention that we were going to look back on this game as one of the greats, but there was no need. It was understood.

The second half kicked off and the game quickly began to read like a scriptwriter had orchestrated the series-by-series action. Ole Miss went up 10 points—the largest difference at any point in the game—when Bo Wallace hit Evan Engram for a 50-yard touchdown. They had run a pass play that was similar to one they used a couple times in the first half, but made a halftime adjustment whereby rather than staying home to block, Engram delayed before sliding up the seam. It worked; Engram was open, beat the safety who was late coming downhill, and scampered to the end zone. *Auburn 14, Ole Miss 24.*

Auburn faced a 3rd and 11 on the heels of Ole Miss's scoring drive. And again when it looked like Ole Miss was ready to take control of the game, Nick Marshall extended the play with his legs. Eventually Duke Williams broke coverage, and Marshall found him for a 41-yard completion. Tigers running back Cameron Artis-Payne carried three consecutive plays for 31 yards and then Nick Marshall's 2-yard touchdown run made it a game again. *Auburn 21, Ole Miss 24.*

Ole Miss couldn't move the football on the next drive, and Auburn took possession at their own 4-yard line with 5:45 remaining in the third quarter. The Tigers demonstrated a tactical precision they hadn't shown since the first drive of the game, marching 96 yards on eleven plays. On a 2nd and 9 from the 17-yard line, Marshall found Marcus Davis wide open for a touchdown. *Auburn 28, Ole Miss 24.*

The Rebs' next possession started in the third quarter and ended in the fourth. On the first play of the fourth quarter, Evan Engram slipped out of the backfield late again and was wide open down the seam, running 29 yards before being tackled at the 3-yard line. Bo Wallace barreled over the goal line on the next play. *Auburn 28, Ole Miss 31; fourth quarter, 14:26.*

Auburn connected on a 3rd and long for the third time in the game as Marshall hit Sammie Coates for a 41-yard gain. Coates went up with corner Senquez Golson in the middle of the field and came down with the ball. Six plays later, Cameron Artis-Payne scored from 6 yards out. *Auburn 35, Ole Miss 31; fourth quarter, 10:23.*

People around Oxford liked to talk about the "good Bo" and the "bad Bo," and how there was no way of knowing which Bo Wallace would show up on any given Saturday. In the season opener against Boise State, Wallace threw three picks. The week before the Auburn showdown, Wallace threw an interception into the end zone with less than ten seconds remaining against LSU; Ole Miss was on the fringes of field goal range. They lost 10–7. But when he was sharp, Wallace made Ole Miss as dangerous as any team in the country. Against Alabama, the biggest Ole Miss win in recent memory, Wallace threw for 251 yards and 3 touchdowns with no turnovers. On this night, on the biggest stage, we mainly saw the good Bo. His stat line for the Auburn game read like a Heisman contender: 28/40, 341 yards, 2 TDs/0 INTs; 14 carries for 56 yards and a rushing touchdown. He was almost perfect, but for one crucial mistake. On the next drive, Wallace led the Rebels down the field, completing 5 of 6 passes for 76 yards. Facing 2nd and 1 from the Auburn 6-yard line, Wallace kept the ball. As he stretched for the first down, the ball was knocked loose, and Auburn's Kris Frost recovered. *Auburn 35, Ole Miss 31; fourth quarter, 06:31.*

Auburn tried to play ball control and chew up the clock, running on first and second down before completing on 3rd and 5 to Sammie Coates. Two more runs before an incomplete pass on 3rd and 2 gave Ole Miss the ball back. Auburn wasn't playing to win on that drive; they were playing not to lose. *Auburn 35, Ole Miss 31; fourth quarter, 03:22.*

Because Auburn tried to play it safe, Ole Miss had another chance for a game-winning drive. Starting near midfield, Wallace drove Ole Miss into the red zone, and on 3rd and 3 from the 20-yard line, connected with Laquon Treadwell on a screen. Treadwell broke a couple tackles before being dragged down as he fell into the end zone. From the opposite 15-yard line, it was impossible to tell whether or not Treadwell broke the plane before going down. After conferring with each other, the refs signaled touchdown. The stadium roared for a moment, but the celebration was short-lived. Treadwell stayed down in the end zone, obviously injured.

The referees announced that the previous play was under further review and a cart drove out from the Ole Miss locker room toward Treadwell in the end zone. Everyone looked to the jumbotron for a replay but we saw nothing except for a giant Ole Miss logo. Not showing a replay at the biggest moment of the game must have meant that something went horribly wrong. At the same time the two guys in front of me received text updates, the lady with the headphones announced that Treadwell broke his ankle and might have fumbled before he got into the end zone. Later that night when I watched the replay online, I understood why they didn't show the replay; Treadwell's injury was gruesome. Compounding the hurt was the referee's announcement that Treadwell fumbled before crossing the plane, and that Auburn recovered the fumble in the end zone. Auburn ball at the 20. *Auburn 35, Ole Miss 31; fourth quarter, 01:30.*

In an instant, Ole Miss watched its dream season crumble. The Rebs came within a foot of the game-winning score that would've put them in position to control their own destiny en route to the playoff. If they scored, it was a relative cakewalk to the biggest Egg Bowl in Mississippi history. The old saying goes that football is a game of inches; I doubt there's ever been a more painful reminder for the Mississippi Rebels.

Ole Miss took the ball back with thirty seconds remaining and no time-outs. When their last gasp fell short, fans everywhere within earshot vented their hurt and frustration. Amid the noise, I heard a particularly sad and familiar refrain: typical Ole Miss. This game was typical Ole Miss football. Get all the way to the doorstep of greatness, only to stumble and fall. *Auburn 35, Ole Miss 31; fourth Quarter, 00:00.*

#5 Alabama vs. #16 LSU

November 8, 2014

Baton Rouge, Louisiana

We've all heard about LSU. Everyone knows it's nearly impossible to beat the Tigers at night in Death Valley. They're a raucous, raunchy bunch of Cajuns who provide one of the strongest home-field advantages anywhere in college football. I'd heard enough stories on the road throughout the season to know that there was no way I'd have a dull weekend in Baton Rouge. To offer one example, Georgia fans told me they had seen LSU sorority girls calling a middle-aged Auburn woman a filthy whore as she and her husband entered the stadium. Also, Florida fans told me about their friends having cups of urine and beer thrown on them outside Tiger Stadium. But I'd also heard stories of people having their favorite road experiences at LSU. One of the overnighters from Mississippi State said he had such a positive experience at

LSU that it changed the way he treats visitors in Starkville. The Auburn couple with the AU-themed show car explained that despite how ornery LSU fans can be, they still make a point to take you into their tailgate, feed you the best Cajun food you've ever tasted, fill you with your drink of choice, and get to know you. Now it was my turn to experience Death Valley.

My friend Liz's cousin Tom is a sophomore at LSU, and she put us in touch. Tom had just finished a football preview show he hosts on campus radio when we met up for a late lunch on Friday. Despite being little more than a year removed from life in Homewood, Illinois, Tom was as devout a Bayou Bengal as anyone I met all weekend in Baton Rouge. Before he showed me around campus we discussed Les Miles and how and why people embrace him at LSU, and the history and rituals surrounding Mike the Tiger, the famous LSU mascot. Strolling down Highland Road, we passed through a brick archway with two distinct placards: one of a pelican and the other announcing Louisiana State University. The weather-worn, faded-copper green color caught my eye, and coupled with the overhanging trees down Highland, the campus radiated an eerie energy from the outset.

Across the street on the Parade Grounds, Scott Van Pelt[76] was on-air for ESPN, broadcasting the SVP & Russillo show, though we didn't stop to listen in. Instead, we discussed Van Pelt's quote about Baton Rouge. The quote is a homage that the purple and gold wear like a badge of honor. Speaking about his experience during the 2012 Alabama–LSU game, Van Pelt said, "For three hours on Saturday night, I don't know

---

[76] The best sports personality in the business, bar none.

that there has ever been an atmosphere in SPORTS that I've been a part of that was as memorable to me." Tom tried to explain it to me, what makes the Tiger Stadium atmosphere so great. For all his eloquence, I knew that Tom's explanation, much like Van Pelt's, wouldn't do. I had to see for myself.

⚑

Tiger Stadium boasts one of the top-5 stadium capacities in the country since its most recent addition. Tom and I stood admiring the All-American player plaques outside the stadium when a couple fellows in their mid-forties walked up. They were Cal fans checking another box off their college football stadium bucket list. There's a shared bond between true college football fans, people whose love for the game extends beyond their own school. We stood around for a while trading stories about various stadiums, comparing favorites and the best games we've seen.

After the bucket-listers wandered off, I noticed T-Bob Hebert's name on the 2007 National Championship plaque and remembered hearing about a locker-room incident before the 2011 Alabama–LSU National Championship Game. During the regular season, LSU had beaten Alabama 9–6 in overtime in one of the greatest games in recent SEC history. When they met again for the National Championship, however, Alabama shut LSU out 21–0. Rumors flew around the Internet about LSU's fractured locker room and a pregame incident that involved Hebert, the Tigers' starting center. The local account, according to Tom, is that Hebert, representing half of the locker room, went to coach Les Miles and lobbied for Jarrett Lee to start over Jordan Jefferson at quarterback. Lee was a journeyman fifth-year senior who made smart decisions but lacked an elite arm and athleticism, whereas Jefferson was the more talented signal caller who possessed all the physical tools to be elite, but played inconsistently.

The All-American plaques were separated into two sections, one for twentieth-century players and the other for twenty-first-century ones. As we looked over the recent stars, I remembered watching many of them play: Glenn Dorsey, Patrick Peterson, Tyrann Mathieu. You don't need to be a fan of a school to appreciate their great players, but I think you do need to root for a particular school to appreciate their redemption stories, except for the most extreme cases that can bring a tear to the eye of anybody with a pulse. Tyrann Mathieu's story is one of those run-of-the-mill feel-good stories you'd appreciate if he played for your school. Outside of LSU, he's the Honey Badger: a player with tremendous, highlight reel-worthy defensive and punt returning talent, a cool-looking blond mohawk, and a drug problem that caused him to miss a full season of college ball. Mathieu overcame his drug problem, however, and now he plays on Sundays.

To hear Tom recount the story, you'd think he was channeling the first time he saw the part in *The Lion King* where Mufasa died. There was so much emotion in Tom's account of how Mathieu couldn't stop smoking weed, to the point where he woke up the morning of the national championship game and didn't even care. He just didn't want to play football. Mathieu failed three drug tests in a row and was suspended for the entire 2011 season before leaving Louisiana to train with former teammate and NFL corner Patrick Peterson and straighten his life out. The outpouring of emotion in Tom's retelling isn't unique to him; it's a common characteristic of college football fans. We're suckers for a good story. And if that good story involves one of *our* players…well, it will be drawn out and dramatized until it becomes a part of the mythology.

Mathieu's story follows a familiar pattern. I don't judge the guy for his struggles with drugs, but I wasn't particularly captivated by Tom's story about how he was able to surmount his personal problems. I'm happy for Mathieu like I am for any player who beats the odds and makes it to the NFL. Regardless of how he is or was portrayed in the media, I hope he stays on top during and especially after his NFL career. But I couldn't connect with the emotion in Tom's narrative.

⚑

I jumped the curb and pulled my Chevy onto the lawn behind a church down the street from Frat Row and walked over to the Parade Ground, the main tailgating area, around noontime Saturday. After lapping the field for a bit, I walked into the Mississippi Gulf Coast Tailgate, introducing myself and telling the people there my grandma lives in Long Beach. They invited me in and fed me pastalaya, a pasta-based jambalaya. Maurice and Kristy, a couple from Biloxi, invited me to join them at the tailgate they were headed to next.

As we walked through the quad and saw the various tailgates—including one built from an old fire truck with a built-in grill up top—we talked about Mississippi. Maurice touched on the differences between coastal Mississippi and the rest of the state, including Starkville and Oxford. "Down here, the shrimpers and construction workers hang out with the doctors and lawyers. There isn't that class difference. Nobody really cares. Up there you still see the Old Mississippi y'all think of up north, with people talkin' about hanging black people out of trees and shit."

I recognized instantly that this was the type of conversation I'd never see on a message board or read about in a book. So I nudged Maurice along, and he obliged. "That's a big part of why everyone from the Coast are LSU fans. A) It's only two hours to LSU from the coast and four to Starkville and five to Oxford, so people go to LSU more; and B) it's the same here at LSU, where it doesn't matter where you come from." Kristy added, "If you go to Southern Miss, you're pretty much automatically an LSU fan."

"People care so much about appearances in Oxford," Maurice continued. "In Oxford everybody's got three mortgages on their house so they can make sure their kid has a BMW while he's in college. Then after a while you don't see them any more 'cause they fall off 'cause they can't keep up with the Joneses anymore."

When it comes to Ole Miss, I'm sure Maurice is given to hyperbole. Part of it is that LSU hates Ole Miss more than any other school. I loved the white-collar, blue-collar dynamic between Ole Miss and LSU. It's not hard to understand how different socioeconomic classes and different fan bases look across the line and paint each other in broad brushstrokes. This "us vs. them" tribal mentality is at the core of being human. Highlight the differences, caricaturize and vilify those differences, and convince those around you to choose a side. Race. Class. Religion. Politics. Nationalism. Regionalism. College football team. Whatever.

As we approached the Biloxi Tailgate, Kristy told me about how her brother played linebacker at LSU in the '90s, "when we sucked." One of her brothers' suitemates was Shaquille O'Neal. When she asked her brother about what Shaq was like, he told Kristy: "He was alright, but he hogged the Super Nintendo." Kristy broke off to chat with a couple ladies and Maurice introduced me to his brother Charlie and their friend

Gavin and his son, Gavin. After a few minutes of small talk, we landed on how youth sports has become a year-round obsession in America.

Let me pause here to note that baseball is almost as big as football at LSU and around the SEC. When I say almost, I'm talking about a far-distant second, much like the Vice President is "almost" the most powerful elected official in America. But still, college baseball has a huge following. Gavin talked about how his golf game is shot because of all the traveling tournament teams his son plays on and how it devours their weekends. From what I was hearing, it seems like there are a lot of drawbacks to this current cultural trend. Gavin (the elder) mentioned that he worries about parents pressuring their kids into trying to become the athlete they never were. His philosophy with Gavin (the younger) is that he asks his son on the way home from every tournament if he had fun. As long as his son is enjoying himself, he's happy to scrap his golf game to drive across the South and make the longer trips to Cooperstown and Omaha. As soon as his son says he's not enjoying himself, that'll be the end of travel ball. It's a tough balance between encouraging your kids to participate in the hypercompetitive world of American youth sports but still allowing them the freedom to step back and be kids.

We talked about how the year-round cycle of games and tournaments and clinics is yet another arms race in the world of sports. It seems that with the exception of freak athletes, teenagers are forced to choose one sport if they want a chance to play at the major-college level. Kids spend eight, ten, sometimes twelve months a year developing in one sport from the time they're eleven or twelve. When do the kids burn out and when does it feel more like a job than a sport? The conversation eventually led back to sports and the South. Eventually, we framed the issues around a key question: Does this time commitment and single-sport specialization account for why the South is better in football?

The South's sports prowess cannot be denied. Someone noted that in 2014, Louisiana boasted the most players on NFL rosters per capita, followed by South Carolina, Mississippi, Alabama, and Florida; Georgia also ranked in the top-10. Does this focus on youth sports account for the talent gap? And if so, why are kids and their parents down here willing to put in so much more time and effort?

This led to an even more riveting and controversial conversation about what might account for the better athletes coming from the Deep South: slave selection. It's a well-documented fact that slaves were chosen for certain attributes. The largest and most physically fit black males and females were pair-bonded by their masters with the intention of producing the next generation of large, physically fit slaves. More than a century-and-a-half after the Civil War, are there residual effects of this practice that show themselves on the gridiron today? After all, a majority of major Division-I football players are black. Is it still a factor after all this time? There's no good answer and the act of asking the question might be viewed as racist, but it's a fair question.[77]

---

[77] Many books, articles, and studies have been published in an attempt to draw conclusions about what cultural, religious, racial, physical, or socioeconomic factors might correlate to athletic prowess in various sports. One, I confess I have not read widely enough in these areas to make any semi-educated comment or draw my own conclusions. Two, I believe this topic is so far outside the scope of this book that any attempt to dive further into the discussion would be a distraction and an abject failure.

Our conversation drew to a close when the crew told me I had to eat. There's no point in mincing words: LSU had the best tailgating food anywhere in the SEC. I met Rocky, a man of about fifty, who operated the deep fryer. What was funny about Rocky is that if it weren't for the Southern accent, he could've fit in perfectly down on Taylor Street in Chicago or come straight from central casting on The Sopranos. His coiffed hair, tracksuit, and "hey, how ya doin'?" mannerisms stuck out to me like my "sheee-kaaaah-goah" accent stuck out to them. Rocky insisted I try some of the catfish fresh out the deep fryer and pointed me over to the ribs, boudin, shrimp, full bar, and dozen coolers with about any beverage imaginable.

As we ate, I asked Maurice, Kristy, and Gavin (the younger) about Les Miles. What Maurice said matched up with what Tom had been telling me the day before. Miles is a weird dude, but there's this relationship where he embraces and embodies the strange nature of LSU and the fans love him for it. And the more I listened to Tigers talk about Miles throughout the weekend, the more I realized how apt his "Mad Hatter" nickname is. The man is a walking paradox.

Let's look at his coaching: his teams are a throwback to the old-school, hard-nosed, fundamentally sound style of football that showcases a pro-style running attack and suffocating defense. Run the ball, play defense, and win the turnover battle. It's a mentality and approach to the game that used to be—and to a certain extent still is—the textbook how-to guide to winning football. With the adoption of spread offenses and a generally more up-tempo game over the past fifteen years, though, Miles's blueprint is quickly becoming an artifact. This, however, is only one side of the man. Miles also employs trick plays like a bad magician pulling multicolored scarves and quarters out of his hat. He makes bold decisions at strange, often inopportune moments. When it works, of course, he's a genius; when it doesn't, he's an idiot.

These two components of the Miles coaching philosophy would seem to be so completely at odds. And yet, despite the fact that they're polar opposites, these two guiding principles complement each other exceptionally well. The pro-style offense and stingy defense often cover for his gambles, minimizing the damage when they're unsuccessful. Likewise, the constant threat of trickery and unpredictability from Miles keeps opposing defenses from overcommitting to stop his conservative run-based offense. At the very least, Miles keeps them on their toes.

For a coach who's won 80 percent of his games since arriving in Baton Rouge entering the 2014 season, a coach who's won two SEC championships and a national Championship, Les Miles sure gets second-guessed a lot. I've never understood it, but there's a sizable contingent of fans outside Baton Rouge who consider the man a moron. Many people say that *anyone* could recruit and win with the abundance of talent at LSU. People scratch their heads and guffaw at the rambling and occasionally incoherent responses he'll give at press conferences, and his affinity for eating blades of grass on the field has been well documented. For fans like Maurice and Tom, though, this type of weird is evidence that Miles *gets* LSU. Kristy had her own take on Miles's strange interview quotables: "They're kind of brilliant. I'll hear something he says in a press conference and think, *What in the hell is he talking about?* and then two days later, it'll hit me. I'll get it. It's like when he said 'Death Valley is where opponents' dreams come to die.' I thought, *That's kind of weird*, and I thought about it again a couple days after and was like, *Wow, that's perfect! In a literary, poetic sense, that's perfect.*"

The other fellow manning the grill with Rocky walked over and asked if I was enjoying myself. Then he looked down at my gold Notre Dame sweatshirt and then rubbed my head as he walked away, proclaiming, "I've got the luck of the Irish now!" In the same way that improvisers learn when to cut a scene on stage, broadcasters know how to smoothly transition out of a live interview when it's done, and George Costanza knew to leave on a high (low) note, I recognized that when a middle-aged Cajun man rubs your head yelling "I've got the luck of the Irish!" it's time to go.

⚑

Down Dalrymple I witnessed a full-on Cajun carnival. All throughout Frat Row, front lawns housed full living-room setups with couches and chairs and rugs and lamps. The attire ranged from classy to trashy, men in suits and ties standing next to men in purple and gold Zubaz[78] and rip-off Walmart jerseys. It was just like Maurice said: "There isn't that class difference. Nobody really cares." While I was taking note of this, I heard a familiar song blasting through one frat's sound system: "*When your arms are empty, got nowhere to go / Come on out and catch this show.*" Hearing a semi-obscure song by The Band in the middle of a tailgate threw me for a loop. They're one of my all-time favorite groups, but not terribly well known by people under fifty. The song is about old-timey Southern traveling minstrel shows in America, and the first verse talks about people needing some sort of diversion and coming together under one roof—or tent—to be entertained. It hit me that this song

---

[78] A hideous brand of striped stretch pants worn seriously by mustachioed thirty- and forty-something males in the early '90s, and worn ironically (I think) by many others since.

coming through the speakers in the middle of an LSU tailgate was, in a literary, poetic sense, perfect.

Around the back of the Phi Delt house, I found a cheap makeshift bar with a tent overhead and a high-end speaker system bumping crunk music and hip-hop so loud you had to be a few yards away from it to hear anybody else talk. Much as I'd like to sometimes, I can't connect with this time and place. I've lived it. A lot of us have—it's what the collegiate lifestyle looks like. Today it's fun to watch and be an observer, but I can't bring myself back. Even if I did, I'd be the creepy older guy. You can't go back to the debauchery, the abuse you put your body through on a weekly basis, the shirking of any and all responsibilities, the ability to laugh at things that made you feel terrible about yourself. In hindsight, and after describing it in that way, it's hard to believe that existence was ever fun. But anyone who's been there knows that it is, if only for a little while.

Lou Holtz once offered a simple and profound statement in answering what's special about Notre Dame, which I believe he took from Saint Thomas Aquinas, and that I think also applies to the experience of going away to college. He said, "If you've been there, no explanation is necessary. If you haven't, none is adequate." Going away to college is the closest thing we, as Americans, have to a rite of passage for teens. And at the end of a thousand ridiculous, oftentimes obscene stories, all you can do is shrug your shoulders and say: "You know…college."

Had I been feeling a little more collegiate, I would've unzipped and peed right there in the back yard; maybe in the bushes, maybe right where I stood. But I didn't. I went into the house in search of a bathroom. The only restroom on the main floor was a girls' bathroom, so I walked upstairs where the bedrooms were, and I saw the high-water mark of college. At the top of the stairs, a young man in an LSU T-shirt and jeans was passed out in a chair with vomit all over the front of his Tigers shirt. The bathroom was around the corner, and the line for it spilled out into the hallway. The two frat boys in front of me were discussing hunting and I could hear girls' voices in the bathroom. One girl stumbled out of the bathroom, poked the guy in front of me in the chest, and said, "Unless you have a vagina, you don't get to cut in line." Then she stood uncomfortably close to me and stared for an excruciatingly long couple seconds before staggering away. When I finally found an open stall to relieve myself in, I looked down and saw a couple tampons, crumpled toilet paper, and urine all over the floor. I know this whole scene would and should bother some people, but like I said, I've lived it. You know…college.

Back in the yard, Tom introduced me to his sister, her friends visiting from New Orleans, and his roommate, a former LSU football team manager. The former manager had the single best response to seeing my Notre Dame shirt I'd heard all season. He looked at me as we were introduced, looked down at the shirt, looked back up at me, laughed, and walked away.[79] Nailed it. I was even less inclined to say anything because, unlike the people around campus all watching the Texas A&M–Auburn game, I knew Notre Dame was getting blasted by Arizona State at that moment, 34–3.

---

[79] Music City Bowl, December 30, 2014: Notre Dame 31, LSU 28.

Eventually, I found myself tossing a football around in a circle with the New Orleans girls and a couple frat bros. The scene played out predictably: brother occasionally tackling brother, brother jumping in front of girl to pick off a pass, brother spiking a full beer on the lawn like he'd just scored a touchdown. Somehow I ended up with beer in my hair and a dog asleep on my sweater, and then spent two full minutes listening to some sorority girl tell me about how a guy named Mike in the frat was a douche.

By 5:45, the sun began to set as I walked back to the Parade Ground and toward the stadium. I mentioned the eerie energy of LSU, and for me it was the school's defining characteristic. After dark, lapping the stadium, that vibe was intensified. Part of it was the lack of street light which heightened the effect of the low purple-and-gold soft light emanating from around the perimeter of the stadium. The giant LSU above the north end zone shone down like a yellow-tinted full moon. A gloomy, almost haunted aura engulfed the place, enough to remind me about the time earlier in the day when Maurice pointed out two big mounds—Indian burial grounds.

I'm surely belaboring the point and at the same time not doing it justice, but Baton Rouge is downright spooky during a night game at Death Valley. You could almost forget that you're surrounded by well over 100,000 people if you focused on the strange energy of the place. I've never been so surrounded by people and felt like I was in a ghost town. The closest comparison I can draw is that it's a lot like turning the corner and walking down an empty side street off Bourbon Street in the French Quarter. But much like walking down Bourbon Street, once you set foot inside Tiger Stadium, there's no doubt about where you are, and there's no doubt that you're surrounded by a throng of rowdy, crazed individuals.

I paid more for my seat at this game than I had all season: $150 for a seat on the 45-yard line, 30 rows off the field on the Alabama sideline. For some reason, it was more important to me to have a great seat at this game than any other. And I didn't feel too bad about paying over face considering that this particular seat was going for $500–$600 on StubHub earlier in the week.

Unlike most other stadiums, at Tiger Stadium the yard line numbers are marked out every five yards instead of every ten. From my seat on Saturday night, this felt like a symbol of LSU's emphasis on moving the chains, the three-yards-and-a-cloud-of-dust mentality Miles instilled in Baton Rouge. I'd never been to a stadium where a 5- or 6-yard run on first down was met with such thunderous applause. In football, the name of the game is staying on time and moving the chains. If we're talking about the NFL, you'll hear players and coaches talk about it constantly in their interviews. At the collegiate level, the explosive play is much more prevalent, so it's not as crucial to average four yards per play to "stay on time" with the chains. At LSU, however, the fans understood and were quick to show their appreciation for every lurch forward, possibly because of the team's anemic pass game over the season. And show their appreciation they did. Tiger Stadium gets loud. You don't need to attend a game to know that LSU has one of the strongest home-field advantages in the game; all you need to do is check their home record, and then their home night record, over the past decade. During commercial breaks, the jumbotron would show an actual decibel-measuring device (as opposed to the carnival-style Get-Loud-o-Meters at nearly every other stadium) that usually started in the 90s and most times ended up topping 105.

When the defense would stop Alabama on third down and get the ball back for their offense, the fans bowed to the defense and waved their yellow-gold towels. Everything about the crowd gave me the impression that LSU fans were attuned to the nuances of the game. It's a strange impression to walk away with, especially for a group known as "belligerent drunk Cajuns" by most accounts outside of Baton Rouge. The paradoxical nature of LSU fans is the same one Maurice and Tom assigned to Les Miles. I think I get what they were talking about now. Bellicose fans who throw full beers at fans wearing an opposing team's gear demonstrated a better understanding of the finer points of football than any other fan base I've encountered; those two things shouldn't fit together, but they do.

I've always preferred low-scoring, move-the-chains-and-limit-the-explosive-plays type of football games. The week before in Oxford was as good a game as I'd seen all season, but it was the opposite of that; Auburn and Ole Miss traded haymakers for the entire four quarters. On a chilly November night in Baton Rouge, LSU and Alabama traded body blows for sixty minutes and needed a little longer to settle the score.

I pointed this out during a few of the previous games on my trip, but it bears repeating: Much like no fan base believes their school does anything illegal or immoral in getting recruits to commit or keeping players eligible, no fan base believes their school gets a fair shake from the officials. Every school has a persecution complex. Every. Single. One. The refs are always out to get us. I'm not the only person who understands that this is a textbook propagandist fallacy, but I'm also not the only person who understands why that doesn't matter to a fan. Either a referee is with us or against us, and since no blindly loyal fan would ever willingly admit to their team receiving preferential treatment, the refs are always against us. Even when the world isn't out to get your team, you've got to create an "us vs. the world" mindset. It's an effective mental framework for keeping your tribe hostile toward anyone who's not one of them.

On this night, though, I wondered about the refs. (Objectively, of course.) LSU entered the game to play spoiler. They had 2 losses and one was a throttling at the hands of Auburn. They were out of playoff contention but still extremely dangerous, as Ole Miss discovered two weeks earlier. If Alabama lost, Mississippi State was the last hope for an SEC playoff berth. Auburn lost right before the game kicked off, making Mississippi State and Alabama the only two SEC teams remaining with fewer than 2 losses. There were some obvious missed calls throughout the game that made me wonder. It made me think about the fact that it's in the SEC's vested interest to keep Bama alive for at least another week in the playoff picture. Then again, that might be the paranoid cynic in me seeping through. Again and again, I'm reminded: we don't see things as they are, we see them as *we* are. Regardless of whether the refs nudged the game in Alabama's favor, the fact is that LSU owned time of possession and controlled the tempo all night, holding the ball for forty of the sixty minutes in regulation. LSU was the better team and still couldn't get the job done.

Alabama running back T. J. Yeldon fumbled inside his own 10-yard line with a minute to play in the fourth quarter and the score tied 10–10. When LSU recovered Yeldon's fumble, the stadium was deafeningly loud. If you could've harnessed the electric energy from Tiger Stadium at that moment, it would've lit up the entire city of Baton Rouge. A questionable personal foul penalty against LSU killed their chances of punching one into the end zone, though, so the Tigers settled for a field goal to go up 13–10 with fifty seconds remaining. LSU's kicker put the ball out of bounds on the subsequent kickoff, a huge gaffe which gave Alabama the ball at the 35-yard line. In those final fifty seconds, the explosive Alabama offense that had been bottled up all night came out. Quarterback Blake Sims finessed the ball downfield with no time-outs and led the Crimson Tide to a game-tying field goal. Regulation ended on the subsequent kickoff when Alabama backup linebacker Reuben Foster lit up LSU running back Leonard Fournette. It was the exclamation point on an already emphatic statement from Alabama in that final minute. In the lull between the end of regulation and the start of overtime, I knew. And I think the people around me knew, too. Sometimes you can flat-out read the energy of a moment in a stadium. LSU didn't have enough bayou voodoo magic left to pull this one out.

Alabama actually put together a 45-yard scoring drive, if you include the 20 yards' worth of penalties offensive lineman Leon Brown racked up. There was a break in the action when a player was injured and the training staff rushed the field to attend to him. During the pause, the student section started into a "Fuck You Saban" chant that couldn't have been any clearer. The chorus of students bellowed with all the frustrated anger of a fan base that knew their team was about to lose a heartbreaker. Coaches talk about how they can't hear the fans or any other peripheral distractions during a game, how you have to be able to block it out and all that. But I'm certain Saban heard the message during that injury time-out. I'm sure that chant rang clear across the Parade Ground a couple blocks away. It was the only noise in an otherwise silenced stadium.

Alabama scored a touchdown on a pass from Blake Sims to receiver DeAndrew White. When LSU had their turn, they couldn't muster any offense. Alabama left Baton Rouge with a 20–13 victory and lived to fight another day in the playoff race.

Leaving the stadium, I knew that I'd experienced peak college football game-day atmosphere in Baton Rouge. Just like Scott Van Pelt, I could describe how it felt to witness an Alabama–LSU night game in Death Valley. I could tell you about how incredible and utterly peerless it was as a sports moment, but it wouldn't do the experience justice. After all, if you've been here, no explanation is necessary; if you haven't, none will suffice.

#9 Auburn vs. #15 Georgia

November 15, 2014

Athens, Georgia

Squeezing in as many true Southern rivalry games as possible while taking in high-quality top-25 matchups over the course of a season was a balancing act. Sometimes a week would present one of each. On Halloween weekend, I bypassed a historic rivalry for the game with playoff implications. In hindsight, there was no wrong answer: Florida pulled the biggest SEC upset of the season against Georgia, and Auburn survived a back-and-forth barnburner against Ole Miss. What's funny is that none of the three teams that were poised to control their own destiny in the playoff race on Halloween—Georgia, Ole Miss, or Auburn—had any legitimate shot two weeks later. I faced a similar dilemma when No. 1-ranked Mississippi State traveled to Tuscaloosa to take on No. 5-ranked Alabama, while No. 9-ranked Auburn traveled to Athens to play

No. 15-ranked Georgia in the classic series billed as the Deep South's Oldest Rivalry. When I thought a little more, the decision was a no-brainer: I would head back to Athens.

It's a seven-hour drive from the Mississippi Gulf Coast to Athens, and six to Atlanta. I became familiar with these stretches of highway and remembered landmarks from my previous trips: the hilly stretch along I-20 through rural Alabama, the bridge going over the Tallapoosa River—it's incline felt like the slow, clicking ascent on a roller coaster—and the JESUS SAVES signs all along I-65. I liked that feeling of something alien becoming familiar. I spent a couple days in Atlanta back with my friend Alex and his dog Carson before heading to Athens. On Friday morning, I stopped at Mae's Bakery to grab a coffee and say hello. The owner, Beth, came out from behind the counter to greet me and informed me that they caught one of the robbers and had video of the other two trying to use that scared blonde girl's credit card at a department store. Maybe crime doesn't pay.

My first stop in Athens on Friday was The Grill, on College Avenue. It's a 24-hour '50s-themed diner with countertop seating and booths with mini-jukeboxes attached to the adjacent walls. While I ate bacon and eggs, drank cup after cup of diner coffee, and finished my first draft of my LSU weekend, I chatted intermittently with the girl in the next booth. Allie hailed from a small town some forty-five minutes outside Athens and found it ridiculous that I considered Athens a modest-sized college town. "This place is huge compared to where I come from. There's like two stoplights in my town and everybody knows everybody and once you get a reputation, that's how people remember you forever." Though I sensed she was speaking from experience, I didn't press the issue and try to uncover how she was remembered back home. While there are pros and cons to big cities and small towns, I think the biggest drawback of living in a big city is that it can swallow you up and make you feel insignificant. Maybe she'd prefer the anonymity after growing up in a small town where everybody gossips. Maybe I feel like I'd matter more in a small town not surrounded by three million faceless souls. Then again, maybe we all just want something different than what we already know. The grass is always greener.

⚑

The biggest news of the week concerned Georgia running back Todd Gurley II's reinstatement after sitting four games. Gurley's suspension was levied because he accepted money for signing autographs, a violation of NCAA rules. It's hard to look at the Gurley verdict without comparing it side-by-side with Jameis Winston. The same website selling Gurley merchandise also offered signed Winston memorabilia. The difference? Gurley's autographs had been authenticated whereas Winston's had not.

During the four games Gurley sat, Georgia suffered their 2nd loss, eliminating them from the playoff conversation. Gurley lost any shot at postseason awards like the Heisman Trophy or the Doak Walker.[80] Meanwhile, the Winston-led Florida State Seminoles remained unbeaten. During the same time frame, a gambling website accused Winston of participating in a point-shaving scheme with childhood friend and University of Alabama-Birmingham football player Chris Rabb. According

---

[80] The annual award given to college football's best running back.

to the accusations, Winston and Rabb bet that Louisville would be winning by halftime. In that first half, Winston threw two interceptions, and FSU trailed 21–7. It's always something with Winston.

Florida State, the school that finally dethroned the SEC, is led by a former Nick Saban disciple in Jimbo Fisher. During his and Winston's run, the school has been accused of being dirtier than any SEC program. It raises the question: in the modern college football era, do you have to cheat to win at the highest levels, or does winning at the highest levels beget so much jealousy that you're automatically suspect?

⚑

Yik Yak is a social media app where people post messages anonymously—not much longer than a tweet or text, 160 characters or so—and only people nearby can see it. People up-vote or down-vote the comments, and well-liked comments rise to the top of the list, while strongly down-voted comments disappear altogether. Understanding the app's popularity on campuses, I dabbled with it at every school since I discovered it at Tennessee. On Friday night in Athens, it yielded results. And not pretty ones. At Georgia, it turned out, social-media racism ran much thicker than any anti-Auburn sentiment. A black frat's probate hearing on campus Friday evening served as the catalyst for people to display their racist beliefs. The black-white tension was a through line all evening, with recurrent comments like: "You bitch about black people now but bet your ass you'll be grateful for them at the game tomorrow night," and "Yeah same white kids who get racist on here be on Gurley's jock the hardest tomorrow," and "Stop actin like you never seen a group of black people before. Y'all cheer for one every Saturday." Comments addressed to the black community, by the black community at Georgia, had their own acronym: BUGA, for Black University of

Georgia. Most of these comments were a call to not react to racist taunts. The anonymity of this app allows people to show who they really are and how they feel. It was eye opening to see people's candid selves.

I don't know exactly where race fits in the college football conversation, how it ties into fan culture, or how to address the national perception of Southern racism versus the reality I've encountered down here. Being a Northerner in the South, though, it's clear to me that racism, even on college campuses, is an American problem rather than a regional one. Though it's hard to make definitive statements about a topic that makes us walk on eggshells, it's too important to the big picture to ignore.

What is obvious is that the world of big-time college football has made huge strides in bridging the racial equality gap. Fifty years ago, black college students in the South required the presence of the National Guard.[81] Since then, the full integration of black athletes and coaches into the college football culture has been seismic, if gradual. The thought of a black quarterback was at one time inconceivable. It took time to stamp out the racist supposition that blacks weren't smart enough to play quarterback. Condredge Holloway became the first black quarterback to start a game in the SEC when he played for Tennessee in 1972. He later recalled Bear Bryant telling him Alabama "wasn't ready" for a black quarterback during his recruitment. In the 2014 season, half the SEC schools started a black quarterback.

When it comes to key coaching positions, however, a deep racial divide still exists. The SEC didn't hire its first black head coach until 2003,

---

[81] See: Ole Miss Riot, September 30–October 1, 1962 (Oxford, Mississippi); and Stand in the Schoolhouse Door, June 11, 1963 (Tuscaloosa, Alabama).

when Sylvester Croom became Mississippi State's lead man. Again, this is a decidedly American issue, as Croom was one of only four black Division-I head coaches at the time of his hire. In the 2014 season, African Americans held thirteen of the 128 head coaching jobs in the FBS. In the SEC, only two out of fourteen schools' head coaches and only one out of the twenty-eight coordinator positions are black. Sure, it's easy to cherry-pick statistics to support assertions, but we're talking about a gross underrepresentation, especially when considering that roughly half of FBS football players are black.

The line between what's a college football problem, what's a Southern cultural problem, and what's an across-the-board American problem becomes blurred even further when examining graduation rates. According to a University of Pennsylvania study, between 2007 and 2010, only half of black male student-athletes in the seven major D-I conferences graduated within six years of enrolling, compared to 67 percent of all student athletes. However, the exact same 17-percentage-point differential exists in comparing all undergraduate students at the same schools: 73 percent graduate within six years, while only 56 percent of black undergraduate men do. While we can clearly see a racial divide running through the college football world, it's probably symptomatic of deeper social issues that I, like many others, am ill-equipped to assess. That's not to absolve the racial injustices we see in the world of college football, but rather to acknowledge that it's not fair to adopt the extreme view that college sports are evil because they're exploiting the black athlete. Exploitation of a student-athlete occurs in those instances where young men incapable of handling a college course load are admitted to and kept eligible at major universities simply because of their athletic prowess. That's pretty close to a textbook definition of exploitation, and it happens far more often than we'd like to admit.

Is it fair to say that black student athletes are being used by the higher education system? Probably not, at least not in such a broad brush statement. Is it fair to say that there's a huge gulf between black experiences and white experiences on college campuses and across the country? Probably. How does that manifest itself in the world of college football?

ESPN's 30 for 30 documentary series[82] produces feel-good documentaries like *Ghosts of Ole Miss* and *The Color Orange: The Condredge Holloway Story*.[83] The films show what racism on campus felt like forty or fifty years ago, and how far we've come in terms of racial equality. The problem is these documentaries also talk about racism like it's an artifact of some bygone era; like it's not a living, breathing thing, like it's something we can look back on and say: "Phew, I'm glad that's over." Late Friday night, I watched *The Youngstown Boys*, a 30 for 30 about former Ohio State running back Maurice Clarett, his coach Jim Tressel, and their journeys both during and after OSU's 2002 National Championship season. Clarett's take on the state of affairs in the NCAA is that it's still a decidedly cruel and racist system: "I didn't have a degree, so the same people who were askin' me for my autograph just a year

---

[82] A popular documentary series that has been airing on ESPN since 2009. The films have mass appeal, in large part, because beyond sharing sports stories, they have strong human-interest angles. Humanizing the athletes behind the stories is always compelling to sports fans (and even non-fans).

[83] As you may recall, *The Color Orange* is one of the documentaries produced by country superstar Kenny Chesney.

before were tellin' me, 'Nah, you can't have a job.' The system is designed to put you back in the inner city. It pushes you back to the hustlin' and the street life."

⚑

In the spring of 2014, before my trip, I befriended a fellow college football nut on Twitter named Matt. We hit it off so well that during the summer we wrote about SEC football together on a blog. I met Matt and his crew at their tailgate behind Boggs Hall early Saturday afternoon. We caught up for a bit and he introduced me to his friends and girlfriend. One of the curious things about their tailgate is that I only met a couple UGA grads in the whole bunch. They were a ragtag group of Atlanta transplants. I met girls who attended Iowa and Miami (OH) and another girl from Connecticut. For the most part, they were nominal Georgia fans who drove over to Athens for a good time. It brought to mind a point fans at other schools made numerous times throughout the season. Athens is only an hour away from Atlanta, a city that's home to professional teams in three major sports. State pride begets allegiance to college teams for so many Southerners, and Alabama, Arkansas, Kentucky, Mississippi, and South Carolina house a grand total of zero pro sports teams. So it hasn't been unusual for an Auburn, South Carolina, or Mississippi State football fan to point to the Falcons, Braves, or Hawks to explain why their team's win-loss record means more to them than Georgia's does to the Bulldog nation. It's an interesting point. Then again, for my money, UGA's Sanford Stadium rivals LSU's Tiger Stadium for the most intense, deafening game-day atmosphere in the SEC. So, it's hard to say how much weight to give the claim.

Matt told me he'd seen Big Dawg, so we took off to find and take a picture with him. I knew exactly who Matt was talking about, of course.

I'd seen the character before on TV, with his black overalls lined with various patches from bowl games and Georgia slogans. Of course, Big Dawg (real name: Mike Woods) isn't known for his overalls. It's the intricately painted Georgia Bulldog atop his bald head that made him one of Georgia's best-known fans. (Sadly, he died in January 2017.) When we found Big Dawg, he was leaning into the passenger side of a pickup truck talking with friends. Matt and I weren't the only ones waiting to take a picture; three ladies—two women in their forties and a little girl—waited as well. One of the women explained that she'd taken pictures with Woods before—a lot of people have—but never with her daughter.

It's fascinating how a super fan can become something of a celebrity. Examples abound in the sports world: Ole Miss has the man who dresses up as Colonel Reb; the New York Jets had Fireman Ed, who would get up on his buddy's shoulders in his fireman's hat; the Chicago Cubs had Ronnie Woo Woo; and so on. Mike Woods was a gracious man. He took pictures and chatted with us for a few minutes. When I asked him how he started painting the Bulldog on his head, he told me his dad did it first. From 1980 to 1987, his father was the Big Dawg. Woods took over in 1990 and hasn't missed a game since. A strange inheritance to be sure, but one that shows yet another way fandom is passed from one generation to the next.[84] Twenty-four years straight with a giant Bulldog painted on top of your head without missing a

---

[84] Big Dawg's son, Trent, will pick up the mantle beginning in the 2017 season.

game? That's absurd. But I suppose when you're that committed, there's nothing ridiculous about it.

A little later, I met up with my Airbnb hosts, Andy and Angela, at their tailgate at the Presbyterian Student Center on Lumpkin Street. Married Georgia alums in their mid-thirties, they fell in love with Athens during undergrad and never left. Everyone was huddled around the big screen watching the Alabama–Mississippi State game when I arrived; Alabama was winning 5–0. Andy declared that this was the de facto National Championship game, and a couple people nearby agreed. While I thought it presumptuous, I'd long since given up on trying to challenge Southerners on their implicit beliefs about SEC superiority. We clustered around a fire pit that kept swirling smoke in our faces no matter where we stood as Angela explained the history of their tailgate. They've been pregaming at the Center for years. She pointed to two people she's been friends with since high school in our sightline. Angela paused, and shared an insight. "It's funny, we're all friends and have been coming to the same tailgate for years but once we get here, the black people all make their way to one side and the white people make their way to the other." I looked around and saw that it was mostly true.

She and Andy introduced me to their friend Christian—one of the few black guys on the "white side" of the tailgate—and we started talking about the Auburn–Georgia game. He said he didn't know who was going to win because he didn't know which Georgia team was going to show up: the one that phoned it in against Florida and lost, or the one that bounced back the following week and hung 63 points on Kentucky in Lexington. He made a valid point. Georgia looked like a Jekyll-and-Hyde squad all season long. The same can be said for Auburn, though. So the question was: which Georgia team and which Auburn team would show up on a freezing-cold November night in Athens? As a fan and observer, it's one of the most intriguing things about watching college football. How can a team look completely different from week to week? It's easy to understand when a team lays an egg against a garbage opponent because they didn't get up for the game, or when a team has a letdown after a huge rivalry game that made it hard to carry the emotional burden and focus through to the next week. On the whole though, so many factors go into what we see as the final product on Saturdays that it's hard to predict when almost any college football team will be "on" or "off."

After waxing incredulous about Mississippi State being the No. 1 team in America, Christian made the comment that it isn't the top-tier schools (Alabama, Auburn, LSU, Georgia, or Florida) who really need to be paying players—it's Mississippi State and Ole Miss, who have to scratch and claw to try and keep up with the traditional SEC big boys. "They're the ones who need to go out and buy some kids. Stud athletes want to come to programs like UGA and Bama because we've been doin' it at a high level their whole lives. Doesn't mean it never happens here, but you know what I mean." He then shared a story from his time at Georgia in the early 2000s. Christian hung around with some guys on the football team and saw them driving around in cars he knew they couldn't afford. When he asked his scholarship buddies about it, they told him about the sweetheart leases they got for the cars. "Man, they'd be paying like five or ten dollars a month. I guess eventually the school found out, so they just ran the car dealer out of town, made him sell his dealership. Georgia didn't report it; they just took care of it themselves."

An hour later at the Dawg Walk, the Georgia buses pulled to a stop. The players rocked the first bus back and forth, chanting from inside. The black-and-red-clad onlookers were stirred into a state of hysteria. Clouds of warm breath billowed up from the wails of the huddled masses on either sidewalk on a 30-degree night. The players exited the buses high-fiving fans as they strode to the players' entrance of Sanford Stadium. When the players had passed, I looked up at the overhang from a parking garage and saw a sign the size of a bed sheet:

Free at Last, Free at Last

Thank God Almighty

3s

Free at Last.[85]

Auburn won the coin toss, elected to receive, and promptly drove down and scored the opening touchdown of the game. After a TV time-out, Todd Gurley II[86] came out to return the kickoff. I was standing in the student section near the end zone where Gurley paced, awaiting the kick 5 yards deep. He barely had to move for the ball; it came right to him. I knew that after four weeks watching from the sidelines, there was no way TG3 would take a knee. Gurley exploded out of the end zone and into a crease in his blockers' return wall. As if shot out of a cannon, he

---

[85] I'm not sure that's what Dr. King had in mind, but it was amusing nonetheless.

[86] Somewhat confusingly, Gurley—whose full name is Todd Gurley II—is often referred to as "3" or "TG3" because of his jersey number.

took off down the left sideline. Todd Gurley raced 105 yards for a kick return touchdown on his first play back from suspension. This was the fairytale ending to his Georgia career Todd Gurley deserved, and the fairytale ending Georgia fans deserved from their best running back since Herschel Walker. It's the story people would've told for the next couple generations at Auburn–Georgia tailgates: "And on the very first play back from that BS suspension…" But fairytales don't exist in real time; they only exist in their retelling after the fact. The referees called holding on Gurley's kickoff return, and Gurley (and the fairytale) came back.

Georgia should have scored three times on their first possession: the Gurley kickoff, an Isaiah McKenzie drop on a wide-open deep ball, and a fake-punt touchdown pass that was called back because of an illegal man downfield. It didn't matter, though—Georgia had all night to rack up points. Auburn never scored again. Georgia routed Auburn 34–7 in an anticlimactic chapter of the Deep South's Oldest Rivalry. Gurley and freshman sensation Nick Chubb split carries all night and both ran successfully on the Auburn defense. Gurley gained 138 yards and scored a touchdown while Chubb rushed for 144 yards and two scores. Late in the third quarter, Chubb broke a big run, and at Auburn's 10-yard line he barreled full speed into one of his blockers; the impact pinballed both his blocker and the Auburn defender behind him three yards backwards. Chubb regained his balance, eluded two more tacklers, and fought his way into the end zone. The replay showed Chubb stepping out of bounds as he caught his balance at the 10, and the touchdown was called back. But it didn't matter; everyone in the stadium was dumbstruck by Chubb's display of freak athleticism and raw power. You could almost hear the gears spinning in people's heads as they began dreaming about big moments to come in 2015 and 2016 with Nick Chubb running past, through, over, and around opposing defenders.

With a few minutes remaining in the fourth quarter, Todd Gurley tore his ACL on his 29th carry of the night. Nobody in the student section was overly concerned when it happened; it didn't look like a bad injury. When Coach Mark Richt announced that TG3 had torn his ACL in the postgame press conference, I remember being overwhelmed by a wave of sadness for Gurley. I don't know why. Players tear their ACL all the time, and these days repairing it is a fairly common procedure with a six-to-nine-month recovery timetable. I reflected back on that 95-degree day in late August when Gurley seemed destined to walk across the stage of the Downtown Athletic Club to accept the 2014 Heisman Trophy. Was this really how it was supposed to end? I caught myself wondering: "What if he's never the same runner again and his NFL career flames out and he's spit back out into the real world and goes down in football history as a might-have-been?" I remember thinking about Boobie Miles, the fallen star running back from Buzz Bissinger's modern classic *Friday Night Lights*. When I was fifteen and read that book for the first time, I felt the sadness Bissinger conveyed as he described how all the promise Miles's future held evaporated in an instant when he suffered a major knee injury.

I remember internalizing the heartbreak in Bissinger's portrait, feeling how unfair it was that this kid's future hinged on his physical ability, how unfair it was that all of a sudden Boobie Miles became yesterday's news in that West Texas town, how unfair it was that all the preferential star treatment disappeared. I felt the impact as Boobie came crashing back down to earth. I had no way of knowing what was in store for Todd

Gurley,[87] and I'm not sure why I thought of Boobie Miles when I heard Todd Gurley tore his ACL, but this is my story, and that's what happened.

Around 3 am, I pulled into a Steak 'n Shake in Athens. While I sat at the counter waiting on my burger, I overheard a couple guys talking about the game. One of them said, "I mean, it sucks that Gurley got hurt but whatever, it doesn't even matter. Chubb is a BEAST!" Something about that comment cemented in my mind the major drawback of college football, at least for the players: they're utterly replaceable. That's why these kids need to be getting paid. That's why I have absolutely no moral qualms with "student-athletes" collecting as much money as they possibly can under the table while they're being recruited and while they're playing on campus. Gurley was already yesterday's news in Athens. The sun hadn't even risen the day after Gurley played his final collegiate game, and the guy who'd been touted as the Second Coming of Herschel since midway through his freshman year was written off by fans salivating over the next freshman sensation who's only six months removed from high school.

---

[87] Gurley's story had a happier ending. He rushed for 1,106 yards and 10 touchdowns in his rookie season with the St. Louis Rams, and was named 2015 NFL Offensive Rookie of the Year.

#8 Ole Miss vs. Arkansas

November 22, 2014

Fayetteville, Arkansas

On the Sunday after the Deep South's Oldest Rivalry, I decided to suck it up and trek nine hours back to Memphis, where I would stay with my friend Anne for the week. I knew that the November part of my schedule would take a toll with all the miles. Savannah to Oxford to Baton Rouge to Athens to Fayetteville to College Station to Tuscaloosa in twenty-nine days promised to be exhausting, as the weather turned cold and the early-season excitement gave way to the grind of a fifteen-week schedule.

It rained all the way from Athens to Birmingham, where I met Ashley, an old Chicago friend, for dinner at Lloyd's Restaurant off Highway 280. Ashley recently moved back to Birmingham, where she was born and raised. As we caught up over fried chicken, turnip greens, fried okra, and hushpuppies,[88] she told me all the things she missed about the South and all the ways she's falling in love with home all over again. In the middle of our conversation, I blurted out something I'd been thinking for a while but hadn't told anyone: "When this trip's over, I'm not going back to Chicago. I don't know where I want to go, but I'm not gonna live in Chicago anymore." She nodded like she understood why. In a car with a broken CD player and no satellite radio, I often sat in silence contemplating the kindness of strangers who became friends in a matter of hours. I pondered the idea of leaving my home permanently, leaving behind family, friends, community. And somewhere along the way, I made peace with knowing that the city I've always called home will be a place I only visit from now on.

Ashley and I made plans to get together Sunday after the Iron Bowl, and I braced myself for another five hours of highway driving. She overruled my objections and paid for our Sunday dinner. I thanked her, filled up on gas, topped off my gas station coffee with French vanilla creamer, and made for Memphis in the pouring rain.

It rained or threatened to rain all week, and I couldn't clear my head enough to write anything coherent. I sat at Cafe Eclectic, a coffee shop on Highland Street and near the University of Memphis, for hours each afternoon trying to snap out of it. It felt like the harder I tried to get any work done, the more hopeless the task became. My arms and legs had started going numb on account of a pinched nerve from all the driving, and I felt the weight of the road crashing down on me all week. Long

---

[88] I'm still not sure exactly what hushpuppies are, but they involve fried dough and are delicious.

walks with Anne's three 80-pound dogs—Mango, Murphy, and Mo—helped some, as did long talks with Anne. Still, I needed to snap out of it. So I left Memphis a day early and spent Thursday night in Little Rock at a hotel watching, but not paying attention to, the games on TV. North Carolina beat up on Duke, Kansas State held on for a close win over West Virginia, and I took a hot bath and slept ten hours, hoping the fog enshrouding me and the weight on my shoulders would finally fall away.

It stormed the whole two-and-a-half hour drive up to Fayetteville, but as I approached the city, the sky framed the lingering fog around the Boston Mountain Range in a way that calmed my nerves. For the first time all week, I felt at ease. I arrived on Arkansas's campus in the early afternoon.

I hate how ignorant this is going to make me sound, but when I think of stereotypical hick towns where there's nothing else going on around campus—no culture, no outdoor activities that don't involve guns, no indoor activities that don't involve booze—I thought of Arkansas. I thought of a couple other places, too, but I thought of Arkansas. I don't know why, but I did.

Fayetteville, Arkansas flipped my expectations on their head completely within a matter of minutes. One of the first things I saw was a bank inside of an old railway car. I turned down Dickson Street and parked. Dickson was a standard college town main street occupied by bars and restaurants, coffee shops and book stores, and even a little enclave of food trucks—Southern soul food, pizza, and a Grateful Dead-themed spot.[89] What I saw were all the trappings of your average college campus. So I had a hard time figuring out exactly why I felt so attracted to Fayetteville right away. I loved how many small, locally owned businesses populated the town. There's a combination of two distinct cultures that mesh and find this great balancing point at the University of Arkansas. Yeah, it's a college town, and sure, it's got a Southern football culture and all that goes with that. But there was something that reminded me of everything great about small city America. It felt like a smaller Portland, Oregon, but with fewer hipsters and better weather. And Razorback football, of course.

The Lights of the Ozarks unveiling ceremony was that afternoon. It's an annual tradition in the main downtown square in Fayetteville meant to herald the town's Christmas lights display. There's something to be said about the square, too. Much like Oxford, Fayetteville's square centers around one freestanding building set apart from everything else. But Fayetteville's downtown square is much less ostentatious than Oxford's. Two-and-three-story brick buildings housed storefronts with oversized front windowpanes on the ground floor and apartments above. Two local news anchors were out to cover the event, testing their mics and coordinating shots with their camera crews. Volunteers lined the streets making last-minute adjustments to the lights and garland.

---

[89] Typically a good sign.

I'm not used to certain rites and rituals in smaller towns and cities. One of those things is having local news stations out to cover a kitschy community event like the unveiling of the town's Christmas lights. It's fair to say that I liked Fayetteville from the start.

After the ceremony kicked off, I left campus to settle in at my Airbnb a couple miles away. As I drove, I noticed the brilliant red sky over Fayetteville at sunset. I'm smart enough to know that it's not natural, that it's something they do on the night before home games, but all the same I'd rather not know how it's done. The same way that knowing the sleight of hand behind a magic trick ruins it, knowing how the evening sky glowed that night might have broken the spell Fayetteville cast upon me on an otherwise grey November day.

🏴

On Saturday, I woke up to another downpour from an overcast sky. It rained all morning and into the early afternoon. Truth be told, I wanted no part of the tailgating scene at Arkansas. I still felt sick and sat around watching the early games on TV until close to kickoff. Only then did I drive over to Donald W. Reynolds Razorback Stadium. I scalped a ticket for $30 on the walk to the stadium, proceeded to the 50-yard line 30 rows off the field, and parked myself there. I don't think I even looked to see where my ticket was because I knew the game wasn't a sellout. And if a game isn't a sellout, you can always find yourself a cushy seat near midfield if you're so inclined.

Razorback players competing in their final home game embraced Coach Bret Bielema in the tunnel behind the north end zone before running out to greet their families at midfield. Every school has a Senior Day ceremony before the final home game. It's a well-deserved sendoff to players who put four or five years of hard work into a program. By itself, the pregame event doesn't merit mention. In the context of Arkansas football over the past few years, however, the moment took on a greater significance.

2010 and 2011 were tremendously successful years under then-coach Bobby Petrino. Arkansas capped those seasons with Sugar and Cotton Bowl victories, respectively, and the Razorbacks finished 2011 ranked fifth in the country. Petrino's tenure in Fayetteville held immense promise: a 21–5 record posted in his last two seasons, and year-to-year improvement (5–7 in 2008; 8–5 in 2009; 10–3 in 2010; and 11–2 in 2011) signaled even greater success in the future. Then it all fell to pieces.

In early April 2012, Petrino wrecked his motorcycle some twenty miles outside of Fayetteville. On the back of his motorcycle was Jessica Dorrell, a twenty-five-year-old former Arkansas volleyball player and Petrino's then-girlfriend. Days before the crash, Petrino had hired Dorrell to an administrative position within the football program. Petrino lied to Athletic Director Jeff Long about Dorrell's involvement in the crash as well as the nature of his relationship with Dorrell. Petrino was summarily fired, and collegiate coaching journeyman John L. Smith was hired as Petrino's interim replacement. The Smith-led Razorbacks stumbled to a 4–8 finish in 2012. After Arkansas let Smith go, they hired Bret Bielema away from Wisconsin to be their next head coach. Things went from bad to worse, however, as the Razorbacks finished 2013 with a 3–9 record, losing nine straight to close the season.

When you consider the roller-coaster ride these players had been on—coming in and tasting success, being nationally relevant and a part of the BCS Championship conversation, and then suffering through two coaching changes and two atrocious seasons—the pregame celebration on Senior Day seemed all the more poignant. High highs, low lows.

⚑

Arkansas allowed signature wins to slip through their fingers numerous times during the '14 season. Against Texas A&M, the Razorbacks led 28–14 entering the fourth quarter; they lost 35–28 in overtime. Arkansas had the ball late in the fourth quarter against Alabama, down by one, only to have Alabama's Landon Collins intercept a Brandon Allen pass and secure a 14–13 Crimson Tide victory. The next week, Arkansas led Mississippi State 10–7 until late in the third quarter, when the Bulldogs put the final 10 points on the board to win 17–10. At the time of those games, Texas A&M, Alabama, and Mississippi State were all top-10 teams. It would have been easy for players, coaches, and fans alike to believe themselves cursed and pack it in for the season after any of those devastating losses, but they never did.

There was a punch-you-in-the-mouth toughness about the 2014 Arkansas team. As one ESPN commentator wryly noted in the week leading up to this game, the 5–5 Razorbacks are the best 5-loss team in the country. In many ways, the Ole Miss–Arkansas game represented a meeting between teams headed in opposite directions. Mississippi peaked in early October, when they beat then-No. 3-ranked Alabama. Fans in Oxford rushed the field, and actually took the goal posts out of the stadium with them (an event so memorably recalled by the Alabama super-fans I met with in Knoxville, Matthew and Jackie). Since then, Ole Miss had lost to LSU and Auburn, eliminating them from playoff contention. Although they entered the game ranked eighth in the playoff standings, it felt—to me, at least—the ranking was more a function of the media's fawning over SEC teams than an accurate reflection of the Rebels. Meanwhile, Arkansas was riding high. The week before, they shut out a ranked LSU team, 17–0, for their first conference win in two years.

⚑

The Razorbacks capitalized on early turnovers and miscues by the Rebs and built a 17–0 first quarter lead. The early Arkansas scores were a combination of opportunism and riding out the wake of whatever adrenaline surge spilled over from Senior Day into the opening stages of the game. After darting ahead to a quick lead, Arkansas's offense stalled out for the remainder of the day. Arkansas had a one-dimensional offense. They finished the day with 8 of 15 passes completed for a whopping 152 yards, but when you play mistake-free football and your opponent doesn't, that's all it takes. Ole Miss turned the ball over six times, including two Bo Wallace interceptions in the end zone. The second was returned by Rohan Gaines 100 yards for a touchdown. The pick-six made the score 27–0 late in the third quarter. They added a field goal early in the fourth to cap a 30–0 shutout, making the 2014 Arkansas Razorbacks the first unranked college football team ever to blank ranked opponents in consecutive weeks. This was also their second straight SEC win.

As the rain poured down, washing away the bitter taste of two years' worth of losing, I observed jubilant fans all around me. The four fellows behind me were every group of post-collegiate bros you've ever met: mid-twenties, drunk, loud, belligerent, alternately hilarious and obnoxious. It started at kickoff. They had nicknames for nearly every player on the team and yelled "Getchu some" every single play. When Alex Collins stood in the backfield, they shouted "Getchu some number four." When Jonathan Williams lined up behind Brandon Allen, it was

"Getchu some J-Will." And when punter Sam Irwin-Hill came on to punt, they'd shout "Getchu some Sam Hill."

I flipped between thinking they were the funniest guys on the planet and wanting to strangle them to the applause of everyone around us at least ten times during the game. They were cartoon versions of themselves, caricatures of Southern rednecks, like Yosemite Sam decided to grace Fayetteville with his presence. The best part was that they always talked in twos, which gave their comments the effect of echoing in stereo. After the refs called a blatant penalty against Arkansas the following exchange unrolled: "What?" "What?"; "Don't make us come down there!" "Do NOT make us come down there!"; "You've got to be kidding me!" "You've got to be kidding. Are you kidding me?"; and, of course, "Wooooo!" "Wooooooo Pig Soieeee!"

A father and his young son occupied the seats to my left. In the lulls between the bros behind us hollering, I could overhear their conversation. The boy couldn't have been more than seven or eight and the dad was around my age, probably thirty. Throughout the game, the dad explained football to his son. On a 2nd and 11, the dad explained that Arkansas had to get all the way to the second stick on the chains to make a first down, not the one right in front of the down marker. When a scrum ensued after a Bo Wallace fumble, the dad explained that the guys in the pile were fighting for the ball and when an Arkansas player emerged with the ball, the boy jumped up and high-fived his dad. Being a college football fan is part of the family heritage for so many in the South. Listening to the boy ask questions that his father patiently answered, and watching the two celebrate together after a big play, choked me up a bit. It felt like I was watching a sacred ritual, a familial bond being strengthened with every excited question, every patient answer, and every celebration. Fathers and sons connect on all sorts of common ground. It just so happens that in the South, being a college football fan is the ubiquitous connection. It's no wonder the roots run so deep when the seed is planted so early.

I introduced myself to a pair of Arkansas grads a couple seats over to my right in the downtime between Senior Day festivities and kickoff. We made small talk and traded high-fives and jokes throughout the game. Phil and John attended Arkansas together in the early '90s and had returned for a reunion weekend of sorts. The funny thing was how everything reminded them of their college days. When House of Pain's "Jump Around" played during a time-out they gave each other the "this is our jam" look, fist-bumped and took turns spitting lyrics. Watching Phil and John affected me, too. I started thinking about how I'm halfway between college and where these two are in their lives. Detailed memories of my first weekend away from home at Marquette University returned to me as if they'd occurred last weekend. It freaked me out, like the passage of time does any time I stop and think about it. I recalled that first weekend in Milwaukee in 2003 like it was yesterday, and realized that I'm going to blink my eyes and be where these guys are, in my early 40s, trying to figure out where it all went. It's a good thing the rain poured down all day because the thought made me teary-eyed.

At John's suggestion, I headed to Hugo's for a bite to eat after the game. Hugo's is a basement den burger bar with wood-paneled walls and a low-hanging ceiling. I found the last open wooden stool at the bar and ordered a Swiss and bacon burger. Then I watched the game cast of Notre Dame losing again—this time to Louisville—and thought about what meaningful takeaways I could mine from a game weekend where

I did no tailgating. I felt I already knew a fair amount about the Arkansas fan's condition through conversations I had had with fans on hogville.net over the spring and summer. The extract of any good fan base can be found on message boards talking year-round shop about the team, and the good people on hogville.net openly shared their opinions about what it's like being an Arkansas backer. One of the biggest things I gathered was that Arkansas fans feel Murphy's Law[90] applies to them more than any other fan base. A poster named Big Papa Satan described it for me in terms that I was uniquely qualified to comprehend: "Being a Razorback fan is a bit like being a Cubs fan, in the sense of any championships won were a long time ago and the times they've gotten close, strange, heartbreaking things have happened. As a result, Arkansas' football program could be described as snakebit."

In a follow-up message he elaborated on the many times and ways Arkansas football has made fans throw up their hands in despair: "Snakebit is where things can go south to the point where you're yelling, 'My God, what else can go wrong?!' And something inevitably does, whether it be the refusal to kick a field goal that would've won you a national championship and finding a way to lose the game… a fumble when you're undefeated and you have #1 on the ropes, or a coach tanking a national championship spot because he, as a grown man around fifty, can't fathom a few eighteen year olds having no respect for him, setting off a civil war in the fan base… As I said, snakebit."

The distinguishing feature of a fan base that feels snakebit is that they point the finger inward, rather than blaming others for their failures. I

---

[90] Anything that can go wrong, will.

never once heard about getting screwed by refs, others conspiring against them, or any forces outside Arkansas's control dictating their fate to them. Then again, maybe that's exactly what I heard. When the breaks beat you down so completely over a long period of time, maybe you attribute it to something greater than "the other guy." Maybe you attribute it to forces beyond your control, like a curse. (Perhaps it involves a billy goat.) Being a Chicago Cubs fan, I've always been curious about the phenomenon of fans believing their team is cursed, as if the gods have turned their backs on their team. It's as if the idea of Calvinist predestination lives, breathing its dogmatic superstitions into today's sports world. The New York Yankees, 27-time world champions, are the elect of Major League Baseball. They believe they'll win—or purchase—a title every October. And up until 2016, the Chicago Cubs, 100-plus years removed from their last World Series, were the smote, scorned by the gods of baseball and destined to stumble and fall before the finish line year in and year out (oftentimes straight out of the blocks). If the analogy fits, then the SEC equivalent would be Alabama as the New York Yankees and Arkansas as the Chicago Cubs. You could point to Vanderbilt or Kentucky, but Vanderbilt anchors their identity to academics and the city of Nashville, and Kentucky hangs their hat on a premier basketball program. Both schools are, almost by definition, less invested. Arkansas only has their Hogs to call upon.

I don't know how to look at it: Are Arkansas football supporters a special breed of fan, a type who combs through their own shortcomings for answers to their problems? Might they be—*gasp*—introspective? Or do they feel the weight of all their disappointments is so far beyond their control that they bypass the typical persecution complex and go straight to something supernatural? Maybe that's a question better left for a sports psychologist.

One of the events Big Papa Satan alluded to plays a prominent role in understanding modern Arkansas football history. It all started when Houston Nutt was hired as Arkansas's head coach after the 1997 season. In his first season, Nutt led the Razorbacks to an SEC West co-championship with Mississippi State. Nutt's star rose and fell over the next seven seasons, with back-to-back 9-win seasons in 2002–03 followed up by 5–6 and 4–7 campaigns in 2004 and 2005, respectively. Entering 2006, the stage was set for a make-or-break season in Fayetteville.

The 2006 Arkansas team was arguably the school's most talented in a generation. Future first-round NFL picks Darren McFadden and Felix Jones headlined an impressive backfield stable that also included future Cleveland Browns 1,000-yard rusher Peyton Hillis at fullback. For a conservative run-first, run-second and maybe-pass-but-probably-run-third coach like Houston Nutt, the 2006 backfield was a lifetime's worth of prayers answered all at once. In addition to what was probably the best running back tandem in the nation that year, Arkansas had both an influx of both young talent and progressive new football philosophy.

During that 4–7 2005 season Arkansas fans would rather forget, most of the local football hype revolved not around the Razorbacks, but a high school team down the road. Springdale High School is practically within spitting distance of the University of Arkansas, a mere fifteen minutes from campus. And in 2005, everything about the Springdale program was eye-popping. Five big-time Division-I football prospects—known as the Springdale Five—all played on one team. Mitch Mustain was the top-rated quarterback in America coming out of high school, ranked ahead of both Tim Tebow and Matthew Stafford. Wide receiver Damian Williams was a top-100 player, and receiver Andrew Norman, tight end Ben Cleveland and offensive lineman Bartley Webb were all three-star prospects with numerous big-time Division-I offers. Springdale went 14–0, won an Arkansas class 5A state championship, and finished as the No. 2-ranked high school team in America.

The catalyst behind Springdale's success was an innovative coach who designed a spread, no-huddle offense that devastated opponents on Friday nights to the tune of 7,000 yards. You may have heard of him. His name? Gus Malzahn.

The tale of what happened next has been covered ad nauseam within Arkansan circles. While the intersection of these two football programs only fifteen minutes apart could have been the best of times, they turned out to be the worst of times for Arkansas football fans everywhere.

Four of the Springdale Five signed with the University of Arkansas—Webb accepted a scholarship to play at Notre Dame—and Gus Malzahn was hired as Arkansas's Offensive Coordinator. Between the two-headed monster of McFadden and Jones and the promise of finally stretching the field vertically in the pass game and tormenting SEC defenses with Malzahn's Hurry-Up, No Huddle strategy, Razorback fans believed 2006 would bring their first SEC championship. The starry-eyed among the fan base even thought Arkansas could win their first national championship since 1964.

Alas, it wasn't to be. Almost from the start, the marriage between Nutt and Malzahn was a rocky one. The process of overhauling the offense was a garbled mess, with Malzahn's spread cobbled in bits and pieces on top of Nutt's traditional ground attack. A couple pass concepts and protection schemes here, a little tempo and spread formation there, but the offense was never really properly installed.

On the surface, the promise of 2006 looked to be coming to fruition. After being thrashed by No. 6-ranked Southern Cal in the season opener, Nutt named Mitch Mustain starting quarterback and Arkansas started to roll over the competition. Mustain won seven straight games as the starter and all was well in Razorback Nation. Until it wasn't. The locker room anxieties mounted as the tousle over offensive control continued. This manifested itself on game days, when Nutt would relieve Malzahn of play calling duties. With one offense installed from previous years and another partially installed, mix-ups in terminology for plays and blocking schemes were far too common for a big-time collegiate program. The net result was a mushrooming tension within the Razorback locker room.

Much has been written on the subject, but it's hard to know exactly how everything played out behind the scenes and who's to blame. Like any story where the main parties disagree, there are two accounts, and the truth probably lies somewhere in between. But some indisputable facts help color the story. A local writer followed the Springdale High team in 2005, chronicling their pursuit of a state championship. Along the way, he found and added some juicy tidbits about the recruiting world and, germane to such a discussion, Coach Houston Nutt. Specifically, the book revealed that Mitch Mustain was uncertain about committing to Arkansas, calling Nutt a "dork" and generally ripping his future coach; nothing jaw-dropping but noteworthy nonetheless. Curiously, this information went public, at least within the Arkansas football world, close to the time Mustain lost his starting position. Another verified fact is that the tension between coach and quarterback had a negative effect on an already fracturing locker room. Multiple players confirmed the impact. Mustain and Nutt discussed the issue with the media, and their accounts couldn't differ more. Nutt claimed it was no big deal, that he and Mustain talked through their issues and that was the end of the book blurb-related tension. Mustain claimed Nutt took the whole ordeal personally, and looked for any opportunity to bench his starting quarterback and write him off altogether. To this day, Gus Malzahn has stayed quiet on the subject. If he bore the same resentment toward Nutt that Mustain did, nobody other than those in his inner circle ever knew about it.

On Arkansas's first offensive possession against South Carolina in week nine, Mustain threw an interception. Nutt benched Mustain, and the freshman never started another game for Arkansas. With Casey Dick as triggerman the Razorbacks went on to win that night against the Gamecocks, and the next two games against Tennessee and Mississippi State, leaving Arkansas with a 10–1 record and ranked sixth in the BCS polls.

Had the Razorbacks won their next two games against No. 8-ranked LSU and the SEC Championship game against No. 4-ranked Florida, they would have played for a national championship against Ohio State. But, characteristic of the snakebit Arkansas football team, then came the point where the proverbial rug was pulled out from under them. The Razorbacks lost to LSU and Florida before falling to Wisconsin in the Capital One Bowl. Fayetteville, Arkansas, never saw a more disappointing 10-win season. The expectations were sky-high, with good reason, but the promise went unfulfilled.

Many pointed the finger at Nutt, saying he was too egotistical to allow a coordinator with a bright new scheme to come in and do his job and too petulant to shrug it off when an eighteen-year-old kid said some mildly disrespectful things about him. Any way about it, the Springdale connection severed at the end of the season. Gus Malzahn took the offensive coordinator job at Tulsa, where his offense led the country in total yardage in 2007. Mitch Mustain and Damian Williams transferred to Southern Cal, where Mustain was buried on the depth chart and Williams thrived, eventually making his way to the NFL. Andrew Norman followed Malzahn to Tulsa. A year after being heralded as the next big thing in Arkansas football, the Springdale crew had all departed, with the lone exception of tight end Ben Cleveland.

In retrospect, many people believe Malzahn was only hired in order to lure Mustain and company to Fayetteville and that Nutt had no intention of handing over the reins of his offense. It represents a drama-filled chapter in their history filled with lots of might-have-beens. Maybe it's because might have been is the most painful form of remembering that many Arkansas fans are happy to put the Springdale Five era behind them.

A year later, after an 8–5 record in 2007, Houston Nutt was fired and Bobby Petrino was hired away from Louisville. His offenses at Louisville were exciting and prolific enough to start the merry-go-round of hope and disappointment, with its buildup of increased expectations and eventual letdown into cold reality. Hearing Arkansas fans explain their recent history and what it means to feel snakebit, I pictured Lucy pulling the ball out from Charlie Brown over and over again.

An objective observer would have to look at Arkansas football right now and see a program on the rise, a program that's an impact player or two away from being a 9- or 10-win team in the SEC. I departed Fayetteville thinking that the Bielema era had finally turned the corner, blanking consecutive ranked opponents and earning bowl-eligibility in the process. But given the program's history, I suspect many Arkansans see the Hogs starting to win and then ask themselves when the other shoe's going to drop.

LSU vs. Texas A&M

November 27, 2014

College Station, Texas

College Station, Texas, the home of the Texas A&M Aggies, is a place where military culture and football tradition are inextricably linked. Considering that Texas A&M boasts the largest corps of cadets on any United States college campus outside the service academies, it's not surprising that everything about the campus smacks of military tradition and history. Come to think of it, Texas A&M has a long-standing tradition behind just about everything they do.

One such tradition was playing a night game on Thanksgiving weekend.[91] Historically, A&M would play Texas every year on this date, much like the Iron Bowl, Egg Bowl, Florida–Florida State, Ohio State–Michigan, Clemson–South Carolina, and so on. It's one of the great college football traditions that teams play their archrival—often an intrastate rival—on the last weekend of the regular season. So when A&M left the Big XII in 2012, they also left behind their biggest rivalry game. Understandably, Thanksgiving weekend hasn't felt the same across Texas these past few years.

According to A&M fans, the story of how Texas A&M ended up joining the SEC was driven in large part by ESPN signing an exclusive contract with the University of Texas for the Longhorn Network. When conference expansion was the hot-button issue in 2011, numerous scenarios floated out to the public, including both Texas and Texas A&M joining the Pac-10 conference (now the Pac-12) and both schools staying in the Big XII and adding new members. But according to Aggies, it was the condescending way that former Texas Athletic Director DeLoss Dodds interacted with former A&M Athletic Director Bill Byrne that led to Texas A&M joining the SEC. In essence, Aggie fans say, Dodds told Byrne "don't worry, we'll take care of you, too," all the while keeping A&M at bay in the expansion dialogue. Fans liken the

---

[91] For over seventy years (1918–1988), the Texas A&M–Texas game was played on Thanksgiving night. The schools renewed the Thanksgiving night tradition in 2008, but when A&M left the Big XII after the 2011 season, they attempted to keep the tradition as their own. When Texas A&M played LSU at home in 2014 and 2016, both games took place Thanksgiving night. However, LSU refused to schedule the games on the same night when the schools played in Baton Rouge in 2015 and 2017.

relationship between Texas and Texas A&M to Alabama and Auburn's or Ole Miss and Mississippi State's, where there's a built-in dynamic of big brother-little brother, one that often leaves A&M feeling disrespected. The way Texas handled the expansion conversation was the final straw in a long and antagonistic relationship between the schools.

Many traditions built into the culture at Texas A&M specifically address the University of Texas. At the start of the fourth quarter of A&M games, fans throw their arms across one another's shoulders and lock legs, with the left leg going in front of the person to your left because—and I swear to God I'm not making this up—"no man left behind." The crowd then rocks side to side, alternate rows moving in opposite directions. This coordinated swing is known as sawing, and the rationale is that they are "sawing off" the horns of Bevo, the Texas Longhorns' mascot.

Even the name Bevo, according to Aggies I talked with, originated when A&M students branded "13–0" into the Texas mascot in 1916, commemorating the 13–0 final score of the 1915 matchup. Texas was humiliated, so the account goes, and transformed the score into a word. A quick Internet search debunks the tale as folklore, but again, and as per usual in fan culture, there's no point in letting the truth get in the way of a good story.

To give another example, as the cadets march into the stadium, there are chants dedicated to insulting Texas. Aggies refer to Texas as t-sips, short for or tea-sippers, because Aggies claim the majority of Texas A&M enlisted in World War II while students at the University of Texas were busy sipping tea. The big city-small town, white collar-blue collar, liberal-conservative, high culture-agriculture dichotomy between Texas and A&M, so common among intrastate rivals, magnify the schools' differences. The similarities are minimized to ensure hatred between the schools. I'd come to see this as a well-worn pattern at this point in my trip; South Carolina and Clemson love to play up these tensions, as do both LSU and Mississippi State with Ole Miss. But, nowhere else in the SEC are the contrasts sharpened to such a jagged-edged point to be aimed at their rival like they are at Texas and Texas A&M.

If one were to patch together a coherent story about Texas based on A&M's Texas-themed traditions, it would read something like this: the Longhorns are condescending effeminate liberal hippie jerks who think they own the Lone Star state, and the Aggies are the all-American, crew-cut wearing, family-values-touting, quiet force for all that is good and just in the world, an unassuming underdog who has had enough of playing second fiddle to an oppressive university. To an outsider this characterization is amusing, if farcical. But it also has a logic to it. Who wouldn't want to paint themselves as the unassuming protagonist who finally rises up to thwart the evil force holding them down?

Without the annual Texas–Texas A&M game, however, the tension that powers the story described above is deflating. Indeed, one of the major drawbacks to conference realignments is that it often ends decades-long rivalries and leaves schools like Texas A&M without any traditional rivals on their schedule. The closest thing A&M has to a rival in the SEC is the LSU Tigers. The schools have played over fifty times, and they seemingly stand for very different things. The common perception is that LSU is the nastiest place to be an opposing fan on game weekend, and Texas A&M (along with Auburn) the friendliest. Still, it takes time for a rivalry to develop, and it's often a generational process. Texas A&M fans think LSU might develop into an archrival, but it will certainly take a full generation of playing every year on rivalry week before that happens. For the time being, the Yell Leaders—we'll get to them soon enough—have to rely on tired jokes about LSU fans smelling like corn dogs and being trashy Cajun folk in order to arouse in Aggie fans *some* sort of dislike for the Tigers.

During the spring I spent time on TexAgs.com, a fan site covering the Aggies. One fan reached out and we struck up a dialogue that carried over to e-mail and the occasional phone call throughout the spring and summer, culminating in him and his wife inviting me to stay at their home over Thanksgiving and show me around Texas A&M. David and Virginia are all-in Aggie backers, empty-nesters living in College Station after years in Austin and Marietta, Georgia. Their four daughters, all A&M graduates, all thought they were nuts for inviting a complete stranger from the Internet into their home.

Bearing kolaches from the Czech Stop, a famous bakery in West, Texas,[92] I arrived in College Station Tuesday evening. David, Virginia, and I sat around getting acquainted. An early topic was BBQ around the South and thoughts on the various styles and flavors. Though I enjoyed the South Carolina vinegar-based sauce on pulled pork sandwiches, I'm partial to the brisket burger at Fox Bros and ribs at Fat Matt's, both in Atlanta. The dry-rub ribs at Central BBQ in Memphis,

---

[92] Kolaches are round sweet roll pastries, usually containing fruit in the middle. If you're ever anywhere near West, Texas, be sure to stop through Czech Stop. You won't regret it.

however, are my absolute favorite. They wanted me to have a local comparison, so we went to Fargo's Pit BBQ in Bryan, Texas, a nationally ranked BBQ spot. Their ribs were as good as any I'd had, but their sliced brisket was dry and unremarkable.

⚑

There's a strip of bars on campus known as the Northgate area, but it seems small considering that Texas A&M boasts an enrollment of over 50,000. Forty years ago, supposedly, there was only one bar anywhere on campus, and though you were allowed to have a rifle in your dorm you weren't allowed to have alcohol. Deep in the heart of Texas. What A&M's campus lacks in aesthetic beauty, it compensates for in sheer size. Texas A&M boasts enormous tracts of land. Before Texas A&M was founded, the surrounding East Texas area was largely undeveloped. Even the name "College Station" stems from the fact that a train station had to be established at the point along the railway route nearest Texas A&M's campus. Students were jumping off the slow-moving train near A&M because it didn't stop until Bryan, Texas, some fifteen miles up the track. Railroad officials very wisely decided that wouldn't do, and constructed a makeshift train stop. Because the town had no name, they decided to call it College Station. The name stuck, or so the story goes.

Despite all the background and detailed information I learned about A&M, I didn't do anything special or significantly different with my time in College Station than I did at any other school I visited. The truth is, people in the Texas A&M community know almost everything about their school's history, and are more than willing to tell you all about it.

⚑

Sports Illustrated and ESPN were both on campus the week I visited. They were covering the fifteenth anniversary of the bonfire collapse that killed 12 students. While the university no longer has any official connection to the annual event, the student body has ensured that the tradition lives on. The Student Bonfire takes place about twenty miles north of campus in an enormous field where knee- and waist-high weeds line the bumpy, gravel-strewn ground that serves as parking for the event. The tradition has deep roots, and serves as one of the ties that binds Texas A&M together.

To assemble the bonfire students cut down trees and layer the logs vertically, and an outhouse—formerly known as the "tu frathouse[93]"—is placed atop the structure. Since LSU is the new Thanksgiving opponent, a purple-and-gold outhouse is now perched above the logs with phrases like "Geaux Home" on the outside of what is now being called the "litter box." A speaker's voice resonated across the fields to the makeshift parking lot. When I got closer I saw students, parents and children, husbands and wives, circled around the bonfire at least ten deep. A kettle corn stand and commemorative T-shirts for sale gave the bonfire the same atmosphere as a neighborhood carnival or Fourth of July block party.

Making my way through the crowd, I noticed a group of four younger-looking students, likely underclassmen, wearing matching green helmets. I stopped to ask what was up with the helmets. They took turns explaining their helmets' significance, how it reflected their class year or

---

[93] Inverting the UT for University of Texas and keeping the letters in lower case are both deliberate signs of disrespect.

what groups or clubs they belonged to; I followed along as best I could. I gathered that all four were freshmen, and when I asked how they already knew about all these detailed A&M traditions, they began to explain Fish Camp.

Fish Camp is a retreat that all freshman, transfer students, and graduate students—basically, all new Aggies—are required to attend. The purpose is to learn all about the history and traditions of Texas A&M and find a community and support system, because without one, a campus of over 50,000 can feel overwhelming and intimidating. Ronald, one of the freshmen with a helmet, extolled the benefits of the retreat: "We learned that there's tradition in everything here. And for the most part, it's pretty cool. Even these helmets: they're 90 percent tradition and 10 percent safety. They couldn't stop a pencil, but they're decorated for different things that identify you as part of various groups to other people working on the bonfire. It's just part of the culture here."

When I asked how they put the bonfire together, and what specific jobs they did, the group explained that since they're all freshmen, they mainly chopped down trees: "It's not an all-freshman thing, like hazing, but it's mostly freshman doing the chopping." Safety is obviously the name of the game so that what happened fifteen years ago never happens again. According to Ronald, "They'd gotten to the point where [the bonfire] was layered like a wedding cake and logs were stacked on top of logs. It was dangerous for years before the accident happened. The bonfire used to be ninety, a hundred feet tall. They used a million pounds of wood in those bonfires."

Somehow I managed to find my friends David and Virginia in the darkened crowd of roughly 9,000 Aggies, and they drew my attention to Bus 12, a refurbished yellow school bus decorated in maroon and white parked behind us. Hunter Goodwin, a former Texas A&M and NFL lineman (and co-owner of TexAgs.com), addressed the crowd from the overhead deck to begin the bonfire lighting ceremony. I circled the bus, taking note of all its bells and whistles and greeting the fans on the back deck. Along the driver's side windows I introduced myself to Ellen, the bus owner's daughter. She invited me inside. The seats were configured diner-style: two booths facing each other with a table in the middle. Collages of Texas A&M football pictures sat beneath a plastic veneer covering the tabletops. While Ellen's father, Roger, was busy controlling the music being pumped out to the crowd through the speaker system before and after Goodwin's address, Ellen and I stepped outside to talk where we could hear each other over the noise. We were the same age, and Ellen's a former student at Texas A&M, class of 2007. I should explain the former student thing. It's Texas A&M verbiage, according to Ellen. "We say 'former student' and not alum because no one's an ex-Aggie. You're always an Aggie."

Ellen described so many of the Texas A&M traditions in the course of our conversation that I'm sure I forgot half of them. We talked about the origins of Bus 12: how her Dad bought an old school bus, rehabbed it in 2006, and how it's been a fixture on campus ever since. Their family has no generational ties to the university, but her older brother Brent enrolled at A&M two years before Ellen, and when she visited, she fell in love with College Station instantly. When I asked her what drew her in, she highlighted the tradition and the sense of community. Much like the freshmen I talked to, she went into detail about the Fish Camps and how the school does so much to make newcomers feel welcome.

There's so much about Texas A&M that sticks out. The school has one of the top-5 highest enrollments nationally yet still manages to foster a sense of community unmatched anywhere in the SEC. Interestingly, there isn't a huge drinking culture on campus, which isn't a bad thing in Ellen's point of view. "Other schools I visited seemed like they were a party atmosphere, Greek life, and then some school spirit on game day. It was different here. It was like the school spirit was always there and the other stuff took a back seat. That's why I ended up here."

As the conversation carried on, we walked around to the other side of the bus and caught the end of Goodwin's speech about protecting the traditions that matter and holding tight to values that Texas A&M believes in. I met Ellen's husband Jesús and her brother Brent, and we watched the ritualistic procession of torches into the bonfire area. I was dumbfounded by how the crowd stood stone-still. Jesús must have seen the look of astonishment on my face, because he leaned in and whispered: "That's the thing about traditions here, we're reverent about them: when it's time to be quiet, we're all silent, and when it's time to be loud, we're all really loud."

When the specially appointed upperclassmen threw their torches on the logs and the bonfire began to blaze, the heat blew everyone back a couple steps. The crowd cheered wildly and everyone looked on in amazement for a few minutes, taking pictures and video before conversation kicked back in. When that happened, Jesús and Ellen schooled me on the cadet corps on campus and the function they serve. "Up until the 1960s, military training was mandatory on campus. If you were a student, you had to. You didn't have to enlist afterwards, but you had to be in the corps while you were enrolled," Jesús said by way of explanation. "It was General Rudder who changed all that. He was the Texas A&M president in the late 1950s and '60s. He made military training noncompulsory and allowed women and blacks to enter the school."

James Earl Rudder was World War II general and a former Aggie. He led the near-suicide mission at the Battle of the Bulge, and after the war he returned to College Station. If one person had the capacity to enact the seismic changes A&M went through at the time, it was General Rudder. In any place where tradition is held in such high regard, change is the scariest thing in the world. People fear change in general, but people who find immense comfort in routine and tradition fear change more than most. So it's not surprising that General Rudder's unpopular reforms met belligerent opposition. A lesser man, Ellen declared, would have crumbled and been unable to see such wholesale changes through to fruition in a place like College Station. "People picketed and protested outside Rudder's house at the time. And the first graduating class with women in it—there were about ten—put their pictures in the yearbook in the shape of a question mark. But if it weren't for Rudder's vision, the school would've collapsed. It couldn't have survived as a military institution. We wouldn't be 50,000 strong now."

The bonfire raged on, the only light in the night sky except for the soft glow from a low-hanging yellow moon. Ellen's father, the man who owns Bus 12, stepped away from his emcee duties and joined us. Roger was an engaging man from the outset. When we were introduced, his handshake was firm and he looked me in the eye. He explained later that he believes little things like making eye contact and delivering a strong handshake are becoming relics in modern society, and he loves how Texas A&M teaches their kids to do these things. Come to think of it, most people I met in College Station did the same when we met. I grew up with these manners and they're not lost on me, but it felt like the people I met at A&M inherently trusted me *because* I did these things.

What was compelling about Roger was his unflagging belief in what Texas A&M stands for. As a result, his conversational tone came off a bit preachy, even though I don't think he meant to be. It was clear that the man loves Texas A&M with all his heart and was super-excited to tell a guy like me—an outsider who's never visited—all about it. Interestingly enough, Roger never attended Texas A&M, making him something like the alpha male of T-shirt fans. He beamed as he told me he was Texas A&M Parent of the Year while Brent and Ellen were in school and how everything about A&M fosters community. He talked about meeting with various mothers' clubs and how they would raise money for scholarships and send care packages to all the kids at A&M from their home county.

In short order Roger touched on most of the things he loves about A&M: he loved how the conservative A&M values align with his own; and he loved that the university teaches its students to stand up for what they believe in, which, for him, included opposition to abortion and same-sex marriage. I didn't understand what anti-gay and anti-abortion rhetoric had to do with school spirit and the traditions and values fostered by the Aggie community, but Roger's passion burned like the bonfire raging over his shoulder, and his words bled into different topics so quickly that I never bothered to ask what the hell he was talking about.

After the Student Bonfire was Midnight Yell Practice, another tradition unique to Texas A&M. I had seen a watered-down version of it on the steps of the South Carolina state capitol back in August. I thought it was a strange phenomenon back then, but it's on a whole other level under the lights at Kyle Field. The easiest way to describe it is as a pep rally. In essence, that's what Midnight Yell Practice is: five male students dressed in overalls (but short-sleeved white shirts and white pants on game day) taking turns leading chants that the fans all know and addressing the crowd with typical rah-rah chest-thumping. They also sprinkle in a series of hand signals, which are passed back among the crowd, row by row, before the next chant begins. I'm sure learning the hand signals is on the agenda at Fish Camp.

The A&M Yell Leaders roared into their microphones about how the Aggies were going to wipe the floor with LSU to the thunderous applause of over 20,000 people. Because it was the last Yell Practice of the year, the head Yell Leader read a long poem written by some former Aggie. The poem was about the Aggie players and band meeting Saint Peter at the gates of heaven. It had the reverent tone of a eulogy, and the hushed crowd seemed truly moved. I found the whole ritual strange. I stood on the third deck scanning the first and second decks filled with A&M fans, and I couldn't wrap my head around it. There's even a whole science behind how they stand, leaning forward with their hands on their knees; supposedly, it maximizes the air pressed from their lungs. When they finished with the "Beat the Hell Outta LSU" chant and slapped their right biceps with their left hands repeatedly in a "screw you" motion, I lost it. I stood there laughing uncontrollably, looking down on this Aggie football staple. This was one tradition I'd *never* get.

Around 1:30 am, I picked up the best drive-thru tacos I've ever had in my life from a place called Fuego and headed back to David and Virginia's house. We discussed the book I'm writing, Texas A&M, and how the Aggie community has impacted their lives. We discussed porous Aggie defenses and where we think college football is headed. We discussed family and friends, God and service, political and social issues. We talked about life. I was grateful to be sitting in a living room in

College Station, Texas, in the wee hours of Thanksgiving morning with people I'd met only thirty-six hours earlier, opening up to one another, sharing ideas and laughs. I might not have learned everything about Southern fan culture, but when it comes to Southern hospitality I can say I've met enough people like David and Virginia along the way to know I've experienced it in full. At a certain point, Virginia looked down at her watch and asked, "Do you all know what time it is?" I looked at the clock above the dining room table and announced: "Oh my God, it's five o'clock in the morning!" "I haven't stayed up this late since I had a newborn in my arms," said David. And with the sun coming up, we all finally headed to bed.

⚑

It's amazing how many people stick around College Station on Thanksgiving. Students I talked to didn't think twice about it. To walk around the tailgate, you wouldn't know it was a holiday. On a sunny day with temperatures in the low-60s, it definitely didn't feel like the Midwestern Thanksgiving I was used to. David and I watched the Lions beat up on the Bears early in the day and I called home to wish everyone a happy holiday, but otherwise it felt like any other SEC game day to me. David and Virginia introduced me at their friends' tailgate, and after chatting for an hour, I went off wandering. I'd done this over a dozen times now this season and it never got old. Walking around a campus aimlessly on game day as a curious spectator and observer became a much-enjoyed ritual.

Near the Alumni Center, I found Brent, Ellen, and Jesús by Bus 12. The four of us cruised around campus in their golf cart. A bit later, we dropped the cart off and walked through the corps dorms. At the entrance underneath the archways leading to cadet housing, a cannon fired off a shot so loud my ears rang for two minutes straight despite the fact that my hands were cupped over them. The cannon blast signaled the start of Step Off and Walk In, a tradition where all cadet companies march into the stadium to their own chants. I hit my saturation point with all the military traditions during the Step Off and Walk In. Listening to chants that sounded so choppy and robotic ("I'm a Steamroller, Baby" sounded like "I'm-a-steam-ro-ller-bay-bee") and other ones that insinuated male Texas students are girls finally put me over the edge. Was it just now, or had something grated on my nerves the whole time I'd been on campus? Finally the thoughts hit me: these "traditions" were all rhythm and no soul, and outdated like a little drummer boy in modern warfare. I hated how stereotypically masculine and mechanized this all was.

When the last formation of cadets passed, Ellen, Brent, and Jesús looked at me with eyebrows raised high, as if to say, "How 'bout that? Wasn't that incredible?" I felt bad. I had met nothing but over-the-top friendly, outgoing, and kind people who made me feel welcome in their community, but all I could focus on was the robotic cumulative effect of all their traditions. The whole scene was kind of like a middle school student writing a paper chock full of exclamation points. If every sentence ends with an exclamation point, nothing is exclamatory. If every tradition is sacred and important, none of them really matter.

I headed to the stadium and found a $10 ticket in the north end zone. Tickets get cheap for non-marquee games, especially later in the season. And, if I'm being honest, I almost felt like I'd overpaid by halftime. The game was a snoozer, and I didn't find anything remotely interesting until halftime. But at halftime, I was entranced by the Fightin' Texas Aggie Band. Entirely befitting everything I've learned about Texas A&M,

the band moved with military precision and executed their turns at crisp 90-degree angles. The grand finale was a four-way shuffle where band members formed an X going out in all four corner directions from midfield before converging upon one another and navigating a perfect weave, all while keeping the beat. Of all the traditions at Texas A&M, that was the one that left me awestruck. I've never been all that interested in halftime shows, and until this trip I always used halftime to hit the bathroom and grab a Coke from the concession stand. But I tried to pay attention as I went around the SEC. A&M's band, along with Tennessee's, was the most intricate and precise halftime show around.

LSU led 20–7 at the end of the third quarter, which surely said more about the Tigers' inability to convert yardage and time of possession into points than it did about any resiliency on the Aggies' part. LSU ran for 384 yards and held the ball for over forty-one minutes, yet somehow still found themselves in a dogfight at the end. Texas A&M continued to hang on in a game where they were seriously outplayed, and the crowd of over 105,000 sought out any opportunity to get behind and lift their team. For example, on the Aggies' first offensive play of the second half, they hit a slip screen for a first down—and the crowd roared like they had just hit the pylon on a national championship-winning drive. As hard as something like this is to prove or know, I'm sure it wasn't a sarcastic cheer. You'll often hear these kinds of responses when a home team is playing like hot garbage and finally does something right. The Aggies showed a genuine excitement for finally having something to cheer about.

Again, the internal conflict boiled up. How do I feel about Texas A&M? I didn't experience this kind of ambivalence at any other school. I hated how hokey all their traditions were and the fact that their cheers were all choreographed and led by a boy band, but I loved how the fans were behind their team for sixty minutes and looked for any opportunity to provide a home-field advantage. I hated how homogenized the culture is, but I loved how genuine, hospitable, and outgoing all the people in the homogenized culture were.

A&M mounted a comeback in the fourth quarter. The Aggies finally put together two solid drives that resulted in 10 points. Despite dominating every facet of the game all night, LSU clung to a 20–17 lead with seven minutes to play. Texas A&M's defense stood firm and forced the Tigers to kick a field goal with two minutes left, making the score 23–17 and giving freshman quarterback Kyle Allen and company the chance to stage a last minute, come-from-behind victory. The Aggie offense completed 2 passes and had the ball at midfield. After two incomplete passes, however, the game effectively ended on a controversial no-call. On 3rd and 10, an LSU defensive linemen jumped into the neutral zone before the snap. As quarterbacks are taught to do on defensive offsides, Allen threw up a jump ball downfield.[94] The pass went into double coverage and was intercepted. No flag ever came though; the game was over. LSU ran out the clock and left College Station with the victory.

Back at David and Virginia's house, I met their daughter Michelle and her husband Craig. The five of us stood around the kitchen island rehashing the game and the state of Texas A&M football heading into the off-season. I imagined families standing around kitchens and living rooms all throughout Aggieland that night doing the same. In a way,

---

[94] The idea is that it's a free play, so it doesn't matter what the quarterback does.

that was our Thanksgiving dinner, discussing what coaches need to be fired and which units underperformed, the underclassmen who represent a bright future, and recruits who might be able to come in and help out as freshmen. Not knowing nearly as much about A&M as everyone else there, I mostly listened.

The four of them felt the good thing about a 7–5 season is that other schools wouldn't try to poach Coach Kevin Sumlin this off-season, as was the case in 2013. In a lot of ways, this time of year is every bit as exciting for all the off-the-field drama as what we wait all year to see on Saturdays. The head coaching carousel rides from late November through January. In general, schools who fire a coach need to find a replacement by the first week of January in order to reassure the commits in their recruiting class, aggressively poach players committed to other schools, and make final pitches to uncommitted players.

The dead period in recruiting—the time between Christmas and early January when coaches are prohibited from initiating contact with recruits—serves as the calm before the storm. Once that period is over, the final month leading up to National Signing Day in early February is chaos. There's so much hope for the future projected onto these high school seniors, and following the recruiting trail down the home stretch is an intoxicating experience for fans. It's no wonder recruiting services and websites have become such a profitable marketplace over the past twenty years. Die-hard fans, myself included, get high off imagining the next program-changing blue-chippers coming in to put our team over the top next fall.

College football, especially at the D-1 level, is a results-driven business. And as we sat around the kitchen, the family agreed that while the Aggies may have elite talent coming in to help the defense next season, their coaching wasn't good enough. They liked defensive coordinator Mark Snyder, but being a good guy isn't what you hire a coach for; you hire them to get a job done. Sure enough, the next day Snyder was fired as defensive coordinator. I set out for Tuscaloosa the next morning with the coaching carousel already spinning behind me.

#15 Auburn vs. #1 Alabama

November 29, 2014

Tuscaloosa, Alabama

The road rolled past in shades of black asphalt and grey concrete with yellow lines pinging my brain like Morse code, interminably, week after week, town after town, and I would look for ways to pass the time and keep boredom at bay. On the ten-and-a-half-hour drive from College Station to Tuscaloosa on Black Friday, I had plenty of time to think about what the Iron Bowl means. The Iron Bowl is the annual meeting between Alabama and Auburn, two of the best teams in all of college football and arguably its fiercest intrastate rivals. The winner of the Iron Bowl has gone on to win four of the last five national championships; the fifth was lost on a touchdown with eleven seconds left. So, when I think about big-time college football in the South, and must-see sporting events in general, I think of the Iron Bowl. Still, I've come to learn that with all the major Southern rivalries, it's always about more than the game. There's a mythology surrounding the Auburn–Alabama rivalry that somehow overshadows a game that regularly lives up to its tremendous hype. My limited understanding is that the rivalry isn't about one day—it's year-round, and permeates all facets of daily life, from office politics to family dynamics, throughout the state of Alabama. When I conceived of this trip, the first game I locked into my schedule was the Iron Bowl. You can't claim to know the SEC, have an opinion on rivalries in the South, or begin to fathom the passion of Southern fans without seeing it.

The 2013 Iron Bowl might have had the most thrilling end to a college football game ever played, with respect given to Cal–Stanford[95] and the dozens of game-winning Hail Marys over the years. For the few who don't know, Alabama and Auburn were tied in the closing seconds of regulation and headed for overtime. Alabama was driving in an attempt to kick a last-second, game-winning field goal. T. J. Yeldon caught a pass with seconds remaining and stepped out of bounds as time expired. Officials reviewed the play and ruled that Yeldon stepped out with one second left on the clock. Alabama lined up for a 57-yard field goal. When the kick fell short, Auburn defensive back Chris Davis caught the ball a yard shy of the back line of the end zone and returned it 109 yards for a game-winning touchdown. Auburn won 34–28, claimed the SEC Championship game the following week, and played for the BCS National Championship. Alabama accepted a Sugar Bowl bid, and Oklahoma beat the Tide convincingly. To hear Alabama fans' version of events, the Crimson Tide went into the tank after the Iron Bowl loss

---

[95] November 20, 1982: "The band is on the field! The band is on the field!"

and didn't care about or show up for the Sugar Bowl. How do you bounce back and play another game with heart after losing your own Super Bowl in such excruciating fashion?

Alabama entered this year's game as the top seed in the playoff rankings and sporting a 10–1 record, while Auburn ranked fifteenth and had an 8–3 record. Auburn's offense was potent enough to play spoiler against anybody, though, and the fact that they were playing Alabama would make their spoiling that much sweeter. As clichéd as the saying is, there's truth in it: records truly don't matter when archrivals meet.

⚑

I was staying with James and Gina, the couple who had hosted me during my first Bama game in late September. We drove to campus together around noon. Much of the earlier part of the day felt like déjà vu. We parked in the same spot we did in September and walked their dogs, Jack and Rocky Balboa, down Paul W. Bryant Drive zigzagging our way through alleys and past apartment complexes. As we approached their usual tailgate, I saw many familiar faces from the Florida game in September, even though I'd forgotten most of their names. James introduced me to his buddy Chad, who I hadn't met at the first game. When Chad asked me about my first trip to Tuscaloosa, he appeared genuinely interested. So I was honest with him about feeling unwelcome and out of place for the only time all season. He suggested that the Notre Dame shirt I was wearing might've had something to do with it, as the older generation—the Bama backers who were around through the '70s—have a lingering hatred for the Irish. In trying to explain why I experienced such heavy blowback, Chad, who is an Alabama alum, discussed the stereotype that Bama grads are good people and sidewalk fans are trash. In his view, being a decent Alabama fan isn't about whether or not you're an alum. What matters is how you represent the university—how you treat people and carry yourself—while you're wearing Crimson Tide gear. That made a lot of sense. We dissected the stereotypes—the Finebaum Show-calling nuts and the uppity elitist frat stars—and how they don't apply to most of the fan population. "Neither of those represent what Alabama stands for, and they're both an embarrassment. But the public perception doesn't see the snobby frat guys. They only see the ignorant hick fans. Us and Mississippi will never shake those stereotypes. They're not true for the majority but that's just how people see us." In the same way that some people on the road will hear me say that I'm from Chicago and ask about murders and crime and how dangerous it is, some people are always going to see people from Alabama and Mississippi as uneducated country bumpkins. It's hard to shake stereotypes.

University Avenue was packed with people shuffling along in both directions, the foot traffic too dense for normal strides. Scalpers, college kids, and stuffed shirts alike stood around selling tickets. This is the sweet spot for ticket sales, three to four hours before kickoff. It's fun to watch, like a trading floor spilled over onto a college campus. I stood around Denny Chimes for a few minutes watching the show and then I took a closer look at the structure. I noticed it the first time I was here, but hadn't taken time to peruse. On the back, the names of every Alabama team captain since 1947 are engraved in the concrete along with their hand and shoe prints. Turns out, Tuscaloosa's version of the Hollywood Walk of Fame stands beneath a mini-bell chime tower on University Avenue.

The thing about the Quad is that it seems to stretch on for days in every direction during a tailgate. I walked through it, working hard to find my buddy Bob's tailgate. I met Bob when he was trying to buy tickets for his kids at the Alabama–Tennessee game. We traded texts and he gave me a general area to search for his tent. The problem was that trying to find one person at random behind Denny Chimes is roughly the same as finding a 50-yard line ticket lying on the ground. So I was searching, but at the same time, I wasn't in any rush.

Wandering around a game-day tailgate scene alone made me feel so small and insignificant, but the experience also never failed to amaze me. It's easy to feel like somebody within your community, especially if you contribute to that community in any constructive way. But go to a town that normally houses 100,000 people when 180,000, 200,000 people are condensed inside a two-square-mile area, and you'll find you don't really know anyone. Finding your bearings is like contemplating the universe; you can't help but feel miniscule. In that moment, when I felt tiny and awestruck by the blur of faces belonging to people dressed in crimson, white, and houndstooth, I understood that the most appealing part of being a die-hard fan is belonging to something bigger than yourself. I saw it in the swirl of school colors, the mass of tents and grills, coolers and spreads, lawn chairs and big-screen TVs. For some fans, tailgating and attending the game is a fun way to spend a Saturday afternoon, but for others, this "thing" swallows them whole. It becomes their identity.

I'd given up on finding Bob and his tailgate after walking through the Quad for half an hour. I was headed back toward the front of Denny Chimes when I stopped for a second to decide where to wander next. Just then, Bob stepped in front of me with his hand extended and a smile on his face. The ticket found me. We shook hands and made small talk and walked back into the Quad to his family's tailgate. Bob's one of those people who has a way of making a stranger feel like family. He called me son, and even though I doubt he's more than fifteen years older than me, somehow it fit. He introduced me to his friends Jason and Jessica and wandered off to find his wife. Jessica thought Bob was crazy for inviting a total stranger to their tailgate. That's one of the by-products of Southern hospitality I've noticed: every time someone goes out of their way to make me feel welcome and included, there's one member of their family who thinks they're nuts for inviting Stranger Danger over.

Jason and Jessica both attended Alabama and started dating while Jessica was still an undergrad. They've been married a few years now. Neither knows anything other than Alabama; they were born in Alabama, grew up as fans, became students, and are now young alums with season tickets. They're going to raise a family in Alabama and watch their season tickets creep closer and closer to midfield as the years go by. Jessica said she was a lifer before she had a choice in the matter: "They brainwash you and you're a fan for life by the time you're two." There was neither pride nor bitterness in Jessica's declaration; it was matter-of-fact. It's as if Jason and Jessica both knew that they never had a choice in being Alabama fans. They've accepted it as a certainty, like death and taxes.

The biggest rivalry in all college football carried with it the biggest price tag for tickets, according to the StubHubs of the world. I found a ninth-row upper deck seat on the 30-yard line for $100. To reach the upper deck, you have to walk up a spiral concrete structure. There's a triple-length golf cart that makes trips up and down to take people who can't, shouldn't, or don't want to walk up the steep curves. At the top, I stopped to take it all in for a minute. A backlog of people stacked on top of each other as the line into the seating area stood still. Fans of both teams jittered and shuffled their feet in place waiting for the line to move. After a couple minutes, the traffic jam broke up and we all headed to our seats. The people around me were anxious and eager to chat. I got the sense they would've done anything to distract themselves as the thirty-five minutes until kickoff ticked off second by excruciatingly slow second. On my left was a man in his mid-forties named John. Like most of the people I met here, he's a lifelong Alabamian. Born and raised a Bama fan, John's a teacher in some small lakefront town in northern Alabama. The unique thing about John is that his pride in being from the state of Alabama superseded his pride in being a Crimson Tide fan. He gushed about the kind, outgoing, and genuine people of Alabama. When I told him I'm a teacher thinking about relocating from Chicago, it's like I was a blue-chip prospect. He started giving me a sales pitch trying to get me to commit to Alabama.

On my right were Courtney and Marie, young Alabama grads in their mid-twenties. When I asked about their shakers, or pom-poms, it quickly led to a conversation about superstitions. I've always been aware of superstitions as they relate to sports. I know how silly they are, and still I've fallen prey to thinking they matter. I remember the Chicago Bears–Arizona Cardinals game on Monday Night Football when I was in college, the "They are who we thought they were" game,[96] during which my buddies and I all switched seats at halftime. My friend Pat

---

[96] October 16, 2006: The Arizona Cardinals led the undefeated Chicago Bears 20–0 at halftime. The Bears staged a comeback and won 24–23. But the game is best remembered for the postgame press conference meltdown of Cardinals coach Dennis Green.

even changed into jean overalls at halftime. On some goofy, childish level, we believed our front-room halftime adjustments had something to do with the comeback victory. Superstitions are completely illogical and have no bearing on the outcome of any game, but that doesn't stop fans from giving them power.

Courtney throws her shaker in the trash after an Alabama loss. She discarded the pom-pom she waved during the Ole Miss game in October but had been using the one in her hand for every game since. As bad as she might be, her uncle's superstitions are on a whole other level, Courtney explained. "First, he wears the same outfit every week. It's funny seeing him in the same shirt in pictures year after year. Second, he drives through the same Milo's[97] and orders the same fried chicken meal every week on his way to the tailgate, and third, if Alabama loses, he changes his underwear and socks. Otherwise, he wears the same ones."

To someone who's not a fan, superstitions must seem like bizarre occult rituals or the make-believe of small children playing, but what Courtney described makes perfect sense to me. Even though I've given up on all of my game-day superstitions, I cast no judgment toward those still holding on. I've given a lot of thought to why we have superstitions, and I've decided that they make fans who have no real connection to the team and no bearing on the outcome of games feel like they're a part of the black magic that results in a victory. When the emotion we feel as fans overrides our common sense, it's often not enough to just be a spectator cheering our team on; we need to feel like we make a difference. So we tell ourselves ridiculous stories, tell ourselves that if we wear a

---

[97] A fast-food chain in Alabama.

certain thing, stand a certain way, or eat or drink a particular meal or beverage, we provide the wind at our team's back on game day.

Just like Jason and Jessica told me about being brainwashed into Alabama fandom from the time they were toddlers, Courtney saw the same thing firsthand growing up: "My little brother was, like, two and I remember one of the first words he said was 'Aubie.' He got it from my Aunt and Uncle who are Auburn fans. My dad was furious. He had sit-downs with my brother to correct this. I remember it was a huge problem for my dad. He couldn't have his only son growing up an Auburn fan."

That's one of the things I kept hearing about down South that I don't ever remember hearing about as a child in Chicago. We don't have nearly the same level of indoctrination at such a young age up north. I've met dozens of people on this trip who explained that their formative memories were of wearing the jersey or plastic helmet of the team they love as adults, or sitting on their daddy's knee watching the ball game on Saturday afternoon at age three or four. With the exception of people who move down south later in life and get baptized through years of total immersion, a person can only really absorb the culture by being born into it. When learning that Alabama is good and Auburn is bad or vice versa happens at the same time as learning the alphabet and words like "mommy" and "daddy," how can you be a casual fan? It's nearly impossible. The only way out is to rebel completely and do the opposite. That's why you see so many lone Auburn fans in an Alabama family or vice versa. It's no wonder there are so many black sheep in college football families. When we want to break out of a learned behavior, the easiest thing to do is its exact opposite.

Alabama tried an onside kick to start the game, which caught everyone in the stadium off guard. Auburn recovered, and on their first play from scrimmage turned the ball over on a fumbled swing pass. As far as starts go, this one foreshadowed the twists to come on a chilly late November night in Tuscaloosa.

<u>1</u>

An 8-yard T. J. Yeldon touchdown run capped a lightning-quick five-play, 35-yard drive, and the Iron Bowl was off and running. *Alabama 7, Auburn 0.* Auburn moved the ball 72 yards in twelve plays before having to settle for a field goal. *Alabama 7, Auburn 3.* Blake Sims hooked up with Amari Cooper on a 17-yard touchdown pass to cap another five-play drive. *Alabama 14, Auburn 3.* Auburn finessed the ball down the field with ease, 68 yards on eleven plays, before having to settle for another field goal. *Alabama 14, Auburn 6.*

Auburn can move the ball on anyone, but during the season they frequently found ways to come up short in key situations. Against Mississippi State, Auburn failed to convert three first-half turnovers into touchdowns, settling instead for field goals. The 12 points they missed out on (including extra points) might have come in handy and changed the momentum in a game where they lost by 15. Being great between the 20s but coming up short in the red zone, where it matters most, was the story of Auburn's season. Alabama's offense, meanwhile, hummed when it wanted to. Most of the season it scored at will. The Crimson Tide defense wasn't the stout defense of 2009, 2011, or 2012, though. It wasn't as good as it'd been in recent years, but it managed to get the job done with the offense setting the tone, unlike typical Alabama teams under Saban. All of which is to say: in so many ways, the first quarter served as both a microcosm of both teams' seasons and a slow burn building to the volcanic eruption about to occur over the next forty-five minutes.

2

Another long Tiger drive (fourteen plays, 73 yards) sputtered deep in Alabama territory and resulted in a field goal. *Alabama 14, Auburn 9.* Blake Sims threw an interception at the start of the next drive, setting up Auburn with great field position. On the second play of the drive, Auburn struck with a 34-yard touchdown pass from Nick Marshall to Sammie Coates. *Auburn 16, Alabama 14.*

It started to feel a bit uncomfortable inside the stadium when Auburn took the lead. I remember feeling conflicted; as someone writing a book on SEC football, I needed Alabama to win and win again in the SEC Championship, otherwise there's no SEC team in the inaugural playoff. But as someone who was welcomed with open arms at Auburn and shunned at Alabama, I was pulling for Auburn in earnest. Alabama receiver Christian Jones's 29-yard punt return shook the stadium out of its lull. Sims completed passes of 15, 13, and 21 yards on the first three plays of the possession to put the Crimson Tide inside the 10-yard line. And on 4th and goal from the 1-yard line, T. J. Yeldon broke into the student section end zone. The crowd erupted, and the shakers shook as that ever-catchy Alabama fight song boomed from the Million Dollar Band in the corner of the end zone. Alabama reclaimed the lead and the momentum. *Alabama 21, Auburn 16.*

Auburn took over with 1:26 left in the half. After a 7-yard run by Nick Marshall on first down, Marshall hit Sammie Coates deep again, this time for a 68-yard touchdown. The quarter of the stadium filled with Auburn fans screamed and shouted while a silent gloom enshrouded the rest of the crowd. The ups and downs of an Iron Bowl are accompanied by wild mood swings—maybe stronger than I've ever witnessed in sports—that reverberate through the crowd. When I think of Auburn scoring inside of Bryant-Denny Stadium, the expression "deafening silence" immediately comes to mind. *Auburn 23, Alabama 21.*

Rather than running out the clock with fifty-four seconds remaining in the half, Alabama decided to try and put a drive together. Auburn corner Johnathan Ford sat on a curl route and intercepted a poorly read pass by Blake Sims. Auburn had the ball with thirty-seven seconds before halftime. Marshall hit Sammie Coates again—Coates abused the Bama secondary—on first down for 40 yards, bringing the Tigers down to Alabama's 1-yard line. Then, clock management issues hit. I couldn't contain the Auburn fan within. I screamed expletives as Auburn ran the ball with Cameron Artis-Payne on 1st and goal for a loss of 2 yards, letting the clock run down to 00:04 before calling time-out. When I remembered where I was, I felt compelled to explain to the people around me that I was upset with poor clock management on general principle. In case they weren't aware, I restated the obvious, "y'all got a huge break there, that was absolutely brutal," before Auburn kicked a field goal as time expired in the first half. *Auburn 26, Alabama 21.*

Half

At halftime the mood on the concourse was somewhere between dejected and conspiratorial. I don't mean conspiratorial in the usual sports sense of "the refs are out to get us." I don't think even the most biased Alabama fan would think that SEC officials would go out of their way to try and make the only team with playoff aspirations lose. I mean conspiratorial in the sense of guys putting their heads together over cigarettes and whiskey-topped Cokes concocting a plan to resolve the defensive and quarterback problems Alabama faced in the first half. I felt like a spy who'd successfully infiltrated an intelligence cache behind enemy lines. I peppered the group with questions so I could to hear more and more of their armchair coaching. They were just so damn entertaining.

"Jesus, the defense is all over the place out there."

"Right, what do you think we gotta do to fix that?"

"We need to cover Coates, and Collins has to stay back and cover deep."

"We gotta keep Marshall contained and lock down Coates."

"Yeah, yeah, you're right. But what about Sims? He's turnin' the ball over."

"Oh Jesus, we gotta run the ball."

"You think we should pound it between the tackles?"

"More Henry. More Yeldon. Then when it loosens up let him find Cooper."

We bantered on like this for a good five, ten minutes. I'm almost positive none of the five of us knew each other. Standing around the concourse, we stumbled upon a strategy session for the second half, and when we'd decided what all of Alabama's halftime adjustments ought to be, we departed as if we were breaking a huddle. We all walked away, if not in different directions, then at different speeds. Everyone went their own way. But before we walked off, everyone but me exchanged a "Roll Tide."

I walked back to my seat laughing and thinking of that ESPN commercial with the best man giving a wedding speech: "Y'all don't even know he was a virgin until he was 28, but now...Roll Tide." And it's real, it's all real! I think I felt the way Bill Murray described when he talked about being in the announcer's booth with Harry Caray at Wrigley Field and opening his mini-fridge to find it stocked with Budweiser. People assumed Caray drank his way through Cubs games for years, but nobody knew for sure. Murray is said to have remarked, "It was like waking up on Christmas morning and finding out Santa Claus is real." That's how this makeshift powwow felt to me. Total strangers huddle up at halftime of the Iron Bowl, concoct some in-game adjustments, and part ways with a "Roll Tide." I spent the last few minutes of halftime back at my seat with a shit-eating grin on my face that I couldn't explain to the Alabama fans around me. I didn't know how, and even if I could, they wouldn't have understood why it made me so happy.

3

On Alabama's second offensive snap Blake Sims threw another interception, this one to Jonathan Jones. Auburn marched down and scored in three minutes, hitting pay dirt on a 5-yard pass from Marshall to Quan Bray. At this point, the Auburn cheers felt almost inappropriate, like starting chants in the back row of a funeral. That's how sharp the contrast between Alabama fans' distraught and stunned silence and Auburn fans' giddy cheers felt. *Auburn 33, Alabama 21*. Alabama needed to respond with a score. The Tide put together an eight-play, 75-yard drive in three minutes and a reinvigorated crowd was back into the game. *Auburn 33, Alabama 27 (extra point blocked)*.

What happened next, in the course of four plays, marked the turning point in the game. Auburn had walked the ball down the field with little resistance. Inside the red zone, Auburn had a 3rd and 5 at the 16-yard line, and on that play Duke Williams broke wide open near the Alabama sideline and headed into the end zone. There wasn't a defender within yards of Williams, but he couldn't pull in what would've been a touchdown pass from Nick Marshall. Auburn kicked a field goal, their fifth of the night. *Auburn 36, Alabama 27.* On Alabama's first play from scrimmage after the field goal, Sims hit Amari Cooper for a 75-yard touchdown. *Auburn 36, Alabama 34.* At that point, I knew. I think most people in the stadium knew, too. Some games don't have a definitive turning point, but this one would've been obvious to even a non-football fan. It all happened in four plays. The game was still exciting until late. Auburn didn't quit, and they were still winning when the game turned on them, but the Tigers lost then and there.

<u>4</u>

Alabama leaned on Auburn and began to pour it on. The climax already happened late in the third quarter, and the fourth was the inevitable conclusion coming to fruition. Blake Sims scored on an 11-yard run early in the fourth quarter. *Alabama 42, Auburn 36 (two-point conversion good).* Blake Sims threw a 6-yard touchdown pass to DeAndrew White halfway through the fourth quarter. *Alabama 48, Auburn 36 (two-point conversion no good).* Derrick Henry scored on a 25-yard run with under four minutes remaining in the game. *Alabama 55, Auburn 36.* Corey Grant scored on a 5-yard run with twenty seconds left. *Alabama 55, Auburn 44 (two-point conversion good).*

On the heels of that missed third-down pass and subsequent field goal, Alabama racked up 28 straight points in less than fifteen minutes. When it was time to kick into another gear, Alabama found a way to do just that. All-American receiver Amari Cooper had another 200-yard game with 3 touchdowns. I realized that I witnessed all three of his 200-yard receiving games in person over the season. The game itself ended up being the highest-scoring Iron Bowl in the rivalry's history: 99 points. Alabama beat Auburn 55–44 and was headed to the SEC Championship in Atlanta.

More than the intensity and the back-and-forth of an exciting Iron Bowl game, what I'll remember most fondly for years to come is the spectacle of fans interacting with "Sweet Home Alabama" and "Dixieland Delight" when the songs played over the loudspeakers at commercial breaks in the second half. I heard them both in September during the Florida game, but the experience was completely different at the Iron Bowl. Everyone knows the fan lyrics and the interplay between the actual songs and the echo and reverb of the better part of 102,000 people singing the custom-made fills was one of the most incredible, awe-inspiring sports related moments I've ever experienced.

As "Dixieland Delight" trickled in during a fourth-quarter commercial break, the pom-poms cracked sharp as a whip; you could hear the snap playing in time, in near-perfect harmony. My jaw fell open and my eyes welled up. It was everything I've ever loved about sports and sports fans.

> *"Spend my dollar - ON BEER*
>
> *parked in a holler 'neath the mountain moonlight - ROLL TIDE*
>
> *Hold her up tight - AGAINST THE WALL*
>
> *make a little lovin' - ALL NIGHT*

a little turtle dovin' on a Mason-Dixon night – FUCK AUBURN

fits my life - AND LSU

oh so right - AND TENNESSEE, TOO

my Dixieland Delight."

After the 2014 Iron Bowl, the song was officially banned from games at Bryant-Denny Stadium. Part of the reason is that in the following verse, after nearly every line, the student section yelled FUCK AUBURN. Political correctness does a lot of good in society. It shames and teases out necessary changes, but sometimes being PC overextends its usefulness and robs us of good clean fun; this is one of those times. Please don't be confused: there's nothing at odds about excessive cursing and good clean fun in this case. Regardless of the profanity, or maybe precisely because of the profanity, seeing "Dixieland Delight" during an Iron Bowl should be on any sports fan's bucket list. Instead, it's being taken away because of the fear of offending people or giving Alabama a black eye. I'm not an Alabama fan by any means, but it made me sad that one of the most beautiful in-game traditions anywhere in sports is being sucked out by righteousness.

SEC Championship

#16 Missouri vs. #1 Alabama

December 6, 2014

Atlanta, Georgia

I wasn't even remotely excited for the SEC Championship game. Part of the reason was that I already knew the outcome. There wasn't a doubt in my mind Alabama would win and move on to the College Football Playoff. The larger part of it, though, was the venue. The game took place at the Georgia Dome in Atlanta. I'm not knocking the Falcons' home field in any way. In fact, I found the stadium impressive. But I'd grown so accustomed to, and fond of, college campuses that the venue would inevitably be a letdown. Lack of game-day atmosphere dimmed my spirit unquestionably. I missed the fields of trampled grass and densely packed tents, each filled with fans in lawn chairs watching the early game on the big screen, with grills and spreads across long Alabama or Missouri tablecloths. I missed knowing that whatever game I was attending was the only show in town; that there were no other big-city attractions, no exciting nightlife. I loved that all season long, every Saturday afternoon or evening, I was immersed in an event whose singular focus made the town double in size. And strange as it is to say, I missed the overwhelming, almost debilitating anxiety that would overtake my system week after week when I first realized that I was completely surrounded by strangers; strangers I had nothing in common with except a love of college football; strangers who all shared one common, unifying bond that I wasn't a part of.

I parked down the back alley behind the College Football Hall of Fame, where a lone black-and-gold tent stood in the parking lot. The faded asphalt of the lot and the multilevel concrete parking garage in the background made this group of Missouri Tigers look completely out of place. They weren't in their natural habitat. It was like seeing animals at the zoo: there's nothing alarming about it, but you know that they don't belong there. These Tigers belonged on a college campus. The crew had trekked from Columbia and surrounding towns down to Atlanta for a game they were trying to convince themselves their team had a chance of winning. If that's not dedication, I don't know what is.

After exchanging pleasantries with the group, I spoke at greater length with two of the tailgaters, Kevin and Rob. Kevin was a couple years younger than me, and Rob was in his mid-thirties. The first thing I asked was how they felt about Mizzou's chances. Both stammered a bit before Rob responded, "I think if [defensive ends Markus] Golden and [Shane] Ray can get a pass rush going early and keep them out of rhythm, we'll have a chance." Kevin nodded vigorously and chimed in, "Yeah, we definitely have to get after their quarterback. And we really need [quarterback] Maty [Mauk] to come out hot. He's really up and down, we need him to have a big game and extend plays with his legs. If Maty has a big game, we've got a good shot."

"You guys don't sound too confident," I suggested, offering the obvious. Rob agreed: "I mean, we've got a good team but Bama's tough, man. We can win, but we need a lot of things to go right for that to happen." Most Missouri fans I met throughout the day spoke with the same tone of cautious optimism, which belied a feeling of resignation not too deep beneath the surface. No Tiger fan could bring themselves to say the Tide would roll, but homerism can only take you so far.

We talked about how both analysts and fans overlook Missouri when I mentioned my surprise at Mizzou making it to the championship game. Both Kevin and Rob felt Missouri got no respect and it had been that way since they joined the SEC. "We came in at the same time as A&M and we've been to two SEC Championship games. They haven't been to one, but they're the legit team because of Johnny Football? Gimme a break," Rob bellowed between long slugs of his Jack and Coke. I asked if that's because Mizzou plays in an Eastern Division that hasn't been nearly as tough as the West the previous three seasons. Kevin was quick to counter: "I guess that might be part of it, but we beat A&M two of the last three years, so I don't really see it."

I refrained from asking the last question I wanted to because I could tell I was hitting a nerve. They weren't annoyed with me as an individual, but with the fact that nobody respects the Missouri Tigers program. Almost all committed fans see their team in a more favorable light than others and become defensive about perceived slights, but this was a unique case because those slights were actually real, and they manifested themselves in a uniformly negative national perception. Of course Rob and Kevin were annoyed; their team is a 10–win afterthought. The last question I wanted to ask was, "Would Missouri have made it to the SEC Championship game if they played in the West?" The answer was obvious and the question would've been needlessly antagonistic, so instead I wished their team luck and moseyed on toward the stadium.

It's hard to say whether Missouri was truly underrated and overlooked, or if they simply took advantage of an easy road, being the alpha team in the beta division. Missouri benefitted greatly from their two cross-divisional games this season. They played Texas A&M and Arkansas, the bottom two teams in the Western division, and only won each game by a touchdown. Georgia annihilated Missouri 34–0 in October, but again Mizzou benefitted from Georgia's inability to beat the inferior teams on their schedule (South Carolina and Florida).[98] Still, the Missouri Tigers needed to win six straight SEC games to punch their ticket to Atlanta. Yes, they were the six of the seven worst SEC teams in the conference by record, but Mizzou beat them all in conference with no free wins. They earned the right.

Beer vendors lined the sidewalk between the Georgia Dome and the Georgia World Congress Center, and a carnival-sized pop-up tent sold Alabama, Missouri, and other various SEC merchandise caddy-corner

---

[98] While Georgia had beat Missouri head-to-head, Mizzou represented the SEC East in the conference championship because Georgia had lost two conference games. Meanwhile, the Georgia loss was the only blemish on the Tigers' conference record.

from the Phillips Arena. Otherwise, it would've been hard to differentiate this day from any other Saturday in downtown Atlanta. If it weren't for the crimson and white and black and gold everywhere, these people could have just as easily been milling about in anticipation of a Taylor Swift concert or an Atlanta Hawks game. People sipped cold beers and chomped peanuts and pretzels on the balconies and patios of bars while the scalpers plied their trade. They didn't seem overly optimistic about turning a profit, asking only face value for tickets two hours before kickoff.

The anticipation of kickoff infuses life across college campuses every fall Saturday like dawn breaking in the east. You can hear it in the way voices carry, and feel it in the way people glow when talking about their star players and high hopes for the season in September. I expected it to reach a boiling point by the time Alabama and Missouri fans finally arrived in Atlanta the first Saturday in December, but the atmosphere was flat, like it didn't matter that the sun had already set on every other SEC school. When you take the college game off-campus, it loses the appeal that makes game-day culture so alluring in the first place.

I found a ticket for face value on the 10-yard line fifteen rows off the field in the heart of a Missouri section. An affable couple in their fifties sold me the ticket after making me promise I wouldn't cheer for Alabama. I didn't catch the name of the woman, but the man introduced himself as Doug. When I met them at our seats, Doug's wife started introducing me to their friends as their adopted son from Chicago. Doug's high school buddy, Tim, and Tim's wife Margo occupied the seats on my right. They provided another great example of the split loyalties sports fans sometimes have. Both grew up in Missouri and attended Mizzou in the early '80s. A few years later, Tim's job took them to Tennessee, where they've lived ever since. Both are Missouri and Tennessee fans. Margo raved about the Peyton Manning era and the national championship season in '98, and how those years solidified her status as a Tennessee Vols fan for life. Margo joked about how some years later, she noticed just how many kids—boys and girls—named Peyton attended her kids' grade school: "Peyton must have been the most popular baby name in the whole state of Tennessee in the late '90s." When they talked about Missouri joining the SEC, both expressed a mixture of excitement and conflict. When Missouri plays Tennessee, Tim roots for Mizzou and Margo pulls for the Vols. Another house divided on game day.

It was still forty-five minutes until kickoff, so I bought popcorn and a Coke at the concession stand, and when I came back, Doug, Tim, and another childhood friend were trading high school football stories, reliving old glories, and inquiring about long-lost friends and generally checking in on how everyone's doing these days. Though they were twenty-five years older than me and I've never been to whatever Missouri town they grew up in, it didn't matter. I was part of their conversation. I didn't need to be from that time or that small town for their stories to be entertaining—stories about pulling pranks against their rival during homecoming week, or their crew's hell raiser getting caught by the police in the back seat of a car with the town sheriff's daughter. I laughed with them the same as if their memories were my own.

Alabama won the coin toss and took the ball to start the game. The surgical precision of their first drive cracked Missouri like a series of lead jabs and straight right crosses, leaving the Tigers dazed and slack-jawed: Sims to Fowler for 13; Sims to Cooper for 6; Yeldon for 11; Sims to Cooper for 4; Cooper for 9; Henry for 5; Sims to White for 6; Sims to

Cooper for 10; Henry for 3. And then, the inevitable: Yeldon plunged into the end zone from one yard out. There was no wasted motion, no hesitation, no doubt that Alabama was taking that ball to the end zone. In some ways, having your opponent march downfield in smaller bites like that is more demoralizing than surrendering one explosive play for a touchdown. There wasn't much for Missouri fans to cheer about throughout the first half. Alabama led 21–3 at intermission.

Missouri took their chances on plays that broke down and found quarterback Maty Mauk scrambling for extra time outside the pocket before heaving a deep ball to Jimmie Hunt downfield. This exact formula was the key play on all three of Mizzou's scoring drives. Early in the second quarter, Mauk hit Hunt for 32 yards to put the ball in the red zone and set up their first field goal. On 3rd and 10 on their first drive out of halftime, Mauk saw the pocket collapsing, rolled out to buy time, and heaved another long ball to Hunt for a 63-yard gain down to the 1-yard line. It took all four plays plus a time-out for Missouri to punch the ball in and make the score 21–10. After a defensive stop, Missouri hit another deep ball to Hunt to set up another field goal, bringing the score to 21–13. It was sad to watch Missouri fans bubble with hope. I wasn't watching the game through the eyes of a believer; I saw that the only offense Missouri could muster involved a play breaking down and hitting a 50-50 ball deep. Nearly half their offense came on those three schoolyard football jump balls. So while everyone around me was ecstatic about the game being a one-score affair at 21–13, I was trying to guess the final score in my head. I decided on 38–13.

And at the exact moment when Alabama needed to produce another methodical drive and put points on the board, they did. Sims to Howard for 3, Sims to Vogler for 5, Sims for 6, Yeldon for 1, Sims to Jones for

17, Henry for 8, Henry for 5, Sims to Jones for 17, Henry for 1, Sims to Jones for a 6-yard touchdown. No negative plays, no wasted motion, no doubt they were taking the ball downfield and scoring. Even when the score was close at the end of the third quarter, the game wasn't. Alabama scored twice more in the fourth quarter, for a 42–13 final. The Missouri fans around me headed for the exits in three waves: the first at 35–13, the second at 42–13, and the last when the clock struck 00:00. It's hard to say whether keeping the game close through three quarters earned Missouri football more respect or the final score reaffirmed the notion that they're overrated and their success was mostly a result of a weak SEC East. Either way, I knew Mizzou fans would continue to walk around with a chip on their shoulder long after the game.

In the waning moments of the fourth quarter, the Missouri crowd thinned to the point where I could move toward midfield. I walked down to the front row at the 50-yard line as Alabama rushed the field. Streamers fell from the rafters as the press rushed the field along with the players, snapping pictures and pulling stars aside for interviews. Coach Nick Saban accepted the SEC Championship Trophy. Two college girls climbed down to the front row; one stumbled and almost knocked me over. They were both Alabama students decked out in Crimson Tide gear. Turns out they both had brothers playing in the game. One of the girls was Alabama wide receiver ArDarius Stewart's sister, the other, Missouri defensive back Shaun Rupert's sister. Rupert's sister told me how her brother texted her all week talking trash, saying he's sorry for the whooping Missouri was about to put on Alabama. The three of us shared a good laugh about that. Then they explained how they're essentially the babysitters for a bunch of the guys on Alabama's football team. "You don't know how stressful that is, making sure the boys don't get in trouble, making sure they get home safe on Saturday night," Stewart's sister said. "There's like ten of 'em that we end up watching. They're normal college kids doing what normal college kids do on the weekend, but they get so much more attention, you gotta keep an eye on 'em all the time." College football players walk around a campus as heroes and receive an inordinate amount of attention and preferential treatment. The drawback to the limelight is that every mistake they make is put under a microscope, any misdeed judged as a sign of poor character, rather than a college kid doing foolish things. I'd never stopped to think about the friends and siblings who look after football players in a place like Tuscaloosa. Forget the people on the field—I think I met the real MVPs right there in the stands.

Shortly after the girls walked away, Alabama players began lapping the stadium, shaking hands with and high-fiving Bama fans lined up across the front row. As expected, Alabama was headed to the inaugural College Football Playoff. But somehow, there wasn't enough excitement in the victory. There wasn't so much joy as relief. It was as if the unreal expectations the Crimson Tide Nation puts on its football team had stolen the happiness away from what should have been a blissful moment. I thought back to Paul Finebaum talking about how if anything ever drives Saban out of Tuscaloosa, it'll be the impossible standards set by fans. I stood there overcome with the feeling that somehow the juice wasn't worth the squeeze; that all the year-round hype led to a letdown. I couldn't figure out why, but after spending an entire season building to this moment, I found that once I arrived, the moment didn't deliver.

The Sugar Bowl

#4 Ohio State vs. #1 Alabama

January 1, 2015

New Orleans, Louisiana

At the start of conference championship week, Texas Christian University (TCU) held the No. 3 slot and undefeated defending National Champion Florida State had the No. 4 slot. Ohio State at No. 5 and Baylor at No. 6 sat on the outside looking in. On December 7, the big drama following championship week hinged on which 1-loss teams would earn the third and fourth playoff slots alongside Alabama and Oregon, who had already punched their tickets. Both TCU and Baylor are members of the Big XII conference, which currently has only ten members (the result of various realignments between 2010 and 2013). NCAA rules required twelve teams in order to hold a conference championship game. So, rather than playing each other in a likely play-in game, Baylor squared off against a tough, No. 9-ranked Kansas State squad and won by 12, and TCU demolished a listless 2-win Iowa State team 55–3. Meanwhile, both Florida State and Ohio State played top-15 teams in conference championship games. Florida State held on for a 37–35 victory over No. 11 Georgia Tech in the ACC Championship in Charlotte, and Ohio State dismantled No. 13 Wisconsin 59–0 in the Big Ten Championship in Indianapolis.

Despite the strong resumes sported by TCU and Baylor, Ohio State and Florida State were the obvious picks. Ohio State made a 10-win Wisconsin team look like a high school squad and Florida State, for all their sloppy play, still hadn't lost a game since 2012. When the final rankings came out Sunday night, No. 1 Alabama matched up against No. 4 Ohio State in the Sugar Bowl and No. 2 Oregon squared off with No. 3 Florida State in the Rose Bowl. If a large portion of the country felt TCU or Baylor got screwed out of a playoff spot, the exclusion will only serve to fuel the argument for expanding the playoff to eight teams within the next few years.

Even if conference championships weren't a determining factor, and even if Ohio State hadn't justified their catapult into the playoff by massacring Wisconsin, Florida State and Ohio State still would have received the playoff bids. Why? Florida State and Ohio State are traditional powerhouses that provide sexy story lines the media could run with all through December. Both OSU and FSU sport deep and devoted fan bases—that is, fan bases that travel well and buy tickets and merchandise. Baylor and TCU struggle to sell out home conference games. Money talks.

Much like the Mississippi State game in October, I flipped my sleep cycle completely for the Sugar Bowl. I was flying out to Portland for a wedding the morning after the game, so I decided to stay awake overnight. Having spent the past month with my grandma in Long Beach, where I'd grooved a routine of going to the gym in the morning, writing all day, cooking dinner for and watching movies with Maggie at night, I was grateful to have some excitement back in my life. I woke up at 2 pm and drove the hour-plus to New Orleans, parked in a lot in the French Quarter, and met my friend Angela—the one from Oxford—at Cafe Du Monde.[99] We ate beignets and drank coffee and then strolled the French Market and Jackson Square for a couple hours. Fans lined the sidewalks sporting Bama and Ohio State gear and in fair weather fan fashion, I brought my Notre Dame sweatshirt back out, reenergized and emboldened by ND's win over LSU in the Music City Bowl a couple days earlier. We stopped in one of the daiquiri bars with a few-dozen flavors lined up across the back wall like Slurpee machines in a 7-Eleven. We watched the second quarter of the Rose Bowl before I made my way to the Superdome. Again I was struck by how something significant is lost in moving games to these NFL venues. Fans descend on these cities for a vacation and a party weekend, especially when we're talking about New Orleans on New Year's. But still, the romantic charm of an SEC football weekend vanishes in the presence of big city lights.

Half a mile down Decatur Street I found a shuttle taking people from the New Orleans Marriott to the stadium. The two couples I waited with were Alabama fans. One couple drove in from Birmingham and the other from Hueytown. As the five of us took our seats, we talked about the Rose Bowl's 18–13 score at halftime and naturally that segued

---

[99] An absolute must for any American's bucket list. You'll never find a better home for powdered sugar.

into a conversation about Jameis Winston. The couple from Hueytown had plenty to say about Winston, and coming from Alabama fans, what they offered caught me off-guard. Neither uttered a bad word about Winston. The husband explained how Jameis was diagramming complex plays and breaking down varsity defenses with high school coaches when he was in sixth and seventh grade. Winston's media persecution has been a near-constant over the past two seasons. To read nothing but press-clippings, you'd almost have to conclude he's a great talent and a bad guy. I've wondered, though, if he's being portrayed accurately. Do his reported actions truly indicate the person he is, or has he been railroaded, with every negative story about him played up and exaggerated? Across the board, once you paint a high-profile somebody as a villain, they become too salacious a topic to not talk about. The world needs bad guys. (Or at least the media does.)

The low lights in red and white gave the stadium a funky, haunted vibe, almost like a watered-down version of the spooky atmosphere I encountered outside LSU's Tiger Stadium before the night game. Then again, that might have just been New Orleans. Once inside, I joined the procession of fans ascending the cream-grey ramps to the upper deck. The slight stagger and swerve of adults who'd spent the afternoon in the Quarter was contrasted by the determined march of kids and preteens in Tide and Buckeyes jerseys champing at the bit to catch their first glimpse of the field below. Anticipation hung in the air with a preseason-late-August-level thickness. Both fan bases had been reborn into the playoff and everyone seemed on edge, knowing that a trip to the National Championship was within their grasp.

My seat was in the fifth row all the way up in the north end zone. A mother and her seven-year-old son sat directly to my left. The boy wore a Braxton Miller jersey and excitedly told me he's a big Buckeyes fan, and this was his first Ohio State game ever. His mom explained that their family lived an hour northeast of Little Rock, Arkansas, but her husband grew up an OSU fan and passed the Buckeye gene along to their son. Turned out their seats were actually in the fourth row so they soon moved down. A grandmother and her seven-year old grandson wearing an Alabama T-shirt and holding a souvenir-sized Coke in his hands took their place minutes later. This boy was at his first Alabama game, and though quieter than the other boy he was clearly excited as well. I introduced the boys because I thought they had plenty in common—same age, both at their first college football game supporting their favorite team—but they only said hello, looked at each other's shirts, and went back to whatever they were doing.

As the boys fidgeted in their seats in anticipation of kickoff, their futures came into focus for me. Twenty-five years from now, one boy will be telling his young son about seeing his team win the Sugar Bowl, relaying the indelible beats of the game from memory; the other will be sharing the scars of his first college football heartbreak. Both will be passing this college football birthright along to the next generation. After seeing this play out numerous times throughout the season, I decided that the family bonds created and reinforced by love of this game are one of my favorite pieces of the college football fan puzzle.

I looked down and saw a couple in their sixties gathering their bearings as they walked through the ramp to my left. They walked back and forth checking section and row numbers and all the while I stared at them thinking, "Man, what are they doing here? They're really out of place." Both husband and wife wore Michigan Wolverines sweatshirts. As I tried to figure out what their deal was, it occurred to me that—forget how much I despise Michigan—they were a mirror being held up to me. This is exactly what everyone saw when they saw me walking through their campus in Notre Dame gear. I looked down. I'd forgotten that I was wearing a Notre Dame shirt. When they finally figured out where to go, they made their way to the seats a couple over from me on my right. When I stood to let them by, we locked eyes with knowing smiles and laughed.

Notre Dame hates Michigan. Michigan hates Notre Dame. But here we were in the same boat. Being out of place, outsiders, brought us together. I congratulated them on Michigan hiring Jim Harbaugh and told them I'm happy Notre Dame doesn't have to face him every year. We talked about how we all ended up at an Ohio State–Alabama game in New Orleans. (They were vacationing in New Orleans and decided a Sugar Bowl was a good bucket list item to check off.) And we shared in the experience of the fans surrounding us, whose schools were about to play on the field, the fans who belonged there (and threw darting sideways glances in our direction). I suppose there's something about the regional bond we shared, too. I hadn't ever considered a Midwestern connection until the man, Bob, said: "I know it's Ohio State and our biggest rival but I want them to beat up on Alabama tonight. I'm sick of this 'SEC is the greatest' nonsense, like they play some superior brand of football all over the South." It took a Michigan fan to make me recognize my own sense of regional pride. What a sickening thought.

Fireworks flash-boomed through the Superdome, marking the end of a month's worth of media talk. Thank God. The media coverage had long since hit its boiling point, with every sports outlet dissecting matchups and comparing statistics and schemes and records ad nauseam. Moments before kickoff, someone shouted out the Oregon-Florida State final: 59–20. Though I wondered how the Ducks outscored FSU 41–7 in those final thirty minutes, I was happy the Seminoles were finished. You can take whatever side of the argument you'd like—resilient champion or a heaping pile of fool's gold—but Florida State's luck finally ran out and the Oregon Ducks awaited the Sugar Bowl winner.

Early on, it looked like Alabama would be that team. In a matchup that began playing out a lot like the Iron Bowl, Ohio State—like Auburn—chewed up yardage only to stall out in the red zone and settle for field goals or turn the ball over. Meanwhile, Alabama put the ball in the end zone.

Alabama 0, OSU 3 // Alabama 7, OSU 3 // Alabama 7, OSU 6 // Alabama 14, OSU 6

When T. J. Yeldon scored halfway through the second quarter to extend Alabama's lead to 21–6, Crimson Tide fans danced out in the aisles, shouting and high-fiving each other. Though many in the stadium believed Alabama firmly controlled the game at that point, Nick Saban dispelled the notion in his postgame interview: "We were up 21–6 because of two turnovers and two stops in the red area. So we weren't really stopping them…we weren't really playing and executing the way we needed to even then. I didn't like the feel of the game even then."

Trailing by 15 late in the first half, the momentum began to shift inside the Superdome and the Buckeyes started to wrest control of the game. Ezekiel Elliott scored for the Buckeyes on a 3-yard run with three minutes remaining in the second quarter. *Alabama 21, OSU 13*. Ohio State took possession again after an Alabama punt. The Buckeyes pulled out a trick play to score again with 00:19 left before halftime. All-purpose back Jalin Marshall took a handoff moving right and flipped the ball to wide receiver Evan Spencer, coming back to the left on a reverse. Spencer planted his feet in the middle of the field and threw a near-perfect pass toward the left sideline. The ball sailed over the outstretched fingertips of cornerback Cyrus Jones and into the arms of airborne receiver Michael Thomas, who managed to plant a foot from his acrobatically contorted body within three inches of the sideline. *Alabama 21, OSU 20.*

Somewhere early in the first quarter, a couple took the seats immediately to my right, between me and the Michigan fans. I didn't pay them any mind at the time because of the game. At halftime, I began talking to the man next to me. Al and his wife, both in their fifties, were as out of place as my newfound Michigan acquaintances and me. Al and his wife were in from Brooklyn and Al typified the best Italian New Yorker stereotypes you'd ever want to encounter: coiffed and slicked-back hair, a tracksuit, and a way of talking that involved his entire body. We discussed the betting lines for the second half and life in our respective big cities. In the same way that I was confused by my bond with the Michigan couple, I was surprised to find myself in the same boat as Al. Because we were both from big cities, we shared an unspoken bond. You're wired differently somehow if you were born and raised in a major metropolis. Our demeanors and dispositions were much more similar than I would've suspected. We talked about baseball and when I asked him Yankees or Mets, he shared the ultimate New Yorker response: "You kiddin' me? Mickey Mantle held me when I was a baby." He compared Alabama fans to Yankees fans, talking about how they expect to win every year and that makes them a special breed of cocky. I laughed and told him what I'd been doing the past four months. He nodded. "Oh, so you already know."

⚑

Early in the third quarter, Ohio State scored on a 47-yard pass from Cardale Jones to Devin Smith. Alabama 21, OSU 27. Around this time, an Alabama fan in his sixties stood up from his seat two rows ahead. He stood in the aisle having a conniption: fidgeting, gesturing wildly, pacing back and forth, and most importantly, blocking our view. Al and I hollered at the man to sit down. When that didn't work, Al ripped off a piece of his pretzel and hit the man in the back of the head with it. I died. The Alabama fan whipped around and Al did that thing Italians sometimes do (in my imagination at least), where he bunched up his fingers and said "Ahhhhh." That was literally all he said. Short of saying "fuhgettaboutit," he checked off every box on the caricature checklist. I was in tears, doubled over laughing.

The white-bearded man, already upset about how the game was unfolding, didn't take kindly to the gesture. One thing I've learned about the emotionality of fans is that when they're unhappy, many are eager to find an outlet for their anger. Apparently I was the outlet this man was looking for. He concluded that I threw the pretzel at him, and at every commercial break for the rest of the game he turned around and glared at me. This man, well into his sixties, wanted to fight me. This played itself out in its own melodramatic way: Multiple fans in my section called ushers over to ask the belligerent man to sit down, which led to White Beard leaving to find another usher to grouse at, saying the usher in our section was harassing him and his family. He kept turning around to stare and mumble obscenities at me. And on and on. The angrier the Alabama fan grew, the funnier Al and I found the whole spectacle. Free laughs.

Meanwhile on the field below, Ohio State defensive end Steve Miller intercepted a Blake Sims pass and scampered 47 yards for a touchdown.

Alabama 21, OSU 34. In less than twelve minutes of game time, Ohio State rattled off 28 consecutive points and the Crimson Tide were in trouble. Blake Sims closed the gap to 6 points on a 5-yard touchdown run late in the third quarter. *Alabama 28, OSU 34.*

As college football fans, Northern or Southern, we've all been cast under a spell that compels us to believe that there's something special about the SEC. Whether or not we want to believe it is irrelevant; we all feel it. Part of the feeling is data-driven: The Southeastern Conference has produced seven of the past eight national champions, and the South produces NFL players at a greater rate per capita than anywhere else nationally. Part of it is an indefinable mystique hovering around the conference and the region. Whatever it was, the effect in the Superdome on New Year's Day was that entering the fourth quarter, it felt like everyone in the building believed Alabama would find a way to win the Sugar Bowl and advance to the National Championship game.

Most of the action in the fourth quarter took place in Ohio State territory. Alabama had Ohio State pinned back inside their 10-yard line three times. The first two times, Alabama forced punts and took possession in Buckeye territory. It seemed inevitable that Alabama would score and win 35–34. But the Tide couldn't move the football. Ohio State picked off a Blake Sims pass the first time down and forced a punt the second time. With five minutes remaining, Alabama downed a punt at the 5-yard line and Ohio State took over on offense. Four plays later, running back Ezekiel Elliott broke through the line and scurried 85 yards for the game-winning touchdown. *Alabama 28, OSU 42 (two-point conversion good).* Alabama made the finish exciting, scoring once and getting the ball back with a chance to score again in the waning seconds. But the night belonged to the Ohio State Buckeyes and for the second year in a row, the national champion would be crowned from outside the SEC.

Alabama 35, OSU 42. Fourth Quarter, 00:00.

As Alabama fans headed for the exits in stunned disbelief, the old bearded man glowered at me as his family joined the procession of dejected Bama backers headed home to lick their wounds. He and his family faded away into the reddish-whiteish blur and spilled back into the New Orleans night, as did the seven-year old boys and their families, Al and his wife, and the elderly Michigan couple.

I sat alone in my fifth row seat, letting the moment wash over me. It was over. My season-long SEC journey had come to an end. I remember the moment feeling surreal, like it was unfathomable that an entire college season had breezed by so quickly. I remember telling myself at so many stops along the way to hold on to these moments, to soak them in before letting them pass. As the Ohio State postgame celebration came to an end and I canvassed the empty aisles strewn with Coke cups and half-eaten popcorn bowls and pulled pork nacho trays, and row upon row of vacated seats, I felt a sort of instant nostalgia take hold of me. I'm not ashamed to say that I got teary-eyed as I realized that the ride had ended, the bar had risen, and it was time to step off the roller coaster and back out into a cold and lonely New Orleans night.

Epilogue: The National Championship

#4 Ohio State vs. #2 Oregon

January 12, 2015

Arlington, Texas

What was I gonna do? Spend an entire season going to some of the best college football games in the country, then skip the championship game because no SEC team made it? C'mon now. I'll admit though, it was strange not seeing SEC fans at Cowboys Stadium (now known as AT&T Stadium). I spent three days in Oregon for a wedding after the Sugar Bowl, then flew home to Chicago to see family and friends for five days. It was bizarre returning home. Friends and family all asked me the same questions about the trip. I found myself shrugging and giving non-answers like "it was incredible," and I'd have so much to say that I'd get flustered and say nothing at all. How could I share all of my experiences over a four-month period in a couple minutes? Sometimes the "tell me all about it" prompt isn't very useful.

I could sense that my time in the South had changed me somehow; it had changed how I relate to my family and friends, to the city I'd always called home. The time away, the time on my own, forced me to realize that a big part of why I'd always felt so attached to Chicago is because it's all I'd ever known. When I stepped back into my former life in Chicago for a few days, I found nothing had changed. Everything was as I left it. I talked with my dad about how surreal it felt coming back, feeling that I'd been somehow transformed by the trip and wanted to move away from Chicago long-term. He said, "You already know what's here. It's the same shit. If you want to live somewhere else, go. This'll always be here if you want to come back." I set out to discover what makes Southern college football fan culture great, and ended up questioning how I anchor myself to the world around me. I think it's safe to say I got more than I'd bargained for.

⚑

The flight from Chicago back to New Orleans touched down a little after 6 pm Saturday, and I decided to make the eight-hour drive to Dallas straightaway, the last leg of this long, strange trip. With the cruise control set at 80 mph, I rode through the night down dimly lit highways, I-49 and I-20, sipping gas station coffee yet again, chomping on beef jerky, and racking my brain for possible takeaways from a championship game that didn't include any SEC teams. Around midnight, a Bob Seger song[100] came on the radio. I turned the volume to full blast and

---

[100] "Travelin' Man"

began to sing along, *"Sometimes at night, I see their faces / I feel the traces they've left on my soul / Those are the memories / that made me a wealthy soul,"* and all my worries about "possible takeaways" washed away. I remembered that all the best moments on this trip happened when I was present and unconcerned with "the story."

I spent Sunday watching the Cowboys–Packers playoff game before dinner with my friends Stephanie and Miranda in Dallas. On Monday I drove to Arlington early in the afternoon to survey the scene. Mostly, I reflected on the season as the hours counted down to kickoff and I didn't see much point in chatting up fans. I had made the return trip to Texas for my own sake, to finish what I'd started.

Beneath the decision to explore this subculture I've always been fascinated with, the decision to quit my job and write this book came from a desire to do something great. Just beneath that desire to do something great was the fear of waking up at fifty or sixty and realizing I'd never accomplished anything I was truly proud of. I often meet older folks who offer advice—solicited or otherwise—about what I should do with my life; what they would've done differently if they had to do it over again. I don't want to turn into one of those old men projecting their regrets onto the young people around me.

Standing in the upper deck on the Ohio State sideline, I witnessed Buckeyes all around me live out the experience we all crave so desperately as sports fans: to watch our team win a championship in person. All the while, I thought about Razorbacks and Aggies, Bulldogs and Gamecocks, all huddled around their TV sets already fantasizing about next fall. I thought about the Crimson Tide and the Volunteers, the

Gators and the Tigers, scouring the message boards hoping their school would reel in impact players in the final weeks before National Signing Day. And I allowed myself to drift off and dream about the Fighting Irish bringing a national title back to South Bend for the first time since I was three years old. What occurred to me in my reverie was that while we're all obsessed with the idea of our team hoisting a National Championship Trophy in early January, it's not the end goal we're concerned with so much as its pursuit.

Some months after the 2014 season ended, I sat struggling to decide how to end this story. A friend asked me if it mattered that no SEC team made it to the championship game. "Would this SEC fan culture change if they stopped making it to the title game every year?" Without hesitation, I responded: "Absolutely not." And that's the thing I finally get after spending a season on the road with these die-hards that I wouldn't have understood before my sojourn into the South: It's not about the championships. It's about riding the roller coaster one more time, cycling through the highs and lows of a college football season. The outcome doesn't matter nearly as much as our willingness to pay the emotional cost to ride every season. Sports fanaticism is the most widely accepted form of addiction in our society this side of caffeine.

While we certainly appreciate the beauty of watching our team improve and pull out tough wins throughout the course of a successful season, we're never satisfied. We always want more. Win a national championship on January 12 and two days later, when the recruiting dead period ends, our attention becomes fixed on the future, on securing next year's crop of freshmen.

Remember the Nick Saban interview after Alabama trounced Notre Dame in the 2013 National Championship? I know I do. ESPN's Tom

Rinaldi asked Saban how long he planned to celebrate the victory. Saban replied, "Two days and we're going to start on next year." Minutes after his Crimson Tide won their second consecutive national championship, Saban already had his eyes on a third. Across the board, those of us classified as fanatics share one common characteristic that defines us and sets us apart from the casual fan: we're addicted to the chase, hooked on the dream, and obsessed with its pursuit.

'til next season…

Afterword: A College Football State of the Union

After months on the road, sleeping on couches and backseats of cars, being stuck in coffee shops and game-day traffic, something became clear to me. I came to realize that there are several key issues threatening the sanctity of this game I love. While I am immensely grateful for the opportunity to immerse myself in the world of SEC football, it didn't afford many opportunities to discuss meta-perspectives on the college game as a whole. In fact, I doubt I would've been welcome to tailgate for very long had I pushed these kinds of hard conversations.

To help me sort out my thoughts and observations, I enlisted the help of five professionals in the winter after the 2014 season. (Not those kinds of professionals. I'm talking college football experts.) We discussed the ins and outs of what I believe are the most pressing issues swirling about in the college football ether, gathering storms that threaten to rain down hurt on America's game and do irreparable damage to the sport as we know it.

Depending on how they are resolved, each of these issues has the potential to enhance the competitive greatness of college football or shatter whatever remnants of innocence and purity exist in the country's most popular form of amateur athletics. On one side there is the realization of the sporting ideal, competition for the sake of competition, a true gridiron where will and determination always win out and where a paycheck is not the driving force behind spectacular performance. On the other there is a perverted semi-pro circuit, a farce and a sham and another instance of big business winning out in the end.

As I sought more detached, critical perspectives on college football, the logical choice was to discuss these issues with writers who intimately cover individual teams; that is, writers who find themselves entrenched in the college football world on a daily basis. To this end, I decided to speak with the following five writers at length: Gabe DeArmond, publisher of Power Mizzou, Rivals.com's Missouri team site; Phillip Marshall, senior editor of Auburn Undercover, 247Sports's Auburn team site; Chuck Rounsaville, founder and publisher of Ole Miss Spirit, Scout.com's Ole Miss team site; Andrew Spivey, recruiting analyst for Gator Country, 247Sports's Florida team site; and Bryan Driskell, staff writer and analyst for *Blue & Gold Illustrated*, a magazine dedicated exclusively to covering Notre Dame football (its website is hosted through the Rivals.com network).

Of the writers involved, Rounsaville and Marshall represented the old guard, having covered their teams since 1979 and 1969, respectively. DeArmond, Spivey, and Driskell provided fresher voices, all three having been in the business for less than fifteen years. It was important to me to find a cross section of perspectives from different generations.

What follows is a brief summary of the issues in college football I have questions and concerns about. Below them are relevant responses from the various writers I spoke with, who ever so graciously agreed to give me their thoughts. (Note that my own thoughts and interjections are in italics.)

Issue 1: Round-the-Clock Coverage

An untapped well of fan interest in college football bubbled beneath the surface for decades, but it wasn't until the media started to recognize this yet-unsatisfied demand that the mass explosion of interest really sprang forth. Water bowls of all-you-can drink information were laid out and the great lapping up began, starting with expanded TV coverage and eventually moving on to a bottomless well of year-round Internet-based sports coverage.

DeArmond: ESPN happened. They changed everything in every sport. It started with putting the Hartford Whalers on TV, then Big East basketball, and now fast-forward to what I do. Everything is more and more specialized. People are so fanatical about sports that there's no limit to the amount of product they'll consume.

Without a doubt, the influx of media attention catalyzed the trend toward college sports becoming a major business over the past 25 years. For a career sports journalist like Chuck Rounsaville, the question of how the media game has changed in college football provides a contrast so stark, it borders on redundant.

Rounsaville: Word spreads so fast now. You get information about the team or a player, and you have to post it instantaneously. Otherwise, another Ole Miss site gets the jump on us. The competition made us better. Back when I started this, I published thirty-two issues a year and took summers off. Now it's a twelve-months-a-year, seven-days-a-week job.

It's as if money symbolizes the unquantifiable emotional investment fans put into the team they love. And the more fans put in, the more return on investment they expect.

Marshall: The first major change was the Oklahoma and Georgia lawsuit, which took TV rights away from the NCAA. That allowed for cable TV, ESPN, and so forth. But I can't put my finger on when it became the game it is today. It wasn't like this in the '80s and '90s. It only became huge financially in the past ten to fifteen years. It's as if the Internet and social media took the game to another level. Now the next big thing is the advent of conference networks. SEC schools are raking in a windfall from the SEC Network.

Rounsaville: Back in '82, Ole Miss had an athletic budget of less than $10 million, and they're close to $90 million now. That's on the low end of the SEC, where you see $110–120 million from the Bamas and the Floridas. Competition spikes with that money. Coaches start to earn $4 million a year. Ticket prices have gone up, which means the fan investment has risen dramatically. They're paying a lot of money for a ticket, parking, travel, gas, and putting together a tailgate. For that investment, fans demand a quality product. What used to be entertainment has become way more serious.

Because of the increased clamor for wins and championships, and the fact that message boards have magnified the fans' collective voice, a fan base has more power to affect change today than ever before. The message boards serve as an echo chamber where voicing displeasure with a coach can gain enough momentum to sway an athletic director's decision-making process.

Rounsaville: Message boards are the new coffee shops or neighborhood diners, just with an exponentially larger audience. Back in the day, half-a-dozen guys would sit around the local diner and talk about the team. Now there's such a large community, it presents a very powerful voice. Every idea is hashed, rehashed, and over-hashed on these boards.

Also, fans are expressing their opinions anonymously, so they're not afraid of what they say. It creates an atmosphere of less accountability for your personal opinions.

DeArmond: It's [the message board culture] made fans more knowledgeable for sure. We end up catering to the die-hards of the die-hards. Twenty years ago, nobody knew anything about the recruiting class until the morning after National Signing Day when we'd all read the names of which players we'd signed in the local paper. I thought I was a sports fan until I got this job and met the real fans. I've found it's better to write an article on a backup defensive end than our starting quarterback because my audience already knows everything about the QB.

Rounsaville: The boiling point with this is you take Johnny Vaught, Joe Paterno, or Tom Osborne, career coaches at one school. You don't see that any more and you won't. Frank Beamer at Virginia Tech, Bill Snyder at K-State, those are the last of a dying breed. You won't see those long tenures anymore. That's what the need for instant gratification has done. Look at Mark Richt at Georgia. The guy wins 9 to 11 games a year and fans are calling for his head because they're demanding a national championship.[101]

The instant-information age has created a "What have you done for me TODAY?" mentality. Look at Saban at Alabama. Our expectations lose touch with reality. The same fans who are gonna run him out because he's not winning a national championship every year are the same ones who will worship the Saban statue and clamor for the good ol' days of Saban when the next coach isn't delivering at his level.

Expectations are higher at Ole Miss because 2014 was successful. All of a sudden, everyone here in Oxford is talking about a national championship. Things change quickly.

Our fascination (obsession?) with college sports has allowed for broader TV coverage, and later, Internet message boards, to proliferate over the past quarter century. But what we've found over the past five years is that our thirst might be insatiable. We still want more. The most recent sign is the creation of conference-specific networks.

DeArmond: The SEC Network turned a 70-million-dollar profit their first year. But I think moving forward, we might see the trend start to hurt attendance at games. People can sit home on a Saturday and watch six games at once now. I think we'll get to a point where attendance

---

[101] Richt was fired at the end of the 2015 season, no doubt (at least in part) because Georgia did not win the SEC East from 2013–15. Richt's career record at UGA: 145–51, and 83–37 in conference play.

takes a major hit because of that. But who knows when that might be; it could be decades in the future. We're standing on the ground floor of a building, and we don't know how tall it is. Fans care too much about the outcome of games for this system to go away.

This climate of never-ending facilities expansion has changed the way universities operate as well. Understanding that a major college football program is one of the greatest revenue-generators in higher education, many schools have submitted to the trend toward building. Spurred on by boosters with deep pockets and buoyed by the promise of massive revenue shares, many big-time schools are in a constant state of construction, jockeying for pole position in the race for the biggest, most modern stadiums and sports complexes.

The question that always seems to get lost in the mix is, What's the end game? What are these schools racing at a breakneck pace toward?

DeArmond: The overall donor level thing is the biggest thing. How many new structures are you building? As soon as your stadium renovation is done and the new athletic complex is finished, it's outdated and you have to build a new one to keep up.

Where does this end? We're seeing the bigger schools spending hundreds of millions on buildings, but with the media rights as big as they are—with the SEC Network and ESPN paying for playoff rights—I don't see a tipping point. Every SEC school received something like $24 million in the first year. That'll go up to $30 in year two, $34 in year three. The saturation point comes when people don't care this much, and I don't see that happening anytime soon.

Marshall: The salary war started with Saban getting a $4-million-a-year contract in 2007. Ever since then, it's escalated quickly. You'd have to be blind not to see that money's changed the game in that sense. There was a time when head coaches were upper-middle-class guys, and now they're making millions of dollars a year. If you look at any coach of a top-25 school, they're set for life even if they get canned. How many millions have been paid to get coaches to leave?

We've got all the big-time schools paying top dollar for coaches and now we're seeing schools go into debt with the facilities races. How long can the cycle go on for? We're talking about $750 million on new facilities. Facilities are being built to help recruiting. If it didn't help in recruiting, you wouldn't see it. Plain and simple.

Ticket prices will continue to go up. The universities have to pay for it somehow. The whole system is bound to drive fans away eventually. Now what's interesting is that the whole enterprise falls apart if people stop coming [to games] and the big-time donations stop rolling in.

Issue 2: Land of the Giants

With the recent trend toward super-conferences, and the solidifying of a Power Five conference structure, we're starting to see a process of natural selection separate the field of College Football Bowl Subdivision (FBS) schools into two distinct categories: 1) schools that want to and can afford to be major players, and 2) schools who, by choice or circumstance, step back and avoid becoming football factories.

There's also the conversation about funding the full cost of athletic scholarships. Many smaller schools complain that offering the full cost will give certain schools—mainly Power Five conference schools—an additional competitive advantage over other Division-I FBS schools whose athletic budget won't allow for it. Those in smaller-market FBS schools claim that the bigger schools are using money to throw their weight around and bully smaller Division-I teams out of national relevance.

That it seems the odds have gone from improbable to impossible for a "little guy"[102] *competing for a national championship is easily the sad-*

---

[102] The Power Five conferences are the Pac-12, Big XII, Big Ten, ACC, and, of course, the SEC. Schools from other conferences (the AAC, the Mountain West, etc.) are now considered the "little guys" in college football. During the Bowl Championship Series era, which determined what schools would play in both the National Championship Game and the other major New Year's eve and New Year's day bowls (read: the most prestigious and highest-revenue-generating games), schools like TCU (before they joined the Big XII), Boise State, and Utah (before they joined the Pac-12) would occasionally steal a bid from a major conference by finishing 11–1 or 12–0 in a less competitive conference. Those schools also beat big-time programs over the years (including Oklahoma and Alabama) in BCS games. These moments were the modern-day David and Goliath stories that many fans—myself included—are suckers for. The conference realignment in the early 2010s (which gave us the Power Five and conference championship games) and the recent advent of "cost of attendance" policies have combined to all but eliminate any chance of a little guy finding their way into the College Football Playoff. (Cost of attendance payments are supplemental sums paid to student-athletes designed to cover the difference between a full-ride athletic scholarship and the total cost of living after incidentals like groceries, rent— if housing isn't covered—books, supplies, and transportation. All Power Five

dest takeaway for me. This is the point where I find my own sentimentality overriding the shrewd pragmatism that's making college football a sleeker, more efficient machine. I'm a sucker for underdog stories. I think we all are; it's hardwired into the American DNA.

DeArmond: Money widens the gap between the big-time programs and, say, Mountain West schools. It doesn't matter much to me because I cover and watch a big-time program in a big-time conference, but the days of a BYU or a Navy having a legit shot at a national championship are over. It simply can't happen in today's game.

I could see sixty-four teams in four conferences with two eight-team divisions in each conference. The division champions play in a playoff quarterfinal. The Big XII will probably go away. Teams that want to play big-time football can join one of those four. Boise State would go 8–4 or 9–3 in a power conference every year. They'd compete but we wouldn't see them going 11–1 or 12–0 anymore.

Rounsaville: There's a big gap between the quality of Power Five and non-Power Five schools. We're talking about GM and Hyundai. I know this sounds awful and I'm aware it makes me sound unmerciful, but if a Sun Belt Conference football player was good enough to play in the SEC, then he'd be there. It's like any other competitive market: if you're good enough, you'll get paid more. Sun Belt kids aren't bad athletes, but they're not playing in front of 100,000 people.

---

teams now offer these payments, thus giving schools with larger athletic department budgets even greater leverage.) In short, there will be no more Davids to slay the college football giants.

Marshall: Why does it make any difference to Troy or Youngstown State what Alabama and Ohio State are doing? Why is what the SEC, Big Ten, and Pac-12 do bad for the Sun Belt, Mountain West Conference and C-USA? Troy was never gonna be in the National Championship Game anyways.

I'm more concerned about the impact of money on FCS schools. It's important for them to play one or two FBS schools every year for the money, but some get carried away and they try to do it too much. That starts to exploit players, who know they're going to get beat down just to support the athletic program.

The other five conferences, I don't see how their situations have been seriously affected.

Driskell: The gap between the haves and have-nots is growing, and the Power Five happened to come after Boise State and TCU and Utah acted as BCS-busters in recent years. I'm not sure that's a coincidence.

Issue 3: Money Makes the World Go Round

While cost of attendance (COA) is a hot-button issue right now as it relates to the impact of money on college football, it's an official policy established (that is, worked out) by the NCAA. Boosters providing impermissible benefits to student-athletes and their families is another matter altogether.

Boosters have been around for decades—as have people who earnestly deny their existence. The thing about boosters is that when they come up as a topic, their clandestine nature polarizes the opinions of educated and uneducated people alike. Bring up boosters around a group of college sports fans and you're likely to see the spectrum of responses, from sincere belief to jaded cynicism.

Nowhere was this more evident to me than after talking with the sports writers about the Ole Miss Rebels. Chuck Rounsaville explained that in his thirty-some years covering Ole Miss football, he's become convinced that the University of Mississippi does not allow players to be paid under the table. He was positive. A couple weeks later, I spoke on the phone with Andrew Spivey, who covers the Gators. Without prompting, he brought up Laremy Tunsil[103] and how, at first, the Gators went hard after this can't-miss prospect in their own backyard. Spivey explained that long before Tunsil committed to Mississippi, UF stopped pitching the blue-chipper because it was understood among those in the know that Ole Miss had made living arrangements for Tunsil's mother and

---

[103] The former high school All-American out of Lake City, Florida; Ole Miss offensive tackle from 2013–2015; and Miami Dolphins first-round draft pick (No. 13 overall) in the 2016 NFL Draft. He was suspended seven games during the 2015 season for receiving impermissible benefits. In the hours leading up to the draft, Tunsil's Twitter and Instagram accounts were hacked. On Twitter, a video of Tunsil smoking marijuana through a gas mask was posted. This allegedly led to the Baltimore Ravens passing on Tunsil with the No. 6 pick; the seven spots Tunsil fell in the draft cost him over $8 million. The Instagram posts contained images of supposed text messages between Tunsil and an Ole Miss booster discussing illegal payments to Tunsil and his mother. When asked in his NFL Draft interview if there had been a monetary exchange between him and his coach, Tunsil replied, "I'd have to say yes." Less than a minute later, a reporter asked Tunsil whether he had talked with the NCAA regarding these allegations. An NFL official ended the press conference before Tunsil could respond.

offered her a job in her chosen field. Tunsil's public announcement for the Rebels was a mere formality long before his commitment date. Spivey also explained that this sort of thing is commonplace throughout the SEC and most of the big-time college football world. I confess I'm inclined to believe Spivey's take.

DeArmond: It happens, definitely. They're not dumb enough to hand out briefcases of cash; they've gotten more creative about it. I think the practice is more prevalent at some schools than others. Boosters are more an "area of the country" thing and I think the accusations are overblown. Cost of attendance though, that's a big one. I'm interested to see where that goes and what can of worms that's going to open up. The numbers just came out and Tennessee has the highest number over COA that they can give all scholarship athletes. It's $5,666 per year. Now if I'm [Tennessee Head Coach] Butch Jones, I'm out pushing that hard on the recruiting trail.

We can call it whatever we want but this is another big step in acknowledging that we're not dealing with amateur athletics here; that this is a semi-professional league. Anyone who follows this game knows we crossed that line years ago. Can we quit pretending this is about academics and graduating players? You can call it amateur athletics if you want, but it's a sham.

Fans care about one thing: winning games. Schools trumpeting graduation rates aren't winning enough football games. Look at Bama and then look at Vandy. Yeah, Vandy has a really high grad rate, but when's the last time they beat Bama? Look, that [Ohio State quarterback] Cardale Jones tweet[104] definitely wasn't PC, but he's right. If you're playing at the highest levels, nobody really cares about your education. Most fans only care about you producing on the field.

Fans lamenting the college game's departure from the purity of amateurism and school spirit need to recognize that when our desire to see Ol' State U produce a winner at any cost became our top priority, we became complicit in allowing big business and private money to exert influence on the game and steal away its innocence.

When presented with the choice between seeing our school be successful in football or maintaining academic integrity and providing high-quality young men with valuable college degrees, many choose the former. While it's not an either-or in every case, it does seem that for the most part, we can't have both. I think we, as fans, ought to stop lying to ourselves about the dilemma we're faced with. To take it one step further, we should stop kidding ourselves about the fact that it's a dilemma. We'll take a winner and the illusion of academia every time, and we should stop apologizing for it. Not everyone sees it that way, though.

---

[104] For the tech-savvy, here was the tweet: "@Cordale10 Why should we have to go to class if we came here to play FOOTBALL, we ain't come to play SCHOOL, classes are POINTLESS" [Oct 5, 2012].

For the less tech-savvy: Twitter is a popular form of social media. Cardale Jones posted the above message for all to see publicly. He caught a lot of flack for the "tweet."

Rounsaville: I'll be glad to see [student-athletes] get more money, but they shouldn't make a living doing it. This is a money-driven sport, but for me, the spirit of amateur athletics is still stronger than big money. They can't live on the current stipend. I see six guys living in a two-bedroom apartment. Inequity is living on $700 a month for rent, food, and overall cost of living. Remember that Arian Foster interview?[105] A guy like that doesn't need a percentage of jersey sales, but he doesn't need to go home to an empty fridge either. You can't pay the kids like professionals. That goes against the spirit of college football, but they've gotta give 'em more. This is a full-time, year-round job.

For the record, I know that Ole Miss doesn't do that sort of thing [having boosters pay players under the table].[106] I think the idea of paying

---

[105] The interview he's referring to is from the documentary *Schooled: The Price of College Sports* (2013). It should be required viewing for anyone interested in learning about the darker side of collegiate athletics. In the documentary, former Tennessee running back Arian Foster admitted to taking money from boosters during his time in Knoxville. (He played for the Volunteers from 2004–2008 and the Houston Texans from 2009–2015, and he's the Texans all-time leader in rushing yards and touchdowns.) Foster railed against a system where he'd rush for 100 yards in a college game, see fans from a 100,000-plus capacity stadium lined up—wearing his jersey—for autographs after the game, and then go home to an empty fridge and no money to buy food.

[106] Rounsaville was extremely gracious. He didn't have to take an hour and a half out of his day to talk with someone he'd never met. He also took a personal interest in my book, and in me personally. He asked questions about my background and congratulated me on taking a big risk in life before I

players is overblown universally. Maybe I'm swayed by wanting it to be that way, I don't know, but I've been covering Ole Miss for 35 years and I've seen a ton of four-and-five star players driving around campus in clunkers.

And I think that in the cases where it does happen, it's in the spirit of compassion. A guy sees a student athlete show up on campus with one pair of jeans, sees the inequity of the stipend for the amount of work that kid's putting in, and they're just looking to help the kids out. I think when it happens, it's more a compassionate thing than a competitive thing. It's more taking care of your own than enticing somebody to come to your school.

Marshall: I have mixed feelings on the [cost of attendance] issue. There's a whole lot a young man gains playing college football, especially in the South. A large percentage of those guys wouldn't be attending college and receiving a college degree were it not for their athletic scholarship. I don't buy the destitute card, either. If these kids come from poor families, they have Pell Grants up to $5,000 a year. They can apply for those on top of their scholarships. I don't know. I suppose the cost of attendance should be covered, and probably even a bit beyond that. I hope that if it does happen, the money's distributed evenly. I want to see the third-string offensive guard receive as much as our star quarterback.

---

settled down to start a family. I think that's why I didn't push back at his comment, which I thought was naive; perhaps a more seasoned journalist would have.

A big part of this whole equation is that people want to believe these kids are playing for their school, not for money.

As I'm sure you know, the pressure to win in the SEC is huge. People who do have money aren't going to sit by and watch losing teams for long. Little things like $100 handshakes are really no big deal. That happens everywhere. But when boosters start throwing big money for players, and when the institution plays fast and loose with the rules to keep players eligible, that should get a university in trouble. Absolutely. And I don't believe that sort of thing happens as much as it once did.

I don't see any real sign of guys getting a lot, and I think it comes way more from agents than it does boosters or fans. One time a few years back, I asked Auburn's compliance director if he was given a truth serum and asked how many players on our team were getting paid by an agent, he looked at me and said, "Well I'd hope we had five or six because if we didn't, we're not very good."

Driskell: Part of it is that I think it reflects the sense of entitlement we now see in our country. Regardless of political leanings, you probably feel entitled nowadays, like you're owed something. Even so, I'm okay with players getting paid because these kids deserve it. Why hasn't the NCAA taken care of total cost? These are not normal students. 80,000 people aren't showing up to watch science quizzes.

All but a couple major schools are actually involved in providing extra benefits, from little things to big things to Cam Newton.[107]

You look at a guy like Mark Richt at Georgia. That guy tries his best to keep a clean program, but boosters inject themselves because they're hungry for MORE success. Even though Richt wins ten games a year, he's underachieved in their eyes.

And the surprising thing to me is when schools' boosters are lining up to pay and they still lose. I had a friend who played at Mississippi State in the Jackie Sherill era. After games, there'd be a line of "fans" who would give hundred-dollar-handshakes to the players, and those teams would go 7–5 at best.

Spivey: Don't tell me you're a clean program. If you're a five-star, top-50 player coming out of high school, at least ten of the top programs are coming after you hard. Something is persuading that kid to choose one

---

[107] A footer for those unfamiliar with football: Quarterback Cam Newton led Auburn to a national championship in 2010. He's also the reigning NFL MVP (2015). He planned to transfer to a big-time school from Blinn Junior College in Texas in 2009. It was understood that Newton was going to be a star. There was a massive controversy surrounding his recruitment and there were allegations of Newton's father, Cecil, shopping Cam around to SEC schools. Supposedly, the price tag for Newton was between $100,000 and $180,000. There was circumstantial evidence suggesting Cecil Newton tried to broker a deal with Mississippi State boosters. Ultimately nothing was proven, and Cam Newton was cleared of any wrongdoing by the NCAA. He went on to win both the Heisman Trophy and a national championship that year. The following April, the Carolina Panthers selected Newton as the No. 1 overall pick in the NFL Draft.

over the others. Either A) they grew up a fan, or B) they're receiving extra benefits. I can almost guarantee no big program is 100 percent clean. It's the nature of competitive sports.

In my line of work these days, we spend so much time finding the aunt, the uncle, the second cousin who's really in charge of a kid's recruitment. 90 percent of the time it's an uncle, but now that every big-time kid has a trainer who comes with him on recruiting visits, it's the trainers or the 7-on-7 coaches who are becoming the kid's handlers.

7-on-7 tournaments are quickly becoming the next "big thing" in high school football. They're non-contact passing competitions where each side plays two-hand touch against the other. It's a great way for up-and-coming quarterbacks and skill position players to showcase their skills in hopes of garnering scholarship offers. It also provides an opportunity for eight- or nine-month-a-year football competition. I was vaguely aware that their significance had grown over the past five-to-ten years, but I didn't know much else about their function and impact as high school athletes try to pick up college scholarship offers.

DeArmond: I see how the regional camps and rankings have gotten huge but where I'm at, I don't see the 7-on-7 thing becoming all that big yet. It's not a huge part of the culture here at Mizzou, and I think the comparisons to AAU basketball are hugely overblown. The high school football coach is still the guy you go through around here, unlike high school basketball where it doesn't matter what high school you play for, it only matters who you run with all summer. The AAU thing is so big a lot of high school coaches don't even know where their star player is going to play his college ball until he announces.

In 12 years, I've only covered one 7-on-7 event here at Mizzou. Maybe weather is part of it and I could see where it's much bigger in other parts of the country, farther Southeast, but it's no big deal here.

Driskell: There's this "I wanna play as a freshman" mentality that didn't exist 15–20 years ago. Now coaches make promises and enticements they shouldn't in order to get these top-tier athletes to commit. If and when a kid doesn't get his way, if he's riding the pine his freshman year, he leaves. College football players didn't transfer nearly as much a generation ago. 7-on-7 is changing the landscape. Coaches need to suck up to and keep the guys who run these organizations happy in order to establish a pipeline and have access to these kids. Recently, Notre Dame accepted a commitment from a kid who's a good player and he can compete for playing time at ND. But there was a kid they liked better at the same position, thought he was a better athlete, a little bigger, a little faster, a little more potential. That kid was ready to commit to ND, too. They took the lesser athlete's commitment in order to keep his 7-on-7 organization happy and keep the door open to future athletes from that group.

It's done a lot of good in terms of giving kids exposure and getting their names out there, but it's definitely a flawed system. It weighs these summer camps and 7-on-7 tournaments too heavily. If a kid doesn't run this circuit all summer, it negatively impacts his ranking. Look at guys like [Cincinnati Bengals Pro-Bowl tight end] Tyler Eifert and [Dallas Cowboys Pro-Bowl outside lineman] Zach Martin. They were both low-three-star players. Notre Dame didn't even pursue either of them very hard. They're guys who didn't run the circuit. Same thing with [Carolina Panthers Pro-Bowl linebacker] Luke Kuechly. Fans, for sure, and sometimes even coaching staffs get too wrapped up in recruiting rankings.

Spivey: Coaches down here know they have to recruit the 7-on-7 coaches and if they're in good with a 7s coach, they'll ask him to put specific kids they want to recruit on their roster. Keiwan Ratliff runs Ratpack in Orlando. He's a former UF player, so if the Florida coaches are interested in an Orlando kid, they can just ask Ratliff to take the kid. It gives Florida a leg up on the kid's recruitment.

The 7-on-7 world's influence is getting so big that coaches will be given spots on a university's staff to open up the pipeline. Kevin Beard ran South Florida Express [an influential 7-on-7 program]. He's a former Miami player, and he was hired as a quality control assistant. Now he's the wide receivers coach. That's cleared the way and led to more commits from South Florida Express kids.

I knew about this as an Alabama high school coach, but I didn't know how deep it went until it was my job to know about recruiting. The dirty business of AAU basketball is spilling over into college football through 7-on-7 teams. Handlers guide prospects to a school of their liking rather than where a prospect wants to be.

It's not just 7-on-7 coaches who could provide inroads with top high school prospects. Colleges are finding other similarly creative ways to lure blue-chippers. Ole Miss hired Sean Patterson Jr. as an assistant director of recruiting, in February 2015. Incidentally, Patterson's younger brother, Shea, a bona fide five-star quarterback prospect, committed to Ole Miss the same month. Likewise, Michigan hired former Paramus Catholic HS (NJ) Head Coach Chris Partridge in 2015. The following season, Michigan signed the top ranked player in the 2016 class, defensive tackle Rashan Gary, a Paramus Catholic standout.

Spivey: Byron Cowart[108] was guided away from Florida (and ultimately to Auburn) by his 7-on-7 coach because the coach had a bad taste for Florida on account of a kid he sent there a couple years earlier who's buried on the depth chart at wide receiver.

One 7-on-7 group brought their squad to Florida and the coaching staff really wanted one kid in the group, [current LSU linebacker] Clifton Garrett. UF didn't pay much attention to the other kids, and the guy who ran that 7-on-7 group got mad and has steered his kids away from Florida ever since.

I asked Spivey if he was referring to the Chicago-based Core 6 group headed by Paul Szczesny. (Incidentally, Szczesny and I played high school football together.) Spivey indicated that's exactly whom he was referring to. Since my conversation with Spivey, Szczesny was accused of embezzlement, and as a result his company has been dissolved.

Spivey: You have it now where these 7-on-7 squads are feeders into particular schools. Core 6 kids are typically going to be led to Notre Dame or Ohio State, one travel team in Tampa's kids [are going to be led] to Florida, another travel team in Jacksonville's kids to Georgia. High school coaches are becoming frustrated as they're being pushed aside.

---

[108] The No. 1 player in the country in the 2015 class according to ESPN.

The circuit and the tournaments are only getting bigger. Now they have Nationals. You've got NFA 7-on-7 now,[109] and that only made the process bigger. Before it was only regional and statewide tournaments.

Spivey's was the most damning of all the voices I heard. But a part of me was undeniably drawn to his responses, which rang deeply true to me. More than likely, this was my own cynical point of view attaching to its own confirmation bias. I asked Spivey how, specifically, money infiltrated and corrupted the 7-on-7 circuit.

Spivey: Same way as AAU. Shoe and apparel contracts. 7-on-7 teams are sponsored by Nike or Adidas or Under Armour. These companies are promising kids a $10-million-dollar-deal if they make it to the NFL just for attending a college that wears their brand. It's compelling. Adidas, Under Armor, and Nike start throwing money around and money talks. It starts athletes getting paid and it's taking the amateur status out of the game. A kid is picking his 4–5 year education based on a name brand.

Think about this: until Phil Knight got big and Nike made new helmets and uniforms for just about every game, Oregon was IRRELEVANT.

The companies really reinforce their brands with the amount of swag they give away at these events. Phil Knight sends kids Nike gear in the

---

[109] National Football 7v7 Association. They hold regional tournaments all spring leading up to a national championship tourney in June.

mail just to look at The Opening,[110] and in the process, at Oregon. Look at the All-Star games: the Army All-American game versus the Under Armor All-American game. The Army game lost all its flavor the past couple years because of Under Armor. These kids get six or seven shirts, new cleats, helmets, and gloves at the Under Armor game. They're the prestigious brand right now.

As I processed this information, a number of questions immediately jumped out: "Well, why don't we hear about this sort of thing more often? Why isn't there more smoke if there's fire? Where's the journalistic integrity that compels a writer to become a whistleblower?" Driskell and Spivey had clear, if troubling, answers to these questions.

Driskell: It's not journalism anymore—it's entertainment. There is no more Woodward and Bernstein. Print media is dying as it is. Who's gonna hire you if you're an investigative reporter in sports? The *New York Times*? The culture is "I'm not gonna bite the hand that feeds me."

If any of us reported on any of the shady dealings we see, we'd be blackballed: the company we work for would lose access, and we'd get fired. So I lose my job and the website gets kicked off campus. It's just not worth it.

Spivey: You'd be surprised at [how scared] writers [are] about messing with certain guys and having their sources run dry, afraid of being cut

---

[110] Currently the marquee non-contact showcase for elite high school athletes. Regional events are held across the country, but The Opening Finals take place at Nike headquarters in Beaverton, Oregon, less than two hours from the University of Oregon.

off from the program they report on. If someone from the NCAA asks, "Do you talk with so-and-so?" The answer is no. Always no.

Acknowledgments

There are so many people in my life responsible for putting me in a position where I could write this book. I feel humbled by and indescribably grateful for the love and support I've received along the way.

First, back home in Chicago—Mom, Dad, Ryanne, and all the people I'm lucky enough to call family and friends (I won't even try to compile a list because I know that I'll leave important people off)—thank you for your words of encouragement and for trying not to act surprised when, after not talking about the book for months at a time, you discovered I was planning to finish it after all. Also, to my Dad and Aunt Donna: thank you for offering to help financially before I could even ask. It would have been a lot more difficult to take this trip and write this book without your assistance. Thank you.

Second, all across the South—to Alex Pate, Anne Durkin, David and Virginia Higdon, Dale Braiman, Jerry Price, James Lindquist, Gina Pate, Angela Quadrani, Nancy Mullen, Melissa Reed, Jim Sonefeld, Ashley Barnett, Matt Baumler, Stephanie Tomba, Miranda Rhyne, Holly Harrison Knight, Tom Dobrez, the CrossFit PortSide community in Gulfport, Mississippi (Sara Carter, Melinda North, Beth O'Neil, Allison Cross Edwards, John Byrd and Jacob Moulds in particular), and, of course, my grandma Maggie and her sisters Evelyn and Betty Ann—thank you for your hospitality and making me feel like a little less of an outsider.

Third, in the publishing world—to Adam Rosen, thank you for understanding and clarifying my voice. It was a great comfort to know you understood where I was headed and could help me find the right words to get there. You were the perfect editor for this project.

www.ingramcontent.com/pod-product-compliance
Lightning Source LLC
LaVergne TN
LVHW041538070426
835507LV00011B/817